OUR CHURCH
ONE THROUGH THE AGES

OUR CHURCH

ONE THROUGH THE AGES

REVISED AND ENLARGED

BY

REV. WM. POSTELL WITSELL, D.D.

Rector Christ Church, Little Rock, Arkansas

MOREHOUSE - GORHAM CO.

NEW YORK

1943

Copyright, 1924, 1925, 1930, by
MOREHOUSE-GORHAM CO.

Copyright, 1943, by
WILLIAM POSTELL WITSELL

MANUFACTURED IN THE UNITED STATES OF AMERICA
BY THE VAIL-BALLOU PRESS, INC., BINGHAMTON, N. Y.

CONTENTS

TO THE CHERISHED MEMORY
OF
OUR DEAR PARENTS
CHARLES AND EMMELINE WITSELL
THIS BOOK
IS AFFECTIONATELY DEDICATED
BY THE AUTHOR
IN THE NAME OF HIS BROTHERS AND SISTERS,
AS WELL AS HIS OWN

INTRODUCTION

Those who had the good fortune to read the first or second edition of Dr. Witsell's book will welcome the story now revised and supplemented in the last chapter with an account of recent events and movements, bringing the narrative up to the present moment.

For many others who will take the opportunity offered them by the new publication, the volume comes with fresh significance. It appears at a time when "Our Church—One Through the Ages" is being apprehended as a vital fact by those who claim a spiritual heritage in the Anglican Communion. Of this world-wide Communion the Church of England and the Episcopal Church in America are joint heirs. The sectional aspect of the Church is being steadily outgrown. At the Lambeth Conference of Anglican Bishops in 1920 there emerged a conception of the Anglican Communion in all its branches working as a united body for the reunion of Christendom.

Since that time the Church, with larger horizons in view, has prayed and labored for the realization of this vision. In 1930, at Lambeth, ways were indicated through which to achieve solidarity, first within the membership of our own Church and ultimately in union with still separated Christian Bodies. The background and the present ground for the fulfilment of this hope are clearly given in Dr. Witsell's presentation of his theme. His scholarly approach to the subject and his knowledge gained through wide experience of parochial, diocesan and nation-wide affairs of the Church, give to his treatise peculiar value.

The eventful years which have followed the last Lambeth Conference have shown to him and to other thoughtful Churchmen the opportunity in store for the Anglican Communion to achieve fuller fruition of God's purpose to build on earth a Church universal in its mission, true to its heritage of faith, sure of its promised destiny.

The story of heroic discipleship told by the author of this book, and his appeal in the closing pages for renewal of courageous faith, open doors through which the guiding light of the Holy Spirit directing the Church in ages past is shed upon the years to come.

JAMES DEWOLF PERRY
Bishop of Rhode Island

CHAPTER I

THE ORIGIN OF THE CHRISTIAN CHURCH AND ITS SPREAD IN ASIA MINOR

As it is natural for the traveller, before starting on his journey to ask whither he is going, and as it is customary for the mathematician to give a clear idea of the *quod est demonstrandum,* that is, what is to be proved or demonstrated, before commencing his work, so we wish to let the reader know what is the main purpose of this volume—the goal that we have set for the point of our arrival, the general conclusion of the various thoughts to be found in these pages. It is this: —to show the unbroken continuity of the English Church and its offspring in the United States of America that we know as the Protestant Episcopal Church from Apostolic times to the present day. Prof. W. E. Collins, in discussing the historical method, makes this remark: "There is such a thing as the judicial habit of mind, which endeavors to set aside for the time being all that is not immediately necessary for the purpose in hand, even though it realizes that this is a process of self-limitation; and the historical student has need to cultivate it more than most men. It is a process which brings its own reward." Conformity to this process was found to be an absolute necessity in the fulfillment of the object that we had in mind in sending forth this volume.

This is not to produce a piece of "special pleading," nor is such method fairly open to the charge of assuming arbitrarily certain positions and warping facts to bolster preconceived prejudice, but rather is it the orderly revelation of the record and the placing of the facts in their intelligible relation to one another.

This is a well accepted plan followed by writers of indisputable standing among historical scholars as we have pointed out in our Foreword. For instance, Wakeman in the preface of his "History of the Church of England" writes: "I have attempted in this volume to write a book which may be found more interesting by a general reader and learner than a manual or textbook usually is, and at the same time may do something to stimulate those who are desirous of a comprehensive knowledge of the subject to study it in works of greater size and more solid attainment. My object has, therefore, been to draw a picture of the development of the Church of England rather than to detail her history, to explain rather than to chronicle—in fact, to give an answer, in a short and convenient form, to the question so often asked, How is it that the Church of England has come to be what she is? I have accordingly endeavoured to fix the attention of the reader upon that which has proved to be permanent in the history of the Church, and to avoid burdening his memory with facts and details which, though often very important and interesting in themselves, have not had a lasting influence upon her fortunes."

And Bishop William White was guided by the same considerations in calling his work "Memoirs" instead of a history of the Church (see p. 4).

In accordance with this accepted method of procedure we have given the facts and what we believe to be their natural and reasonable interpretation. Not only out of our own experience but out of the experience of many other clergymen, as well as out of the experience of many of our bishops, particularly those in missionary districts and dioceses, has grown a clear conviction of the need of just such a treatise as this and we trust that it will fill the need.

The Church's unbroken continuity is expressed through the form of her ministry in England and in our American Episcopal Church, consisting of the three orders of bishops, priests and deacons, descending from the primitive Apostolic Church, and through similar continuity of doctrines and methods of worship as outlined in the creeds and the liturgies which have been in constant use from the earliest days to the present hour. A great stream of life has continued steadily forward, although sometimes it has wound about in its course, and on its banks have grown some weeds of error in thought and practice that it was necessary, subsequently, to uproot and cast aside, the Reformation in the sixteenth century being especially such a purifying period. As we pass along we shall find too, that some rank weeds of inaccuracy and absurdity have grown in sections along the stream of thought flowing outside of the Episcopal Church, and have contaminated seriously the mental atmosphere of some, poisoning their judgment and warping their perspective. One of these is the old fabulous statement that the Church of England to-day is a Reformation Church, having been founded by Henry VIII. Another is that, if it was not founded by Henry VIII, then it is a branch of the Roman Catholic Church.

Our method of procedure will be to outline the origin and spread of the Christian Church in Jerusalem and the East and its extension to the Continent of Europe and to the British Isles, thenceforward presenting the clear record of the continued march of the Church in early Britain and modern England and America, showing not only its continuous existence, but also its vigor, zeal and national independence. This, of course, will of itself most effectively dispose of these false impressions and statements, but we shall return to them for some special consideration in order that the reader may have some specific facts with which to meet such misleading, unjust and absurd statements.

Now let us say something which it would hardly seem necessary to say, and that is that we make no pretence to be exhaustive in this presentation of facts. That would be impossible in the limits set for ourselves in these pages. We can only hope to take a sufficient number of typical facts out of the abundant record to make it clear that the Church to which we give allegiance in mind, heart and soul to-day is the Church of St. Paul, St. James, St. Alban, St. Ninias, St. Columba and St. Aidan, Bede and Wickliffe, Ridley and Latimer and Laud. And although for several centuries she was made subject to the *usurped* power of the Roman Papacy largely based on false decretals and unwarranted encroachments, she never lost her identity or the characteristic outlook of her life as a National Church: and when political conditions made it possible, she successfully asserted her independence.

Let us remember also that a fundamental unity pervades these chapters. They are correlated as parts of a mathematical proposition, being built one upon the other, or rather as stages of life and growth of which they are the record. It will not be possible, therefore, for anyone to get the whole unless he gets all the parts. Hence the importance of reading each in relation to the others if one would clearly understand what is herein set forth. The vital importance of such information and instruction as contained in these pages is emphasized by the fact that books used in our public schools are very misleading as to the history of the Church, some instructors even in the higher institutions of learning being inexcusably uninformed or prejudiced on the subject and constantly doing, intentionally or unintentionally, both violence to the facts of history and marked injustice and wrong to a great and noble Church.

The subject may be considered as divided into these parts: First, the General origin of the Christian Church and its spread in the first century East and West. Second, Christianity in the British Isles from its introduction to the invasion of the Northmen. Third, Christianity in the British Isles from the Northmen Invasion to the Norman Conquest. Fourth, Christianity in England from the Conquest to the Reformation. Fifth, the Reformation and onwards to the American Revolution. Sixth, the Episcopal Church in the United States from the American Revolution to the present time.

The Origin of the Church

In dealing with the history of any institution, we

face two lines of thought, that which deals with the outward and that which deals with the inward of which the outward is the expression. The foundation of all institutions is really in an idea or ideas, and the Church is no exception to this general rule. The real foundation of the Church, therefore, is in things seen by the mind and believed in by the heart and soul, but even behind the belief of man we see the origin of the Church in the mind of God. It seems to us that the true and complete projection among men of God's idea of His Church is this—the whole body of humanity redeemed from evil and developed as sons and daughters of God. That, according to the Scriptures, seems to be the Church as God sees it—Catholic indeed, not only in relation to truth but in relation to man, the extension of the Incarnation to the whole race—all men generally, living their lives "hid with Christ in God," as Tennyson sees it, "the one far off Divine event to which the whole creation moves."

Now, so far as our records go, the origin of the Church, as working among men, is seen in the call of Abram as set forth in the 12th Chapter of the book of Genesis. "Now the Lord said unto Abram, Get thee out of thy country, and from thy kindred, and from thy father's house, unto a land that I will show thee; and I will make of thee a great nation and I will bless thee, and make thy name great; and thou shalt be a blessing; and I will bless them that bless thee, and curse him that curseth thee: and in thee shall all the families of the earth be blessed." The Greek word "Ecclesia" which we translate Church means "called out"—that is Abram was called out from the general race of men to be a special servant through whom the knowledge of God should come to all the nations of the earth.

The more definite ecclesiastical organization is presented to us in the book of Exodus. When Jehovah was preparing to lead the children of Israel out of the land of Egypt, along with Moses he raised up a special spiritual ministry, consisting in the beginning, of Aaron the High Priest and his sons, as priests. Their setting apart is recorded in the 28th Chapter, verses 1-3, of Exodus and reads as follows:

"And take thou unto thee Aaron thy brother, and his sons with him, from among the children of Israel, that he may minister unto me in the priest's office, even Aaron, Nadab and Abihu, Eleazar and Ithamar, Aaron's sons. And thou shalt make holy garments for Aaron thy brother for glory and for beauty. And thou shalt speak unto all that are wise hearted, whom I have filled with the spirit of wisdom, that they may make Aaron's garments to consecrate him, that he may minister unto me in the priest's office."

In passing, let us observe that it appears from these words of Scripture that the principle of special ministerial vestments was established at the same time that the ordained ministry itself was instituted.

It is not possible to consider the Christian Church out of its relation to this earlier Church under the former Dispensation any more than it would be possible to consider the history of the American Nation without reference to the English people. The Christian religion is the flower of the old Hebrew faith as the rose is the culmination of the life that is in the stem and the bud. We recall these words of the Collect for St. Simon and St. Jude. "O, Almighty God, Who has built Thy Church upon the foundation of the Apostles and Prophets, Jesus Christ Himself being the head corner-stone," which is recognized as containing words of the Apostle Paul to the Ephesians concerning the Christian Church "built upon the foundation of the Apostles and Prophets, Jesus Christ Himself being the chief corner-stone."

It will be recalled that the original and chief appeal of the Apostles for belief in Jesus Christ was that He is the fulfillment of the message of the Prophets. For instance in Acts 3:22–24 St. Peter is recorded as saying:

"For Moses truly said unto the fathers, A Prophet shall the Lord your God raise up unto you of your brethren, like unto me; him shall ye hear in all things whatsoever he shall say unto you. And it shall come to pass that every soul which shall not hear that Prophet, shall be destroyed among the people. Yea, and all the Prophets from Samuel and those that follow after, as many as have spoken, have likewise foretold of these days." And St. Paul declares (Acts 24:14) "And this I confess unto thee that after the way which they call heresy, so worship I the God of my fathers, believing all things that are written in the Law and in the Prophets." And St. Peter explains the outpouring of the Holy Spirit on the day of Pentecost as the fulfillment of the word spoken by the Prophet Joel, namely: "It shall come to pass in the last days, saith God, I will pour out of my Spirit on all flesh: and your sons and your daughters shall prophesy, and your young men shall see visions, and your old men shall dream dreams: and on my servants and my handmaidens I will pour out in those days of my Spirit and they shall prophesy."

We remember that at first the disciples of Jesus were regarded simply as a sect of the Jews, and at first, too, they were found continually worshipping in their accustomed places along with their brethren in the Synagogue and the Temple. (Jews being spoken of as "brethren.") It was so on the day of Pentecost when they gathered with devout Jews of every nation under Heaven in the City of Jerusalem to observe the Annual Festival. And St. Luke tells us (Acts 3:1): "Now Peter and John went up together into the Temple, at the hour of prayer, being the ninth hour." That is, they were continuing to worship in their accustomed places and going at the appointed hours. And the disciples of the Lord were *first* called *Christians* in Antioch, *after Saul's conversion.*

But, of course, the supreme idea upon which the Christian Church was founded is that Jesus Christ is the Everlasting Son of the Eternal Father. Upon that Truth, Jesus Himself declared to Peter, His Church was to be founded, and we know that upon that truth the Christian Church has rested. It would be extremely interesting to follow the development of the apprehension and expression of the various phases of that idea, but we have neither time nor space for that now. To teach the truth of the Incarnation and to bring man into the fuller life of fellowship with God through His Son, the institution known as the Christian Church was brought into being and in the very nature of things seems essential. For the idea must be embodied and there must be an organization to execute the purpose, if idea and purpose are to exist and be effective among men in this world.

Whitsunday not the Birthday of the Church

Sometimes the day of Pentecost is called "the birthday of the Christian Church." The reader remembers, of course, that that was the time when the Holy Spirit descended upon the multitudes, and a large number, about 3,000 souls, was added to the Lord. To call that the origin or birth of the Christian Church, however, seems strangely inaccurate, for the Church even in its outward organization was already in existence and was *functioning*. In fact it was the *Church Herself, through her commissioned officers,* that was holding this very meeting on the day of Pentecost:

"And when the day of Pentecost was fully come, they were all with one accord in one place.

"And suddenly there came a sound from heaven as of a rushing mighty wind, and it filled all the house where they were sitting.

"And there appeared unto them cloven tongues like as of fire, and it sat upon each of them.

"And they were all filled with the Holy Ghost, and began to speak with other tongues, as the Spirit gave them utterance." (Acts 2: 1–4.)

Again, in the Acts of the Apostles (1:21 plus), we read, "Wherefore of these men which companied with us all the time that the Lord Jesus went in and out among us, beginning from the baptism of John, unto the same day that He was taken up from us, must one be ordained to be a witness with us of His resurrection. And they appointed two, Joseph called Barsabas, who was surnamed Justus, and Matthias. And they prayed, and said, Thou, Lord, Which knowest the hearts of all men show whether of these two Thou has chosen, that they may take part of this ministry and Apostleship, from which Judas by transgression fell. And they gave forth their lots and the lot fell upon Matthias and he was numbered with the eleven Apostles." That is, Jesus had already commissioned His twelve Apostles, and when one fell the organization provided his successor. And this took place *before* the day of Pentecost.

And we know also that the seventy elders had been commissioned to go out to preach (St. Luke 10: 1-20, St. Math. 10: 9-16). And Jesus had also ordained the two great Sacraments of the Church—Baptism and the Lord's Supper. He had already inculcated the fundamental ideas, in addition to the one that we have already spoken of, of the universal Fatherhood of God, the eternal presence and power of the Holy Spirit, the brotherhood of man and the law of love and self-sacrifice.

On the day of Pentecost, the Church in the persons of its representatives was fulfilling its mission, doing the work that it was sent to do, and we read (Acts 2: 37 plus) that after Peter had preached the sermon concerning the Messiahship of Jesus Christ: "And when they heard this, they were pricked in their hearts and said unto Peter and to the rest of the Apostles, Men and brethren, what shall we do? Then Peter said unto them, Repent, and be baptized every one of you in the name of Jesus Christ for the remission of sins and ye shall receive the gift of the Holy Ghost. For the promise is unto you, and to your children, and to all that are afar off, even as many as the Lord our God shall call. And with many other words did he testify and exhort, saying, Save yourselves from this untoward generation. Then they that gladly received his word were baptized: and the same day there were added unto them about three thousand souls. And they continued steadfastly in the Apostles' doctrine and fellowship and in breaking of the bread and in the prayers." We notice that St. Luke says, "The same day there were *added* unto them"—the body was already existing and working and on the day of Pentecost, they were adding to what was already in existence, and energetically fulfilling the task that was their own. Nothing new was created and nothing then brought to birth. Let us recall here these words from "The Anglo-Catholic Movement of Today":

"Jesus Christ, our Lord, had in one sense accomplished at His Ascension in His single person the redemption of man. But in another sense equally apparent in the New Testament, He had only provided in full measure the means for its accomplishment, *leaving behind Him* for the fulfillment of His purpose, *the Church,* which is the New Israel, now freed from all restriction of race—the Church which is His body, indwelt by His Spirit, the home of 'the grace and truth' which 'came by Him,' and the visible organ through which He is to act upon the world."

To these words let us add this quotation from Wells's "Manual of Early Ecclesiastical History":

"The Christian Church is essentially the creation of Jesus Christ. He supplied its fundamental ideas; gathered the first disciples, out of whom He chose twelve Apostles and seventy Evangelists, the first Christian ministry; ordained the Sacraments of Baptism and the Lord's Supper, and taught and commissioned the twelve Apostles to continue His work." All this, be it remembered, was *before* the day of Pentecost which might be called a *great day* in the Christian Church, but not its *birthday*. Let us conclude our comment on this point with these words of Bishop Thos. F. Gailor, "The Church, the Bible and the Creed":

"So our first step in the effort to understand Christianity is to realize that it began as an organized institution, a society distinct from other societies in the world.

"Professor Burkitt, of Cambridge, England, one of the latest and ablest critics of the New Testament, says in his recent lectures, 'The History of Our Lord's ministry is the history of the birth of the Christian Church. *This society was formed by Jesus Christ Himself.*' He proceeds to show, from St. Mark's Gospel, that after the incident of the healing of the man with the withered hand on the Sabbath Day, our Lord broke off relations with official Judaism and *founded His own Society*. As Professor Burkitt says, 'After St. Mark III, 6, a new era in the ministry is opened. From that moment begins the separate existence of the embryo Church.'

"The existence of the Church is taken for granted in the other writings of the New Testament. We read in St. Luke's Gospel (VI, 13) that Our Lord selected twelve of His disciples and named them Apostles. *Here begins the formal organization.* St. Matthew tells us that Our Lord declared that the gates of hell should not prevail against His Church (XVI, 18) and the parables of the Kingdom, while we cannot press their details, all imply the conception of an ordered society, with differentiation of function.'

" 'Our attention is called at the beginning of the Acts of the Apostles to the manifestations of new power resulting from the descent of the Holy Spirit at Pentecost, not upon individuals but upon the *corporate Church* (already in existence, of course—The Author) ; and St. Peter's sermon, after reciting the fact of the Resurrection of Christ, called upon the people to repent and be baptized. Thereupon, the record runs, about three thousand souls were added to them by baptism, and "They continued steadfastly" in the Apostles' teaching and fellowship, in the breaking of bread, and in the prayers.' (Pp. 2, 3 and 6, 7.) That is, they were *continuing* things *clearly* established and recognized.

Sometimes a good deal is said without accuracy or thoughtfulness about the "Mother Church of Christendom," those making use of such terms having reference to the Church in the city of Rome. There were many churches in existence before the inhabitants of the ancient Imperial City ever heard the name of Christ, the Mother Church of all being the Church in the city of Jerusalem. We are told in the first chapter of the Acts of the Apostles, 15th verse, "And in those days, Peter stood up in the midst of the disciples and said (the number of names together were about an hundred and twenty)." That was the first congregation of the Christian brethren. And for the first few years of the Christian era this Church at Jerusalem was the center and power house for all Christian activities. That is abundantly clear from the reading of the first six chapters of the Acts of the Apostles. And we are told that "the word of God increased and the number of disciples *multiplied in Jerusalem greatly,* and a great company of priests were obedient to the faith" (Acts 6:7). And after the conversion of Saul, we are told (Acts 9:23) that he "was brought to Jerusalem" as the Christian center, the Mother of all churches, and that after through the good offices of Barnabas, he was accepted by the Church there, "that he was with them, coming in and going out at Jerusalem." In these words, we have, you see, the picture of what we would call to-day the headquarters of the Church, with her agents and servants going out to the surrounding country, doing the work committed to them, and returning to make their reports and receive fresh orders again.

And when disputes arose a little later, the brethren assembled in Jerusalem (15th chapter of Acts) for the purpose of settling the difficulties with which they were confronted. From Jerusalem, then, the disciples went into all parts, first of Asia Minor and then out into the East. And after the conversion of Saul of Tarsus into the Apostle Paul, Christianity took also a Westward course, that is into Macedonia, Greece, Italy and other parts of Europe.

We learn through his Epistles to the Philippians, Galatians, Colossians, Ephesians, Timothy and Titus of the activities of the Churches in the various parts of Asia Minor. We learn through the same sources of their development in the understanding of Christian thought and the principles of Christian conduct. We read in the 11th chapter of Acts, 19th verse, "Now they which were scattered abroad upon the persecution that arose about Stephen, travelled as far as Phenice and Cyprus and Antioch preaching the Word unto none but unto the Jews only. And some of them were men of Cyprus and Cyrene, which when they were come to Antioch, spake *unto the Grecians,* preaching the Lord Jesus. And the hand of the Lord was with them and a great number believed and turned unto the Lord. Then tidings of these things came unto the ears of the Church which was in Jerusalem and they sent forth Barnabas that he should go as far as Antioch. And who when he came and had seen the grace of God, was glad and exhorted them all, that with purpose of heart they should cleave unto the Lord. For he was a good man and full of the Holy Ghost and of faith, and much people was added unto the Lord. Then departed Barnabas to Tarsus for to seek Saul."

We learn from these passages that about this time the appeal was made chiefly to the Jews, although in the congregation at Jerusalem there had been a sufficient number of Hellenistic Christians, that is, Christians of Greek speech, to cause a dissension about the Greek widows being neglected, leading to the appointment of the diaconate, but from now on we hear more about the presentation of the Gospel to the Gentiles and their acceptance of it. For example, in the 19th chapter of Acts 10th verse: "And this continued by the space of two years, so that *all* they which dwelt in Asia, heard the Word of the Lord Jesus, both Jews and *Greeks.*" And Antioch became an important center of Christian activity.

We recall that emphasis upon the duty of the Church to take the message of Christ to the Gentiles as well as to the Jews was given by the appointment of St. Paul as the Apostle to the Gentiles. In Acts 9:15 we read, "But the Lord said unto him, Go thy way: for he is a chosen vessel unto me, to bear my name before the Gentiles, and Kings, and the children of Israel." We remember, too, that Peter had his special vision, teaching him that no man must be considered unclean, but that *every man in every nation* who wrought righteousness is accepted with God. And St. Peter, speaking to the brethren and explaining that the Gentiles had also received the word of God, said: "For as much then as God giveth them like gift as He did unto us to believe on the Lord Jesus Christ, what was I that I should withstand God? When they heard these things they held their peace, glorifying God, saying, 'Then hath God also to the *Gentiles* granted repentance unto life.'"

And Paul and Barnabas declared in the synagogue at Antioch in Pisidia, "And see how the Lord commanded us, saying, I have set thee to be a light of the *Gentiles* and that thou shouldst be for salvation unto the ends of the earth."

The organization of the Church then, as we see it in Asia Minor in the first two generations of the Christian era, seems to be that of a general institution with the head and center in the city of Jerusalem. As further evidence of this we recall the Council of Jerusalem as described in the 15th chapter of the Acts of the Apostles. St. James, the Bishop at Jerusalem, presided over the Council and summed up the judgment of the assembly. When the meeting of the Council was decided upon, it was determined that "Paul and Barnabas and others of them should go up to Jerusalem unto the Apostles and elders about this question." On another occasion, Acts 21, verse 17, St. Luke tells us that "when we were come to Jerusalem, the brethren received us gladly, and the day following Paul went in with us unto James, and all the elders were present." Of course, the New Testament only knows of the Church as *one,* and only speaks of the general organization as the Church. The plural term "Churches," can only be applied to different *local* units. It was the one Church of Christ located in Jerusalem and Philippi and Ephesus and Corinth.

As we have noted above, the essential elements of continuity in the Church from age to age are her doctrines, or Creeds, Sacraments, worship and ministry. St. Luke (Acts 2:42) describes the marks of Christian discipleship in this way: "And they continued steadfastly in the Apostles' doctrine and fellowship, and in the breaking of bread, and in the prayers." Bishop Gore writes interestingly of this in "The Anglo-Catholic Movement of To-day" (pp. 6–8). "Now plainly a society, which is to stand before the world as one and visible, and which is to approach the world as the representative of the heavenly Christ, but which lacks the links of place and language and race which render nations manifestly one, must have other links of coherence and unity. Accordingly, from New Testament times downward, three such links are evident. The first was the common faith, 'the tradition,' which lies behind the New Testament, which found in time legitimate expression in the Catholic creeds, and

which made its appeal to the Scriptures; the second
was the Sacraments, in which all who would be Christians were bound to participate—which were the
divinely given and necessary instruments of spiritual
grace and at the same time, as being ceremonies of
the society, bound the spiritual life of its members into
that visible fellowship; the third was the Apostolic
ministry, which all must accept, instituted by Christ
in the persons of the Twelve and continued in the succession of the bishops down the ages, linking the different churches together by the fellowship of the bishops
throughout the world and binding the succession of
generations to the Apostolic original.

"These three institutions, the common creed, the
common sacraments, the sacred ministry, all appear in
the early history of the Church as having equal and undisputed authority. They were all retained and emphasized by the Church of England, when it became
separated from the Roman Church. They were familiar
themes with the Anglican divines of the seventeenth
century. The Tractarians set themselves then to make
these elements of the doctrine of the visible Church—
one, holy, Catholic and Apostolic—current coin again
in the familiar thought and speech of men."

Now not only through the preaching of its commissioned officers and teachers, but also through the
conviction, courage, zeal, and sacrifice of the whole
body of believers did the Word of God, the truth of
Christ, glow and grow in the hearts of men. This was
emphasized when the Christians were called upon to
suffer and die for their faith, and

"Met the tyrants' brandished steel,
    The lion's gory mane"

with unflinching courage.

The first persecution of the Church which led to martyrdom was that of the Deacon Stephen. The Apostles before him had been threatened and beaten for speaking in the name of Christ, but no one had lost his life until Stephen was stoned to death. Saul of Tarsus had part in that, consenting to it. St. Luke tells us that at that time there was a great persecution against the Church which was in Jerusalem, and the disciples, except the Apostles, were all scattered abroad throughout Judea and Samaria. In this way, of course, the Gospel spread, because the Christians as they went from place to place in Judea and Samaria proclaimed the truth that was in them. A little later, "Herod stretched forth his hands to vex the Church and killed James the brother of John with the sword." Later, 68 A. D., there was a more general persecution under the Roman Emperor Nero.

Through steadfastness in their faith, and through their unflagging zeal and noble courage the Christians in those early days made a passageway into the hearts of men for the Divine Master, and "the blood of the martyrs became the seed of the Church." And to-day the Church flourishes, can flourish, only by the steadfast faith, the unwavering courage and the ready zeal expressed in the sacrifice of her members in the name and in behalf of their Divine Master, our Saviour Jesus Christ.

As we have stated above, so far as definite historical

records go, the Westward movement of Christianity that led it out of Asia into Europe came under the inspiration and leadership of St. Paul. We shall trace this in our next chapter.

CHAPTER II

In the preceding chapter we have been considering Christianity in Asia Minor and in the Eastward countries. The Four Gospels, the Book of the Acts and the Epistles of St. Paul have been our chief source of information.

We now turn our eyes Westward and follow the journeys of the Apostles over into Europe. The first really historical movement is that of St. Paul into Macedonia. This is described for us in the Acts of the Apostles 16:4-19: "As they went through the cities, they delivered them the decrees for to keep, that were ordained of the Apostles and elders which were at Jerusalem. And so were the Churches established in the faith, and increased in number daily. Now when they had gone throughout Phrygia and the region of Galatia, and were forbidden of the Holy Ghost to preach the Word in Asia, after they were come to Mysia, they assayed to go into Bithynia: but the Spirit suffered them not. And they passing by Mysia, came down to Troas. And a vision appeared to Paul in the night: There stood a man of Macedonia, and prayed him, saying, Come over into Macedonia, and help us. And after he had seen the vision, immediately we endeavored to go into Macedonia, assuredly gather-

ing that the Lord had called us for to preach the
Gospel unto them. Therefore, loosing from Troas,
we came with a straight course to Samothracia, and
the next day to Neapolis; and from thence to Philippi,
which is the chief city of that part of Macedonia, and
a *colony;* and we were in that city abiding certain
days. And on the Sabbath we went out of the city by a
river side, where prayer was wont to be made; and
we sat down and spake unto the women which resorted
thither. And a certain woman named Lydia, a seller of
purple, of the city of Thyatira, which worshipped
God, heard us; whose heart the Lord opened, that she
attended unto the things which were spoken of Paul.
And when she was baptized and her household, she
besought us, saying, If ye have judged me to be faithful to the Lord, come into my house and abide there.
And she constrained us. And it came to pass, as we
went to prayer, a certain damsel possessed with a spirit
of divination, met us, which brought her masters much
gain by soothsaying: The same followed Paul and us
and cried, saying, These men are the servants of the
most High God, which shew unto us the way of
salvation. And this did she many days. But Paul, being
grieved, turned and said unto the spirit, I command
thee in the name of Jesus Christ to come out of her.
And he came out the same hour. And when her masters
saw that hope of their gains was gone, they caught
Paul and Silas and drew them into the market place
unto the rulers." And in chapter 17: 1–14 we learn:
"Now when they had passed through Amphipolis and
Apollonia, they came to Thessalonica where was a
synagogue of the Jews: And Paul, *as his manner was,*

went in unto them, and three Sabbath days reasoned with them out of the Scriptures; opening and alleging that Christ must needs have suffered, and risen again from the dead; and that this Jesus Whom I preach unto you, is Christ. And some of them believed and consorted with Paul and Silas; and of the devout *Greeks* a great multitude, and of the chief *women* not a few. But the Jews, which believed not, moved with envy, took unto them certain lewd fellows of the baser sort and gathered a company, and set all the city on an uproar, and assaulted the house of Jason and sought to bring them out to the people. And when they found them not, they drew Jason and certain brethren unto the rulers of the city, crying, These that have turned the world upside down have come hither also; whom Jason hath received: and these all do contrary to the decrees of Caesar, saying that there is another king, one Jesus. And it troubled the people and the rulers of the city when they heard these things. And when they had taken security of Jason and of the other, they let them go. And the brethren immediately sent away Paul and Silas by night unto Berea, who coming thither went into the *synagogue* of the Jews. These were more noble than those in Thessalonica in that they received the Word with all readiness of mind, and searched the Scriptures daily whether those things were so.

"Therefore many of them believed, also of honourable women, which were *Greeks,* and of men, not a few. But when the Jews of Thessalonica had knowledge that the Word of God was preached of Paul in Berea, they came thither also, and stirred up the people. And

then immediately the brethren sent away Paul to go
as it were to the sea; but Silas and Timothy abode
there still."

In the 17th chapter we also learn of St. Paul's
visit to Athens (17:18–34). We remember that St.
Paul tried to convert the cultured Athenians, using, no
doubt, philosophical arguments and bringing to bear
all the power of his splendid mind, but we have no
record that he was able to establish a Church in Athens.
But it does appear that he learned a very valuable lesson from his experience there.

From Athens he went to Corinth, and using a
different method, a different way of approach, he was
able to establish a flourishing congregation in the latter
city. In first Corinthians 2:1–5 we see what this
way of approach was, and we know that the results
justified the method pursued: "And I, brethren, when
I came to you, came not with excellency of speech,
or of wisdom, declaring unto you the testimony of
God. For I determined not to know anything among
you, Save Jesus Christ and Him crucified. And I
was with you in weakness, and in fear, and in much
trembling. And my speech and my preaching were not
with enticing words of man's wisdom, but in demon-
stration of the Spirit and of power; that your faith
should not stand in the *wisdom* of men, but in the
power of God."

St. Luke tells us, Acts 18:8: "And Crispus, the
chief ruler of the synagogue, believed on God with all
of his house, and many of the Corinthians, hearing,
believed and were baptized," (18:12–17). "And when
Gallio was the deputy of Achaia, the Jews made insur-

rection with one accord against Paul, and brought him to the judgment seat, saying, This fellow persuadeth men to worship God contrary to the Law. And when Paul was now about to open his mouth, Gallio said unto the Jews, If it were a matter of wrong or wicked lewdness, O ye Jews, reason would that I should bear with you: but if it be a question of words and names, and of your Law look ye to it, For I will be no judge of such matters. And he drave them from the judgment seat. Then all the Greeks took Sosthenes, the chief ruler of the synagogue, and beat him before the judgment seat, and Gallio cared for none of those things."

From Corinth he moved to Ephesus and was able to establish a Church there. It was to Ephesus that the eloquent Apollos came, and there "was more fully instructed in the way of the Lord, and he mightily convinced the Jews, and that publicly, showing by the Scriptures that Jesus was the Christ."

From Ephesus St. Paul went all throughout Galatia, and Phrygia, strengthening the disciples that already professed belief in Christ.

On the second visit of St. Paul to Ephesus, he found certain disciples who had not been properly baptized. He baptized them as he thought Christians should be baptized and administered Confirmation, or the Laying-on-of-Hands and so brought them into the full fellowship of the Christian Church (Acts, 19: 1–6). In passing, it is interesting and instructive to recall two other Scriptural references to this matter of Confirmation or the Laying-on-of-Hands. First in the Hebrew Epistle (6: 1–2) we read:

"Therefore leaving the principles of the doctrine of Christ, let us go on unto perfection; not laying again the foundation of repentance from dead works, and of faith toward God,

"Of the doctrine of baptisms, *and of laying-on-of-Hands,* of the resurrection of the dead, and of eternal judgment."

Here we have the Laying-on-of-Hands put in the very middle of those things the writer calls the "principles of the doctrine (or teaching) of Christ," and it immediately follows Baptism in his list.

Then in the Acts of the Apostles we see the practice of the Apostles carrying out what in the Hebrew Epistle is called the teaching of Christ. In Acts 8: 14–17 we find these words:

"Now when the Apostles which were at Jerusalem heard that Samaria had received the Word of God, they sent unto them Peter and John:

"Who, when they were come down, prayed for them, that they might receive the Holy Ghost:

"(*For as yet he was fallen upon none of them: only they were baptized in the name of the Lord Jesus.*)

"*Then laid they their hands on them,* and they received the Holy Ghost."

As evidence of the way that Christian truth was taking hold of the people of Ephesus we read these words from the 19th chapter of the Acts, verses 17–21: "And it was known to all the Jews and Greeks, also dwelling at Ephesus; and fear fell on them all, and the name of the Lord Jesus was magnified. And many that believed came and confessed and showed their deeds. Many of them also which used curious arts brought their books together and burned them before all men, and they counted the price of them and found it fifty thousand pieces of silver. So mightily grew the Word of God and prevailed. After these things were ended, Paul purposed in the spirit when he had passed through Macedonia and Achaia, to go to Jerusalem, saying, after I have been there, I must also see Rome."

The Gospel had also been preached in Cyprus, in Crete, in Italy and in Rome itself. We do not know with exactness who first introduced Christianity into Rome. St. Paul's journey there as a prisoner and his remaining there for a period of two years preaching unceasingly the truth of Christ (Acts 28: 28–30) is the first really authentic statement on record as to the preaching of the Gospel in Rome, but there is ample evidence that Christians were in Rome before St. Paul made his journey thither. For instance, "After these things, Paul departed from Athens and came to Corinth; and found a certain Jew named Aquila, born in Pontus, lately come from Italy with his wife Priscilla; (because that Claudius had commanded all Jews to depart from *Rome*) and came unto them. And because he was of the same craft, he abode with them and wrought, for by their occupation they were tent-makers" (Acts 18: 1–3). Then when St. Paul moved toward Rome from Puteoli he found many to welcome him (Acts 28: 12–16) :—

"And landing at Syracuse we tarried there three days.

"And from thence we fetched a compass, and came

to Rhegium: and after one day the south wind blew, and we came the next day to Puteoli:

"Where we found brethren, and were desired to tarry with them seven days: and so we went toward Rome.

"And from thence, when the brethren heard of us, they came to meet us as far as Appii Forum, and the Three Taverns; whom when Paul saw, he thanked God, and took courage.

"And when we came to Rome, the centurion delivered the prisoners to the captain of the guard: but Paul was suffered to dwell by himself with a soldier that kept him."

The Roman historian Suetonius writing about the Emperor Claudius Caesar says: "He banished from Rome all the Jews who were continually making disturbance at the instigation of one Chrestus," that is Christ. (Claudius, Chapter 25).

St. Paul wrote his Epistle to the Roman Christians before he went there, which shows, of course, that there were Christians there several years before he reached that city. There is nothing in the Scriptures to connect St. Peter with Rome at all, On this point we quote the following from Dr. C. L. Wells: "Not until after the second century do we find a clear and general tradition that St. Peter went to Rome. Not until the third century do the bishops of Rome begin to put forward their claim to be his successors in the Roman bishopric." Irenaeus names the bishops of Rome and places Linus, *not Peter,* as the first. In fact, he does not name St. Peter among the bishops of Rome at all, although he writes of *"that tradition* derived from the Apostles of the very great, the very ancient and universally known Church founded and organized at Rome by the two most glorious Apostles, Peter and Paul." He then gives the list of the first twelve Bishops of Rome, namely, Linus, Anacletus, Clement, Evaristus, Alexander, Telephonus, Hyginus, Pius, Anicetus, Soter and Eleutherius, the bishop of his day. (Irenaeus: "Against Heresies, Ante-Nicene Fathers," pp. 415, 416.) Notwithstanding this statement of Irenaeus as to the "tradition" of Peter's being in Rome, there is no *fact* upon which the certainty of his residence, or even of his visiting there, can be established.

It is quite interesting to recall here these words from the first volume of the "History of the Christian Church" by Jas. C. Robertson, pp. 2–3: "We learn from the books of the New Testament, that within a few years from the day of Pentecost the knowledge of the faith was spread, by the preaching, the miracles, and the life of the Apostles and their associates through most of the countries which border on the Mediterranean Sea. At Rome, before the city had been visited by any Apostle, the number of Christians was already so great as to form several congregations in the different quarters.

"Clement of Rome states that St. Paul himself, in the last period of his life, visited the 'extremity of the West,' an expression which may be more probably interpreted of Spain (in accordance with the intention expressed in the Epistle to the Romans) than of our own island, for which many have wished to claim the honour of a visit from the great teacher of the Gentiles." But it appears to us as most reasonable, if not indeed inevitable and certain, that this great Apostolic Missionary would go on to Britain if he got so close to it as Spain. Then Mr. Robertson adds: "The *early introduction* of Christianity into Britain, however, appears more certain than the *agency* by which it was effected." And the same remark will apply in other cases as seen by the following words of the same author.

"There is reason to believe that by the end of the third century the Gospel had been made known in some degree to almost all the nations with which the Romans had intercourse, although we have very little information as to the details of its progress or as to the agency by which it was effected."

Having now seen the origin and spread of Christianity in the East and its passing over into Europe in general, in the next chapter we will consider its introduction into Britain.

CHAPTER III

As in the case of the beginnings of Christianity in Rome and many another place in ancient times, so it is in regard to its introduction into Britain. No one *knows just when* it took place or by whom it was first preached there. There is clear evidence, however, of its very early existence there.

We recall as matters of interest some of the surmises and traditions relative to that important event, although let it be understood we do not take our stand on any of them as proven history, merely passing them on for what they are worth. Rather do we take our stand upon the clear evidence of the existence of the Church in Britain in very early days,—a Church Apostolic in its teaching, worship and ministry.

It is of interest to note that the land of Britain was known to the people of the Continent as early as 330 B. C. An eminent man named Pythias, who lived in the time of Alexander the Great, made two voyages of discovery to Britain and reported upon its agricultural resources as well as the domestic customs of the inhabitants. We recall also that Julius Caesar undertook a campaign against the Britons at the head of an immense army in 55 B. C., and in his book on the Gallic Wars, described the religion and habits of the ancient

Britons. Still more important for our purpose, is the subsequent invasion of Britain by Claudius Caesar in A. D. 43. This was the beginning of a series of terrible wars between the Britons and Romans which culminated in A. D. 84, when all the land now known as England and Wales, with parts of Scotland, became a Roman Province, ruled by Roman Governors, colonized by Roman citizens and kept in order by Roman legions. Green in his "History of the English People" (p. 20) tells us: "When the Saxon boats touched its coast the Island was the westernmost province of the Roman Empire. In the fifty-fifth year before Christ a descent of Julius Caesar revealed it to the Roman world; and a century after Caesar's landing the Emperor Claudius undertook its conquest. The work was swiftly carried out. Before thirty years were over the bulk of the Island had passed beneath the Roman sway and the Roman frontier had been carried to the Firths of Forth and of Clyde. The work of civilization followed fast on the work of the sword. To the last, however, the distance of the Island from the seat of Empire left her less Romanized than any other province of the West. The bulk of the population scattered over the country seem in spite of imperial edicts to have clung to their old law, as to their old language, and to have retained some traditional allegiance to their native chiefs. But Roman civilization rested mainly on city life, and in Britain, as elsewhere, the city was thoroughly Roman. In towns such as Lincoln or York, governed by their own municipal officers, guarded by massive walls, and linked together by a network of magnificent roads which reached from one end of the Island to the other, manners, language, political life, all were of Rome."

During one of the military campaigns, a very notable prisoner was carried from Britain to Rome, a brave British King whose British name was Caradoc, called by the Romans, Caractacus. Because of his courageous bearing before the Roman Emperor, his life was spared, and he was allowed to return to Britain on condition that several of his family should remain as hostages for his good behavior. Now at this time, St. Paul was a prisoner in Rome, and we know that he had free access into Caesar's household, in which he made several converts. The names of the hostages given by Caractacus are: Bran, Llin, and Claudia, his father, his son and his daughter. It has been said that Bran had been a priest of the heathen religion, but while in Rome, became a convert to Christianity and returned to his native land as an evangelist of Christ. It is also thought that Claudia is the same princess who was married to Pudens, the son of a Roman senator. Now St. Paul, in his second Epistle to St. Timothy, 4:21 writes: "Do thy diligence to come before winter. Eubulus greeteth thee, and Pudens and Linus, and Claudia, and all the brethren." Linus is the Latin equivalent of Llin and the bearer of the name is identified as the first bishop of Rome by Irenaeus and others. It is quite reasonable to suppose that all of these people came under the teaching of the Apostle Paul, as certainly no other Christian teacher in Rome at this time can be compared with him in either prominence or ability, and we have already seen, there is no historic certainty, although good probability, that Peter ever was there. And it is quite probable that they would naturally establish contact between the soldiers and other citizens of Britain who were coming and going between Rome and their native land, and many of them would adopt the religion accepted and proclaimed by the brave Caractacus and his family, of which they had heard in Rome. So that Paul, even if he never set foot on British soil, might easily be the father of Christianity in Great Britain. It has been said, however, that he himself went to the British Isles. For instance, St. Clement, the Bishop of Rome in the last decade of the first century, and a personal friend of St. Paul, wrote that he went to "the farthermost bounds of the West," and of course every intelligent Roman citizen knew that the "farthermost bounds of the West" was the province of Britain. Wakeman writing of the early days of the Church in Britain uses the phrase "extreme limits of Roman Civilization" as describing the British Isles. Here are his exact words: "Still, scanty as such memorials are, they are sufficient to present a fairly vivid picture of what the infant Church in the *extreme limits* of *Roman Civilization* must have been during the last two centuries of the rule of the Roman Emperors of the West." (p. 1).

Eusebius, a noted historian of the fourth century, speaking of Britain, likewise said: "The blessed Paul labored there also." It is very interesting to recall these words of Dr. Dalcho in regard to Eusebius and his testimony on this point. "Eusebius, the ecclesiastical historian, who died A. D. 338, was intimate with Constantine the Great, the first monarch who embraced the Christian Religion. Constantine had lived long in Britain, and was there proclaimed Emperor by the Roman Army. There can be little doubt but that the historian embraced the opportunity which this intimacy gave him, of obtaining information respecting the British churches. This historian states that the Apostles preached in the remotest cities and countries; and after having mentioned the Romans, Persians, Armenians, Parthians, Indians, and Scythians, he adds, that some of them went to the British Islands. Theodoret and Jerome are of the same opinion; and it appears from the testimonies produced by that learned antiquary Bishop Stillingfleet, in his 'Origines Britannicae,' that St. Paul may have been in Britain for any thing that has been proved to the contrary."

Bishop Thos. F. Gailor in his little book entitled "The Episcopal Church" writes: "There is strong enough evidence to make the learned Bishop of Lincoln, Christopher Wordsworth, declare that it is probable that St. Paul himself preached the Gospel in Britain about 64 A. D." Nelson R. Boss, although not ranking as a major historian, yet one whose little book on the Church has passed its 100th thousand, writes: "The early British Church was probably established by St. Paul and had existed in Britain hundreds of years before Roman priests set foot on British soil." It will be remembered that St. Paul in his Epistle to the Romans (15:23-25) writes: "But now having no more place in these parts, and having a great desire these many years to come unto you; whensoever I take my journey into Spain, I will come to you: for I trust to see you in my journey, and to be brought on my way thitherward by you, if first I be somewhat filled with your company.

"But now I go unto Jerusalem to minister unto the saints."

It is most likely, if not practically certain, that if the Apostle fulfilled his purpose to go to Spain, he would also go over into Britain, a well-known province of the Roman Empire. M. W. Patterson reminds us that "Professor Ramsay has pointed out that St. Paul at a very early stage contemplated the Christianizing of the Roman Empire, and that his missionary journeys were carried out *along the lines of the great Roman roads;* the political unity and stability of the Roman Empire, no less than splendid roads, paved the way for the expansion of the Christian Church." The present author has himself ridden over roads in Britain said to have been built by the soldiers of Julius Caesar. However, in spite of all these considerations and quotations we do not state it as an historical fact that St. Paul went in person to Britain, but simply give the tradition as one possible way in which the Gospel might have been carried to the British in Apostolic times. And in spite of what others may say we see no sufficient reason for ignoring it as such. And another historian has written: "In the first century Christianity reached Britain, and began to spread among the Romanized Britons. . . . It is certain that the Romans left the province Christian. . . . From this Church is descended the Welsh Church . . . and the Churches of Scotland and Ireland." Concerning the connection between the old British Church and its offshoots in Ireland and Scotland more will be said later.

There is also a tradition that Joseph of Arimathea, Philip and Lazarus, with twelve companions and Mary and Martha and perhaps other holy women, were put by their enemies into a boat upon the Mediterranean Sea and allowed to drift along whither the winds might carry them. The story goes that they landed on the southwest coast of Wales and established the first Christian settlement, known as Glastonbury. Whether this be true or not, there are very decided evidences that there was a certain Christian settlement at Glastonbury in very early days, reaching back before any settled historic time in Britain. Alfred Tennyson has perpetuated the legend in the "Idylls of the King" from which we quote these words:

> "That Joseph came of old to Glastonbury
> And there the heathen prince, Arviragus
> Gave him an isle of marsh whereon to build;
> And there he built with wattles from the marsh
> A little lonely church in days of yore."

Then he writes thus of the cup

> "From which our Lord
> Drank at the last sad supper with His own,"

which

> "Arimathean Joseph journeying, brought
> To Glastonbury, where the winter thorn
> Blossoms at Christmas, mindful of our Lord;
> And there awhile it bode; and if a man
> Could touch or see it, he was healed at once,
> By faith, of all his ills. But then the times
> Grew to such evil that the holy cup
> Was caught away to Heaven and disappeared."

Along with this goes the fact that the liturgy and customs of the Church in early Britain correspond with the Eastern customs and forms of service, with those of Ephesus and Jerusalem, and not with those of Rome. Some historians believe it most probable that Christianity was carried into Britain from Gaul or France, the inhabitants being not only neighbors but of the same general ancestry in the early days. One has said: "We must read the signs for ourselves, and they point in the direction I have described. They make us a younger sister, *not very much younger,* of the Church of Gaul—a *Church founded from Ephesus— Oriental in its origin, not Western.* I may, perhaps, have time to indicate in my concluding lecture some points which show the *non-Western* connection of the British Church." This was seen when Augustine came in 597 with the Roman liturgy and Roman ecclesiastical customs, e. g., time of observing Easter and manner of priestly tonsure, and found them quite different from the service books and customs of Britain. So different, that he sought advice from Gregory the Pope as to what his attitude toward them should be. And Colman, the defender of the British and Celtic customs as against the Roman in the Council of Whitby 664, urged that the British and Scots had followed St. John, and were satisfied to have their rites and customs on so good a foundation as the teaching and practice of so holy a man as he. Bede describing the controversy between Colman and Wilfrid in this Council attributes these words to Colman: "The Easter which I keep, I received from my elders, who sent me bishop hither;

all our forefathers, men beloved of God, are known to have kept it after the same manner; and that the same may not seem to any contemptible or worthy to be rejected, *it is the same which St. John the Evangelist,* the disciple beloved of our Lord, with all the churches over which he presided, is recorded to have observed." Then again when Wilfrid spoke of the "Picts and the Britons who *foolishly* oppose all the rest of the universe," Colman interrupted him by saying: "It is strange that you will call our labours foolish, wherein we follow the example of so great an Apostle, who was thought worthy to lay his head on our Lord's bosom, when all the world knows him to have lived most wisely." Wilfrid's reply did not deny that the customs then prevailing among the Celts and Britons were founded upon St. John and the customs of the East, but rather tried to explain why he believed St. John would at that time be in accord with the rites and customs he was advocating.

Far above all traditions, however, this point stands out with perfect historical clearness, namely, that however and by whomsoever the Church was established in Britain, there can be no doubt of its full equipment with the three orders of the ministry—bishops, priests and deacons—with its liturgy and its Church buildings by the middle or end of the second century. For example, both the "Anglo-Saxon Chronicle" and Bede write of its existence there in the second half of that century, Bede (p. 9) stating: "The Britons preserved the faith, which they had received, uncorrupted and entire, in peace and tranquillity until the time of the Emperor Diocletian." and Robertson ("History of the

Christian Church," Vol. 1, pp. 217–18) says: "The story of Joseph of Arimathea's preaching, and even the correspondence of an alleged British king, Lucius, with Eleutherius, bishop of Rome, about the year 167, need not be here discussed. Yet within about thirty years from the supposed date of that correspondence, we meet with the statement already quoted from Tertullian, that the Gospel had made its way into parts of this Island which the Romans had never reached." Mr. Geo. Park Fisher, Professor of Ecclesiastical History in Yale University, in his "History of the Christian Church," p. 89, writes: "During Constantine's reign, the Church in Britain emerges most clearly into view. We read of its being represented at the Council of Arles, in 314, by the bishops of York, London, and Lincoln. In the reign of Diocletian it was prominent enough to be the object of persecution, though protected, as far as practicable, by Constantius, the father of Constantine." He also tells us that although "the origin and development of the early British Church are involved in obscurity . . . we may safely conjecture that the Gospel was carried to Britain soon after the Romans gained a firm foothold there," which was in 84 A. D.

Let us recall too, the testimony of eminent men in other parts of the Christian world, not only as to the existence but also as to the orthodoxy and the zeal of British Christianity, which of course carries with it indisputable testimony to its existence. For instance, Justin Martyr, who died in Rome 166 A. D., bore direct and strong testimony to the zeal and orthodoxy of the British Church, and Tertullian in North Africa, about the year 193, wrote as indicated above, "For in whom else have all the nations believed but in Christ? All the coasts of Spain, various nations of Gaul and parts inaccessible to the Romans being now subject to Christ." The only parts in the West then inaccessible to the Romans were the unconquered Picts in the Highlands beyond the fortified walls of Hadrian. Thus does Tertullian show that British Christianity of the second century was so zealous in propagating the Gospel that it had made conquests where even the Roman soldiers were not able to do so. And Irenaeus, in 202, bears testimony to the vigorous life of the Church in the British Isles. He was a near neighbor, just across the Channel in Gaul, which we now know as France. And Origen, writing in 240, speaks of the "establishment of the religion of Christ in the land of Britain."

We know of course, that the Britons suffered very severely during the various persecutions of Christians by the Roman Emperors, particularly in the Diocletian persecution. One man who stands out conspicuously as a witness for Christ at that time was a converted Roman soldier named Alban. Rather than renounce his allegiance to Christ, he suffered a cruel martyrdom about the year 303. The Anglo-Saxon Chronicle puts the date as 286. It is interesting to recall that the site on which our great Cathedral is being built in Washington, D. C., is named after this Martyr of the early British Church—St. Alban's Heights—thus creating a link in sentiment as well as in historic facts and customs between the Episcopal Church in the United States in the twentieth century and the Church in Britain in the third or fourth century.

Throughout the early years of the fourth century, councils of Christians were held in various places on the Continent of Europe. Many of them, so the records go, were attended by representatives of the British Church. For example, in the year 314, in the town of Arles, an important council was held—a gathering of godly men to discuss matters of Christian faith and life. The British Church was requested as a matter of course to send representatives and she responded by sending Eborius, the Bishop of York, Restitutus, Bishop of London, Adelphius, Bishop of Caerleon. These were accompanied by Sacerdos, a priest, and Arminius, a deacon. We feel that Bishop Browne makes a fair statement concerning the representation of the British Church in the great Nicene Council when he writes: "The records of the signatures at the Council of Nicea in 325 are, as is well known, not in such a state as to enable us to say that British bishops were present. But considering their presence at Arles, the first of the Councils, and the interest of Constantine in Britain and his intimate local knowledge of its circumstances; considering, too, the very wide sweep of his invitations to the Council; it is practically certain that we were represented there." There scarcely seems to be any reasonable ground for denying it.

And another English historian writing of the Council of Nicea says, "At this assembly 318 bishops from every part of Christendom were present, and although we cannot nominate those belonging to Britain, we are informed that as soon as the representatives returned with the decisions of the Council, all the British bishops signified their agreement in a letter sent by them to their beloved ruler, and old friend, Constantine the Great."

And Wakeman, speaking of the British bishops, states: "They gave their formal assent to the decisions of the Council of Nicea 325, if they were not present in person."

In 347 in the Council of Sardica and in 359 in the Council of Ariminum the British Church was again represented. It is interesting to note that in preparation for this Council of Ariminum, a treatise of considerable importance was addressed by one of the outstanding leaders of the entire Church in that period, Hilary, Bishop of Poitiers, to the Bishops of Germany, Gaul and *Britain*. He wrote as to men thoroughly familiar with the subtle Arian heresy then dividing the Church and as to men who were wholly sound on the points in dispute. It is deeply gratifying to us to know that our fathers in the faith, the representatives of the old British Church, had such good standing in the soundness of the faith, and in purity of life and in general eminence that they, as a matter of course, were summoned to the great Councils of the Universal Church, were addressed by leading men on most important themes, and had a share in formulating the most far-reaching legislation, and in settling vital matters of Christian faith and practice.

Hence in view of these facts and many others besides, it is not surprising that in the Council of Basle in 1431, a hundred years before the Reformation,—a Council called by those within the Church on the Continent, as elsewhere, whose spirits were stirred within them by the need of reforming the lives of the popes, bishops and other clergy and people of the Church, as well as the customs and teachings of the time—the representatives of the English Church were given their place in the processions and in the seats of the Council as representatives of a Church established in Apostolic times. This then was the judgment of this general Council of the Western Church, when the question of precedence came up—that based upon the date of the founding of the Churches, the British representatives were given precedence over other Churches on the ground of their Church having been founded in Apostolic times.

CHAPTER IV

THE ORTHODOXY AND MISSIONARY ZEAL OF THE EARLY
BRITISH CHURCH

It is interesting to note also the commendation that the British Church received from the early fathers of the Church in other lands because of their unwavering orthodoxy in the faith. For instance, St. Hilary, Bishop of Poitiers, in 358 congratulated "the bishops of the province of Britain on having remained free from the detestable heresy," that is, the Arian heresy. And St. Athanasius, the great champion of the faith in the Nicene Council and in the generation following, acknowledges the British Church among those "loyal to the faith." It is very pleasing to us to know these things of our spiritual forefathers. Their zeal for orthodoxy was also manifested in clear, unmistakable terms in the fifth century, when Pelagius, a Briton who had spent several years in the city of Rome, began to propagate a false theory concerning the free will of man, making salvation a thing that depends entirely upon the human will. Edward Gibbon ("Fall and Decline of the Roman Empire," vol. 3, pp. 319–20) throws some light on conditions in the British Church from the middle of the fourth to middle of fifth century in the following words: "The British Church might be composed of thirty or forty bishops with an adequate pro-

portion of the inferior clergy; and the want of riches
(for they seem to have been poor) would compel them
to deserve the public esteem, by a decent and exemplary behavior. The interest, as well as the temper of
the clergy, was favorable to the peace and union of
their distracted country: those salutary lessons might
be frequently inculcated in their popular discourses;
and the Episcopal synods were the only councils that
could pretend to the weight and authority of a national
assembly. In such councils, where the princes and
magistrates sat promiscuously with the bishops, the important affairs of the State, as well as of the Church,
might be freely debated; differences reconciled, alliances formed, contributions imposed, wise resolutions
often concerted, and sometimes executed; and there
is reason to believe, that in moments of extreme
danger, a Pendragon, or Dictator, was elected by the
general consent of the Britons. These pastoral cares
so worthy of the Episcopal character were interrupted,
however, by zeal and superstition; and the British
clergy incessantly labored to eradicate the Pelagian
heresy which they abhorred as the peculiar disgrace
of their native country." Because of the brilliance of
Pelagius and because of his being a native of the soil,
his heresy began to spread in Britain, even as it did
in other parts of the Christian Church. The native
bishops and other clergy put forth earnest efforts to
root it out, and in combating the errors propagated by
Pelagius, they appealed for help to their sister Church
in Gaul, as was natural, because it was a near neighbor
and because also, as it is thought by many, the Gauls
in France and the Gauls in Britain were of the same

general stock, many historians teaching us, as perhaps the reader knows, that the ancient Britons were descendants of the Asiatic Gauls. Germanus, a very eloquent Bishop of Gaul, was the chief defender of the faith against Pelagianism in Britain, and with his aid and that of another man whom he brought with him, Lupus by name and Bishop of Troyes, the British bishops and clergy were able to extirpate the teachings of Pelagius.

They were not only always zealous for pure faith, but they were equally zealous in their missionary efforts. For example, we recall the sending of Ninian, or Ninias, son of a British chief, to preach the Gospel of Christ to the Scots, or as we should now say, the Irish, for the name of the Emerald Isle in those days was Scotia. He settled among them about the year 400, and labored faithfully among them, a people exceedingly barbarous. Ninian built a beautiful church at Whitehorn, which still stands, but was subsequently forced to leave by the heathen chief. We recall here these words of the Venerable Bede: "For the southern Picts, who dwell on this side of those mountains, had long before, as is reported, forsaken the errors of idolatry and embraced the truth by the preaching of Ninias, a most reverend bishop and holy man of the *British nation,* who had been regularly instructed at Rome, in the faith and mysteries of the truth; whose episcopal see, named after St. Martin the bishop, and famous for a stately church (wherein he and many other saints rest in the body), is still in existence among the English nation. The place belongs to the province of the Bernicians, and is generally called the

White House, because he there built a church of stone, which was not usual among the Britons." The Anglo-Saxon Chronicle (p. 11) also tells us that Ninias "preached baptism to the Southern Picts whose church and his monastery is at Whitherne, consecrated in the name of St. Martin; there he resteth, with many holy men. Now in Ii there must ever be an abbat, and not a bishop; and all the Scottish bishops ought to be subject to him, because Columba was an abbat and not a bishop." And Wakeman tells us: "All over the British Islands during the fifth century Christianity was making its way among the Celts, in dependence upon the individual personal gifts of great men like S. Ninian, S. Germanus, and S. Patrick. Schools were formed round great teachers, homes of a rude religious life established by great saints, churches built and bishoprics founded by great leaders. The magic of personal influence, not the strength of sturdy institutions, was the inspiring force." And very much along the same line is the statement of Bishop Boyd-Carpenter (p. 14): "I have told you how the British occupied the western part of the country; thus the regions which came to be known as West Wales, North Wales, and Strathclyde were Christian. Strathclyde was the country which reached as far as the Clyde; to the north of this were the people known as the Scots, and to the east of the Scots lived the Picts: *these people had received* Christianity *from British missionaries,* and they cherished with special reverence the name of Ninian." And Palladius, also called Patrick, was sent there later on, who also was a native of Britain to prosecute the work among the "Scots *who believed in Christ.*"

Another effort on the part of the British Church to reach out into the heathen world was the missionary work of the famous St. Patrick, whose father and grandfather were clergymen of the British Church. A few items of his personal history will undoubtedly be of interest. He was captured by the pirates and taken to the north of Ireland. After escaping from them, he was educated for the ministry in Gaul, and went back to help free those from the bondage of sin and heathen darkness by whom he had been previously imprisoned in the flesh. He landed at Wicklow in the year 432. He did a splendid work, organized a good system of Church extension in Ireland, and established monasteries for training the clergy, which became centers of education and of missionary enterprise. While some of the following facts are a little in advance chronologically yet it seems not out of place to cite here the evaluations of Patrick's work as given by Patterson and Wakeman: Patterson writes (p. 5): "But in England the British Church retired westwards, together with the Celts (its memories preserved by the ever-living legend of King Arthur): national hatred of the Saxon was so fierce that not the slightest attempt was made by the conquered Celts to win their conquerors for Christ." . . . "The British Church in England contributed nothing *directly* toward the evangelisation of the Anglo-Saxons; indirectly it did, for St. Patrick, the Apostle of Ireland, was a native of Britain, and it was from Ireland that St. Columba came to Iona in Scotland in the sixth century; and it was by missionaries from Iona in the seventh century that the larger part of England was won to the faith of Christ."

And Wakeman describes the results of Patrick's work as the Apostle of Ireland in the years that followed, up to the coming of Augustine. He says (pp. 16–17) that "he (Augustine) did not realize that he was dealing with a persecuted branch of a great Church of the North-west which might well claim to meet even the Church of the West on terms of equality. For more than a hundred years it might well be said that Catholic Christendom had been divided into three great sections—the *Church of the East, with its centre at Constantinople, the Church of the West, with its centre at Rome, and the Church of the North-west, with its centre in Ireland.* With much of barbarism, with much of undisciplined heroism, this Church of the North-west had *developed wholly apart from the influence of Rome* and unaffected for good or evil by its culture or its law. In Ireland its organization was tribal and monastic. Its strength lay in its love of learning, and in its singular power over the human will in consecrating its children absolutely to the service of God. In the sixth and seventh centuries Ireland was the island of saints and the mother of missionaries. From Ireland came S. Columba in 563 to begin, as it has been well called, the noblest missionary career ever accomplished in Britain, in the Island of Iona off the west coast of Scotland. From Ireland went S. Columban and S. Gall to carry the message of the Gospel to the remote valleys of Burgundy and Switzerland. While Rome was engaged in the intellectual struggles of theological controversy, Ireland was sending missionaries to convert the heathen at the very gates of Italy. In Wales the Celtic Church was throwing off the weakness and recovering from the degradation caused by the long struggle with the English conquerors. Organized like the Church in the East and West under territorial bishops, it too had developed, under S. David, Dubritius, and Teilo, a real and true life of its own, *wholly uninfluenced by Rome*. It had great schools of learning at Bangor Iscoed and elsewhere. As in Cornwall, it produced a vast number of local saints, built churches, and hallowed sites in a way which shows it to have had a strong hold over its people. A Church like this, conscious of its own vigour, would naturally resent a claim of foreign authority which treated it as barbarous, and cling to its own customs as part and parcel of its history and methods, however imperfect they might be." And that is exactly what happened when Augustine made his demand on the British bishops for obedience to him and the pope, and for acceptance of Roman customs. We quote here from "The Church in These Islands before Augustine"—Browne, pp. 121–124: "The Scottish accounts make Palladius the founder of Christianity among the Picts in the east of Scotland, Forfarshire and Kincardineshire and thereabouts, Meigle being their capital for a long time. They are silent as to any connection with Ireland. They are without exception late and unauthentic, whatever may be the historical value of the matter which has been imported into them. But all, Scottish and Irish, agree in assigning to the work of Palladius in Ireland either no existence in fact, or at most, a short period and a small result. The way was thus left clear for another

mission. The man who took up the work made a
very different mark upon it.

"I shall not discuss the asserted mission from Rome
of St. Patrick, for we have his own statements about
himself. Palladius was called also Patrick, and to him,
not to the Great Patrick, the story of the mission from
Rome applies.

"Some time after the death of Celestine and the ter-
mination of Palladius's work in Ireland, Patrick commenced his missionary labours; and when he died in
or about 493, he left Christianity permanently established over a considerable part of the Island. That is
the great fact for our present purpose, and I shall
go into no details. It is a very interesting coincidence
that exactly at the period when Christianity was being
obliterated in Britain, it was being planted in large
areas in Ireland; and that, too,—by a Briton. For
after all has been said that can be said against the
British origin of Patrick, the story remains practically
undisturbed. It is, I think, of great importance to
note and bear in mind the fact that Ireland was Christianized just at the time when it was cut off from
communication with the civilized world and the Christian Church in Europe. Britain became a mere arena
of internecine strife, the Picts and Scots from the
north, and the Jutes and Saxons and Angles from
the east and south obliterating civilization and Christianity, and Britain, thus barbarously tortured, was a
complete barrier between the infant Church in Ireland
and the wholesome lessons and developments which
intercourse with the Church on the Continent would

have naturally given. Patrick, if we are to accept his own statements, was not a man of culture; he was probably very provincial in his knowledge of Christian practices and rites; a rude form of Christian worship and order was likely to be the result of his mission. He was indeed the son of a member of the town council who was also a deacon—it sounds very Scotch; he was the grandson of a priest; his father had a small farm. But he was a native of a rude part of the Island. And his bringing up was rude. He was carried off captive to Ireland at the age of sixteen years, and kept sheep there for six years, when he escaped to Britain. After some years, he determined to take the lessons of Christianity to the people who had made him their slave. The people whom he Christianized were themselves rude; not likely to raise their ecclesiastical conceptions higher than the standard their Apostle set; more likely to fall short of that standard. In isolation the infant Church passsed on towards fuller growth; developing itself on the lines laid down; accentuating the rudeness of its earliest years; with no example but its own!"

The Coming of the Jutes, Angles and Saxons and the Effect on the British Church

This brings us to the middle of the fifth century, that is about 450. At this time we see the British Church thoroughly equipped—with Apostolic Orders, with an established liturgy, and a people devoted to orthodoxy in the faith, pious in their lives, and vigorous in their missionary zeal, absolutely free from any outside government; but at the same time recognizing the sisterhood of all national churches, appealing for help, for instance, to the Gallican Church when there was need of such aid. But evil times were now at hand. The Roman army had taken the flower of the British youth out of the land. There were left in the British Isles only the older men and those too young to have had military experience. Invasions from the North by the barbarous Picts and Scots threatened, and even had begun. The British kings appealed to the Roman Emperor for aid in protecting their land. The Emperor was too much engaged with his own troubles, too much absorbed by his own wars to pay heed to local difficulties, and therefore the Britons were compelled to turn to other sources for the necessary help to drive off their invading foes. And in despair, Vortigern, one of the British kings, invited a band of warriors from Jutland, which we now know as Denmark, promising to give them certain grants of land if they were successful in aiding them in their effort to drive away the Northmen. The Jutes came under two brothers, Hengist and Horsa in 449, and the northern enemies were defeated by the allied Jutes and Britons. The Jutes, however, were not satisfied with what they had received, and demanded more. Upon their demands being refused, they took what they desired by force, but not without stubborn resistance from the Britons. And after a short time, the Jutes passed the word to their neighbors, the Saxons, who learned of the fertile land and the opportunity to secure what they desired, and came in force in 477. These in turn were followed by their neighbors, the

Angles, who came in 547. These three tribes, Jutes, Saxons and Angles, kept pushing the native inhabitants farther and farther into the West until at last, after about 150 years, the native Britons were forced to occupy Wales as the land of their habitation. It must not be supposed, however, that these invading hordes had an easy time in driving out the Britons. The natives resisted stubbornly, and the historian Green tells us that "No land was ever held more persistently than ancient Britain, and no invasion ever met with more stubborn resistance than that offered the Northmen by the Britons." Of course, we remember that all of these invaders, Jutes, Saxons and Angles were heathen. They not only took delight in driving out the people and possessing their land, but also in destroying their churches and their religion. Many bishops and priests of the British Church were slain at the altar. And at the end of the sixth century we see the ancient British Church on the west coast of Britain and in Wales and Ireland with a great wall of heathenism between it and its sister churches on the Continent. Wakeman after telling of the invasions of Britain (450–600) and their devastating effects, and reminding us that the British and Celts were driven back into the narrow limits of the West goes on to say: "Toward the close of the sixth century the work was complete. Celtic Christianity had been driven out of sight and almost out of mind over five-sixths of the country. The worship of the powers of nature under the personifications of Woden, of Freia, and of Thor, had succeeded to the worship of Christ, and the days of the

English week are still left to prove how completely the old civilization had passed away."

Just so soon, however, as the British Church was able to recover from the effects of these barbarous wars, it began immediately to establish centers of missionary enterprise. And as the result about 500 A. D. she established the monastery at Llandaff, at Bangor in 516 and St. Asaph, 540. Those episcopal sees and monasteries not only preserved the continuous line of bishops and clergy of the early British Church, but became centers of education, of Church life and of missionary enterprise. In the latter part of the sixth century the British Church showed signs of energy and zeal. They had famous bishops, Dubritius of Llandaff, and Dewi, or David, of St. David's. Study was pursued in colleges or monasteries. Synods were held, and missionary work was undertaken. But it was to Ireland, and not to the Heptarchy, that their missionaries went.

Bede (pp. 67 and 68) tells us, for instance, about the great monastery of Bangor, mother and grandmother of Iona and Lindisfarne, of which he says: "It is reported that there was so great a number of monks that the monastery was divided into seven parts, with a ruler of each, and none of these parts contained less than 300 men who all lived by the labor of their hands." From such strongholds of the ancient Church men like Columba went forth to preach the Gospel in lands we know as Ireland and Scotland and established such offshoots as Iona and Lindisfarne, which in turn became great centers of Christian light and missionary activities. These sees, monasteries and other establishments constitute stones laid in the solid foundation of fact as stated, for instance, by Mr. H. H. Asquith, one time Prime Minister and for so many years one of England's leading and most learned statesmen who in the House of Commons, March 21, 1895, said: "I am not one of those who think . . . that the legislation of Henry the VIII transferred the privileges and endowments . . . from the Church of Rome to the Church of England. I believe that view rests upon imperfect historical information. I am quite prepared to admit, what I believe the *best authorities of history* now assert, *that there has been amidst all these changes and developments a substantial identity and continuity of existence* in our national Church from earliest history down *to the present time.*" We can but ask, when thoughtful, well-read men of high reputation outside of the Episcopal Church freely make such statements, why should loyal sons of the Church seek to deny them or belittle their force and significance?

Some of the results obtained by the activities of the British Christians and their settlement in their new centers will be shown in the next chapter.

CHAPTER V

THE COMPARATIVE FAILURE OF THE ITALIAN MISSIONARIES UNDER AUGUSTINE

At the close of the last chapter, we saw that the ancient British Church with a well supported reputation for being founded in Apostolic times, with a thoroughly established name for orthodoxy in the faith and for zeal in missionary enterprise was cruelly driven from a large part of its own soil by the heathen barbarians from the North, from Jutland and from northwest Germany; but we also beheld the noble faith, splendid loyalty and indomitable courage that were hers still, and how she renewed her efforts in behalf of the faith, sending out continuous bands of missionaries, her children and grandchildren, to the heathen in the North.

It is easily understood that she was estopped, for a while at least, from sending missionaries to the Jute, Anglian and Saxon Tribes. These were thoroughly intractable foes. They despised the religion of the Britons, and would not listen to anything that they had to say. And therefore with clear, practical wisdom, the Britons perceived that their efforts would be more effective among those tribes of the North with whom they had not been at war. And consequently, it was in that direction that they moved at this time in expressing their

missionary zeal. Their situation was quite different from
that of the later Italian Missionaries in Kent who made
no effort at all to reach their nearest neighbors in Sussex who were in no state of enmity toward them.
Partisans of the Roman missionaries should remember
this when they chide the old British Christians for not
attempting immediately to evangelize their heathen
foes.

First, St. Finian of St. David's Monastery went forth
into Ireland. Then St. Columba of Bangor went into
Scotland and established a monastery on the Island of
Iona. As we have written above, this Christian establishment became a lighthouse of Christianity to Northern
Scotland and the smaller islands around it. "In every
highland valley, some one from this place became a
witness for Christ. Even Iceland was not considered
too long and dangerous a voyage for their little boats
to make." And on the northeast coast a few miles from
the river Tweed, another center of Gospel light and
of extensive activities was established by Aidan, a prod-
uct of Iona, this new establishment being called Lindisfarne. From these two centers, Iona and Lindisfarne,
went forth the men who broke down that heathen wall
that separated the ancient British-Celtic Church and her
sister churches on the Continent. This then was the
situation at the end of the sixth century. The Britons
had been driven out of their country—all the land we
now know as England—by fierce pagan foes. They had
retired to the West, chiefly to Wales. Their Church
went with them. They re-established it in their new
home and soon began to found monasteries, centers
of light and fountains of missionary activity, sending

their missionaries to Ireland and Scotland and establishing Christian foundations there. Now between them and the Church on the Continent was this multitude of heathen dwelling in England or Angles' Land. It was now the duty of the Christian world on both sides to demolish this wall of paganism and flood the land with the light of the Cross. The problem was attacked from both sides. To the lasting credit of Gregory the First, surnamed the Great, Bishop of Rome, he sent in the year 597 a man named Augustine with forty companion monks to Britain, to break down that wall of heathenism of which we have spoken, and to connect British Christianity with Continental Christianity. It was a worthy purpose. They made their effort, but as we shall see, they failed to accomplish the thing whereunto they were sent. This does not mean that they did no good or got no results, *but failed to accomplish their purpose,* namely, to Christianize the inhabitants of England and so break down that wall of heathenism that separated the old Church of these Islands from the fellowship of the Church on the Continent. When Augustine and his companions arrived, they went immediately to the county of Kent, whose Queen, Bertha, was a Christian and had married Ethelbert, King of the Jutes in Kent, on the condition that she should be permitted to continue the exercise of the Christian religion. He found in Canterbury, the center of the kingdom of Kent, an old church, built probably in 300 A. D., one of the few old British Churches that had not been destroyed by the heathen invaders. "Bede's Ecclesiastical History" (p. 37) contains this description of it: "There was on the east side of the city a church dedicated to the

honour of St. Martin, built whilst the Romans were
still in the island, wherein the queen, who, as has been
said before, was a Christian, used to pray. In this they
first began to meet, to sing, to pray, to say mass, to
preach, and to baptize, till the king, being converted to
the faith, allowed them to preach openly, and build or
repair churches in all places." He also gives the following account of the reclaiming of another old church in
Canterbury: "Augustine having his episcopal see
granted him in the royal city, as has been said, and
being supported by the king, recovered therein a church
which he was informed had been built by the ancient
Roman Christians, and consecrated it in the name of
our holy Saviour, God and Lord, Jesus Christ, and
there established a residence for himself and his successors. He also built a monastery not far from the
city to the eastward, in which by his advice, Ethelbert
erected from the foundation the church of the blessed
Apostles, Peter and Paul, and enriched it with several
donations; wherein the bodies of the same Augustine,
and of all the bishops of Canterbury, and of the kings
of Kent, might be buried. However, Augustine himself
did not consecrate that church, but Laurentius, his
successor." Canon Robt. C. Jenkins, Canon of Canterbury Cathedral, in his history of the Church in Canterbury (Diocesan History series, p. 15) writes: "The
endowment of the Church of Britain with real property
was probably as early as that of any of the western
churches. The 'quieta pax,' which the Church is said to
have enjoyed until the days of Diocletian, must have
greatly facilitated this kind of donation; and it is not
unreasonable to believe that the appropriation to Chris-

tianity of the temples and even the basilicas of the older worship, carried with it the possession of the lands connected with them, which on the Saxon conquest were reoccupied by a new form of idolatry, and became for the most part the residences of the Kentish kings. The remarkable surrender of all these residences one after another to the Church, made from the time of Ethelbert, would stand almost alone in history, were it not for the supposition that it was *rather a restitution of* what had *originally belonged to the Church* than an actual endowment de novo."

In Kent, Augustine found also the Bishop, Luidhard by name, and the old British liturgy which was different in many minor points from the liturgy used in the Church of Rome, showing again different origins of the Church in Britain and the Church in Italy. We take this interesting passage from Browne's "Augustine and His Companions" (pp. 16–17) : "We learn from a passage in Procopius, quoted by Mr. Freeman in his 'Norman Conquest,' that in the time of the Emperor Justinian, who reigned from 527 to 565, the king of the Franks sent an embassy to the Emperor at Constantinople. The embassy consisted of some of the Franks near the king's person; and along with them he sent some of the Angles, assuming the air of over-lord of their island. Now Eulogius became patriarch of Alexandria in 579, having for some considerable time previously been the head of the monastery of the Deipara at Antioch. He was no doubt often in Constantinople in the time of Justinian; indeed, as he became patriarch eleven years before Gregory became pope of Rome, and Gregory was born about 540, Eulogius may well have been in Constantinople at the time of the Fifth General Council in 553. Thus it is very possible that Eulogius saw and conversed with the Angles who went on the Frankish embassy, and talked about them to Gregory, when he made his acquaintance some years later at Constantinople, either before or soon after 579. Gregory himself was in residence at Constantinople as representative of the pope within twelve or thirteen years of Justinian's death. Eulogius, as we know from Gregory's letters, was deeply interested in missions to the heathen. Thus many reasons combine to suggest that here we have the really first impulse towards the creation of the English Church. If that be so, then not the *British* Church only, but the *English* Church too, owes itself to the East, looks to the foundation-land of Christianity. And if we put the Frankish embassy late in the reign of Justinian—early it could not well be—it may be that just when young Ethelbert came to the throne, and tried his wings against Wessex, and sent to the nearest Frankish king for a wife, just at that very time the Providence of God was laying in Constantinople the train which in process of time sent Augustine to the king of Kent."

Augustine finding the ancient British Church with its fully organized ministry and all of its thoroughly established Christian customs and works, entered into correspondence with Gregory for directions as to how he should treat the Christian bishops and clergy and laity he found already in Britain. He asks, "Why should there be *different liturgies* in use in Gaul and Britain from those in Rome? How are we to act toward the bishops of Gaul and Britain?" Gregory replied:

"We assign no authority to you over the bishops of Gaul, but we commit all the bishops of Britain to you, my brother, that the unlearned may be taught, the infirm strengthened by persuasion, and the perverse corrected by authority." As has been noted by another, this advice was a most unwarrantable assumption of authority on Gregory's part and a breach of the decrees of the General Council of Ephesus A. D. 431, which stipulated that "no bishop shall occupy another province which has not been subject to him from the beginning," and none of Gregory's predecessors had ever asserted any supremacy over the British Church.

Augustine invited the British bishops to meet him in what is known as the "Synod of the Oak," because they met under the spreading branches of an oak tree. Augustine's avowed object in calling the meeting was to ask the Britons to unite their forces with his in the conversion of the Angles, but they began first to discuss other questions as, "When should Easter Day be kept?" because the British Church had followed the Eastern method of observing Easter and not the Roman. And there was also the question of the triple immersion in Baptism, and the manner of tonsure, the Roman monks cutting their hair in the form of a crown, and the Britons wearing theirs in the shape of a crescent. They discussed these questions for a while and then decided to meet again. The British bishops did not know just what to do—whether they should give up their customs and accept those brought by Augustine, so putting themselves in harmony with what was done by the churches on the Continent. In their perplexity they sought the advice of one of their old pious recluses who replied to them: "If Augustine be a man of God, follow him." The British bishops then asked, "How can we ascertain this?" He replied in this fashion, "The Lord saith, 'Take my yoke upon you and learn of Me, for I am meek and lowly in heart.' If, therefore, this Augustine is meek and lowly in heart, it is credible that both he himself bears the yoke of Christ and offers it to you to bear; but if he is stern and proud, it is evident that he is not of God, and that his discourse ought not to be regarded by us." Then the bishops asked: "How can we know this?" and the recluse replied, "Contrive that he and his people may come first to the place of the synod, and if at your approach, he rise up to you, hear him with submission, knowing that he is a servant of Christ, but if he slight you and will not rise up in your presence, when you are more in number, let him also be disregarded by you." Unfortunately or fortunately, as the case may be, Augustine and his companions assumed a haughty demeanor, and when the British delegates arrived, they did not arise. This was enough. The British bishops and their learned companions from the monastery of Bangor concluded that they did not have the spirit of Christ, and therefore would have nothing to do with them. Dinooth, one of the British bishops, declared that they "owed fraternal love to the Church of God and the bishops of Rome and indeed to all Christians, but that they acknowledged no obedience to him whom Augustine called pope." Each Church, British and Italian, went its own way, each to do its own work as best it could.

While the Italian missionaries made some headway in several of the kingdoms, their work was soon undone by heathen reactions, and the missionaries fled to the Continent, with the exception of Laurentius, who remained in the kingdom of Kent. All of the other kingdoms in what we now know as England were now heathen, and this one kingdom of Kent was only partially Christian. Let us now review the evaluation of Augustine's work as given by reliable historians. Bishop G. F. Browne writes: ("Before the Coming of Augustine" p. 7), "The history of the Italian Mission is a history of failure to face danger." And on p. 135, "Thirty-seven years after Columba's death his successors did that for the Northumbrian Angles which the successors of *Augustine* had *failed* to do." And further, this statement from "Augustine and His Companions" (p. 189): "The Christian labors of Augustine and his companions had to show as their actual geographical result the little kingdom of Kent alone. There were many stirrings of Christianity in other parts of the land, and the East Angles were once more Christian, but none of that work was done or was being done from Kent."

Green also makes this statement: "It was not the Church of Paulinus which nerved Oswald to this struggle for the Cross, or which carried out in Bernicia the work of conversion which his victory began. Paulinus fled from Northumbria at Eadwine's fall, and the Roman Church, though established in Kent, did *little* in contending *elsewhere* against the heathen reaction. Its place in the conversion of Northern England was taken by missionaries from Ireland." It is well to remember, also, that Augustine did not *introduce* Christianity even into Kent. He *found* it there. He did much, as we all know, to spread it but he was not the *first* to take it there. Mr. Jenkins, in his "History of the Diocese of Canterbury," says: "To this extraordinary woman [that is, Bertha, wife of Ethelbert, King of Kent], St. Gregory the Great attributes a large share in the conversion of Kent." And other historians likewise point out the large influence that was exercised by Bertha and Luidhart in preparing the way for Augustine and his companions.

Wakeman writes: "In 604, he [that is, Augustine], died, leaving as the practical results of his life the establishment of the Church in Kent and the planting of a mission outpost among the East Saxons in London." And Patterson, although crediting the Roman Mission with "doing much," a rather strong term, if we consider *permanent* results, tells us that: "It is to the Scotch more than to the Romans that we owe the conversion of the English people. It was by the Celtic missionaries from Iona who settled at Lindisfarne that the greater part of England was won for Christ. The century that follows their coming was the most brilliant in the ecclesiastical history of England." Bishop Boyd-Carpenter informs us: "And now came the time which was to try the new work. Penda was the King of Mercia, and joined his forces with Cadwallon, King of the Britons in the West, and attacked Edwin. Edwin was defeated with great loss at Hatfield Chase, A. D. 633. Edwin fell and with him, the work of Paulinus. Paulinus fled to the South, and the Christian faith was for the time crushed out in Northumbria and Mercia. Everywhere heathenism triumphed, and so it came to pass that within forty years of the arrival of Augustine the only place in which his followers held their own was in the Kingdom of Kent." . . . "Thus the Island was practically brought into the Christian faith, the influence of the Roman mission being strongest in the kingdoms of Kent and of the West Saxons, *Celtic* and *British* influence prevailing in all other parts of the country."

Stubbs, in his "Constitutional History of England," (p. 237), says: "The *comparative failure* of the Kentish Mission after the death of Ethelbert and the fact that each of the seven kingdoms owed its evangelization to a different source must have rendered the success of Gregory's scheme problematical from the very first." And on p. 239 Stubbs, writing of the time of Theodore, said: "Roman Christianity had passed away from eastern Britain, leaving few and indistinct traces. . . . The positive paganism of the Anglo-Saxons was, as far as concerns its mythology and ritual, in the most attenuated condition. Scarcely was Christianity presented to them by the seventh century missions when they embraced it with singular fidelity and singleness of heart." The "seventh century" missions, of course, refer to those that had their source and inspiration in Iona and Lindisfarne, children of the British-Celtic Church.

Yet another witness to the same effect is Cutts' "Handbook of English Church History" (pp. 335–6). "The Augustinian Mission was not a *permanently successful* one. It lingered on with various vicissitudes until the time of Honorius. He died in the year 655 and was the last survivor of bishops who traced their orders to Augustine. In time, the Augustinian succession, never large, died completely out." We quote from

Dr. Browne: "As the weary old Italian, Bishop Honorius, slowly dying at Canterbury, looked forth upon the field that had been entrusted to his predecessors, he saw it covered with Christian laborers, but not of his *sending,* the *ministers of a Church not his.* Of all the seven kingdoms there was only one, namely, Kent, which owed its conversion to the mission of Augustine. Of 26 counties in Britain there was only one of which it can be said that it owed its permanent conversion to the mission of Augustine. With few exceptions, England owed its final and permanent conversion to the labors of the Scotic Church," which was the offspring of the old British Church. Finally, let us add these words of another as a very good summary: "Thus the knowledge of the Christian faith had, before the English came, extended over the whole of that part of this island which the English invaders in their furthermost reach ever occupied. It had covered—and it continued to cover, and has never ceased to cover—very much that they never even touched. To convert the early English to Christ, which was the task undertaken by Augustine, a very small part of it being accomplished by him or his mission from first to last, was to restore Christianity to those parts from which the English had driven it out. It was to remove the barrier of heathendom which the English invaders had formed between the Church universal and the Celtic and British Church or Churches. It proved in the end that the undertaking was much beyond the powers of the Italian missionaries; and then the earlier Church stepped in from its confines in the West and did the work."

At this point it will be appropriate and clarifying to

show more pointedly and fully the recognition by trustworthy scholars of the essential connection between the Church in ancient Britain and the Church in Ireland and Scotland, making what has been called the British-Celtic Church. For some meticulous hairsplitters of technicalities may attempt to separate the British and Celtic (early Irish and Scotch Churches) as if they had no connection with each other and endeavor to dissociate the original British Church from the evangelization of the Anglo-Saxons. Such is neither accurate nor fair, for no reliable historian can deny that the original Christianity in the British Isles was what is known as the old British Church. It is equally well established that that Church was driven to the West by the invading Jutes, Angles and Saxons and that this Church sent its missionaries to Ireland or Scotia, and to the Picts of the North or Scotland. The Celtic Church is a child of the British Church. And the *English* Church, notwithstanding what might be said about the Italian missionaries, is the grandchild coming through missionary activities from the centers established by the ancient British Church, particularly St. David's of Menevia, Dubritius of Llandaff and Kentigern of St. Asaph and Daniel of Bangor, just as the Episcopal Church in this country is really the Anglican Church transplanted to the American Continent, and the Dioceses of Tokyo and Osaka are the grandchildren of the same Anglican Church.

In regard to this point, let us call the attention of the reader to these words from the new Schaff-Herzog Encyclopedia of Religious Knowledge, Vol. II, p. 471. "As a result of the foregoing argument, the origin and

early history of the Celtic Church in Ireland seems to
be as follows: Christianity was brought to Ireland from
Britain during the fourth century as a natural outcome
of the close intercourse between southwest Britain and
southeast Ireland." And again on p. 472: "From
statements made by Bede we know that a Briton named
Nynia (St. Ninian) founded a monastery on the pen-
insula of Wigtown, in the extreme southwest of Scotland, about 400, and thence spread Christianity among
the Picts south of the Grampians." On p. 477 the writer
concluded that article, as follows: "Concerning institutions and doctrine, neither tradition nor history offers
any support to the view that the Celtic Church in its
prime almost reproduced the Church of the Apostolic
Age. The British Church of the fourth century was a
part of the Catholic Church of the West, just as Britain
was a part of the Roman Empire. And the *Irish* Church
was an *off-shoot* of the British Church."

The author of the article in Schaff-Herzog quotes
frequently Haddan and Stubbs, whom we suppose all
are willing to accept as knowing something about the
English Church. When, therefore, the British Church
is spoken of as the agency by which the Anglo-Saxon
kingdoms were brought to Christianity it is meant, not
that it was done *directly* by the British Church in its
first establishment in Wales and the West after the
Britons were driven from their native soil, but through
establishments that they effected, and through which
channels the life of the old British Church was continued. The Encyclopedia Britannica contains these
pertinent words: "In the beginning of the fourth
century there was an organized Christian Church in

Britain; and in view of the intimate relations existing between Wales and Ireland during that century it is safe to conclude that there were Christians in Ireland before the time of St. Patrick. Returned colonists from South Wales, traders and the raids of the Irish in Britain with the consequent influx of British captives sold into slavery must have introduced the knowledge of Christianity into the Island considerably before 400 A. D." And Bede, we remember, states that at that time "Palladius was sent to the Scots that *were Christians*."

How interesting are these words addressed to the Welsh Bishops by the present Bishop of London a few years ago. They are doubly valuable because they contain the judgment, not of himself alone, but also of a former Archbishop. "And I cannot conclude better than in the noble words of Archbishop Benson, which I heard myself at the Rhyl Congress: 'But to you, who are our *eldest selves, fountain* of our episcopacy, the very designers of our sanctuaries, the *primeval British dioceses,* from whom our very realm derives its only title to be called by its proudest name of Great Britain, I come from the steps of the chair of Augustine, *your younger ally,* to tell you that, by the benediction of God, we will not quietly see you disinherited.' "

In an account of the Anglo-Catholic Congress held in London in July, 1925, we find the following in the English correspondence to The Living Church, Milwaukee: "Among the many interesting experiences of the Eastern ecclesiastics, who are our guests, the visit to the ancient Cathedral of St. David's in Wales is probably the most memorable. According to tradition, St.

David was consecrated to his archbishopric by the then patriarch of Jerusalem. As the Saint lived when Palestine was still a province of the Empire of the East, there is nothing improbable in his pilgrimage, nor in his recognition by the patriarch when he arrived there. The story was used as a strong argument by the last champions of the old Celtic Church against the right, either of Canterbury or Rome, to deprive St. David's of her ancient liberties. The Archbishop of Wales, who welcomed the Eastern prelates, gave a fascinating sketch of the Welsh Church which he described as the *oldest branch of the Catholic Church* in Britain. He went on to say that for the first time in the history of the Christian Church the prelates of the East had been able to hold converse with the *lineal successors* of those who took counsel with their own predecessors at Arles, Nicea, and Ariminum."

These words from Robertson, Vol. III, p. 13, are pertinent to this point : "In the conversion of the Anglo-Saxons two rival agencies were concerned—that of the Irish or Scottish, and that of the Roman party. Some of the differences as to usage between the Roman missionaries and the native clergy have already been mentioned, among them the variations as to the time of Easter, produced by the adhesion of the Britons to a cycle which at Rome had long been obsolete." British and Celts are, in a fashion, identified, the terms being used interchangeably, as Anglican and Episcopalian are sometimes used to-day.

The same usage of language is found in the articles in the International Encyclopedia under the head of the Church of England. "Largely by means of Irish and

Scotch missionaries (among whom were Columba, Aidan, and Finan) and of Mercians and Saxons, commissioned by Irish born enthusiasts, the Church had been planted more or less firmly in all the English kingdoms. At this time there was no national unity—no one Kingdom of England. Likewise there had not been as yet in the Church any fusion of the *British* and Roman parties, each of them maintaining with great tenacity its own ecclesiastical uses."

Wakeman on p. 6 says: "As the century progressed and the heathen Franks overran Gaul and the heathen Saxon tribes from North Germany made their way into Britain this separation became complete. *The Catholic Church* in the West became practically split up *into two great sections*. One of these had its center at Rome, drew its inspiration from the culture and discipline of the imperial city, its strength from the traditions of an Apostolic see, and exercised an influence none the less real, because often fitful and resented, over her barbarian conquerors throughout Western Europe. The other, *driven back to the islands* and hills of Ireland, Scotland, and Celtic England developed singular powers of personal saintliness and missionary self-sacrifice among her uncultured and undisciplined children. The Romano-British Church then was predominantly Celtic and its poverty may be inferred from the poverty of the British bishops who attended the Council of Ariminum," although Gibbon tells us that many were in better condition than these particular bishops. (Vol. 11, pp. 319–20.)

Boyd-Carpenter tells us: "Thus Columba, who had labored for a generation in the North, died in the very year that Augustine commenced his mission in the South; and when the current of missionary work from the South was driven back from Northumbria and Mercia the Christian zeal of the North, which owed its origin to the Irish missionaries and *through them to the British,* was awake. Devoted men, whose names are worth remembering, worked in Northumbria and carrying on their labors reconquered the hearts of Englishmen for Christ" (p. 29). And he further says:

"We have now almost completed our task. We have seen how the thin streamlet of Christian faith which owed its outlet to the labors of those unknown teachers who first brought Christianity to our shores grew in volume and spread in all directions till the whole land was refreshed by its waters. We have seen how this spreading Christian faith was checked by opposition and exposed to vicissitudes. We have seen how it was driven with the defeat of the British into narrower limits; we have seen also that the faith which once began to flow was never wholly stayed; but even in the times of greatest weakness opened new channels into the neighboring lands. We have seen how from the West, North and South fresh energy came till at length Christianity once more overspread the land and the conversion of England was as complete as the conversion of Britain" (p. 482). Of course, every historical student knows that Aidan, Cedd and Columba, etc., all came from Iona and Lindisfarne, but they also ought to know that they themselves came out of the missionary activities of the old British Church, as we have so clearly seen above.

Before passing on to consider in the next chapter how the various parts of England were brought to the knowledge of Christ, it may be well for us to repeat that at the close of the sixth century, about 150 years after the first invasion of the heathen tribes from the North, the ancient Church is seen through its various centers to be alive with the desire to carry Christianity unto those who had it not, and that it was *existing and* working *without any over-lordship from the outside*. And historians generally agree that at this time "there is nothing in history to show that any bishop in or from the city of Rome had the right to assume the title of universal bishop or claim any authority over other bishops outside of his own province." And we remember that anyone who assumed such a title was termed "Anti-Christ," by one of their own number, Gregory I, called The Great, and one of the best and purest bishops that ever occupied the see of Rome. These are the words he used: "And who is he that usurps this uncanonical dignity? The prelate of a see repeatedly ruled by heretics, by Nestorians, by Macedonians. Let all Christian hearts reject the *blasphemous* name. It was once applied by the Council of Chalcedon, in honor of St. Peter, to the Bishop of Rome, but the more humble pontiffs of Rome would not assume a title injurious to the rest of the priesthood. I am but the servant of those priests who live as become their order. But 'pride goes before a fall': and God resisteth the proud, but giveth grace to the humble.

"To the Empress (for on all religious questions the Empress is usually addressed as well as the Emperor)

Gregory brands the presumption of John as a sign of the coming of Anti-Christ. He uses these very strong terms: 'No one in the Church has yet *sacrilegiously* dared to usurp the name of Universal Bishop. *Whosoever calls himself Universal Bishop is Anti-Christ.*'" (Milman's "Latin Christianity," Vol. II, p. 72.)

We wonder how the supporters of Papal infallibility construe this. This seems but simple reasoning: If Gregory the Great, one of the really true, pious and pure men who have been bishops of Rome, gave it as his judgment that any bishop who claimed to have authority over other bishops outside of his province was Anti-Christ, then either he was mistaken and the claim of infallibility fails, or the long line of Hildebrandine popes have been anathematized by him as Anti-Christ. We recall that the manner of salutation of other bishops by Gregory is in accord with what he wrote to the Empress. For example, he commences the epistle that he wrote to Virgilius, Bishop of Arles, in this way: "To his most reverend and holy brother and *fellow bishop,* Vergilius; Gregory, servant of the servants of God." And the opening salutation in his letter to Augustine is: "To his most reverend and holy brother and *fellow bishop,* Augustine; Gregory, the servant of the servants of God."

We are glad to acknowledge our full debt of gratitude to the noble-hearted, fine-spirited Gregory for his attitude toward the Anglo-Saxons, and to express due appreciation of the efforts of Augustine and his companions, but we must also be true to the old British-Celtic Christian heroes and missionaries such a Ninias, Patrick, Columba, Columbanus, Fursey, Aidan, Cedd, etc. And we must be loyal to the facts of the record in our evaluation of their work and our inheritance from them. In our next chapter we shall proceed to show how the several Saxon Kingdoms were converted to Christianity.

CHAPTER VI

THE CONVERSION OF THE SAXON KINGDOMS BY THE BRITISH—CELTIC CHURCH

We recall that when considering the missionary zeal of the old British Church we illustrated the same by the going of Ninian or Ninias, son of a British Chief, to preach the Gospel of Christ to the Irish about the year 400 and that later, about 432, the famous St. Patrick, both son and grandson of clergymen of the old British Church, went also to the Emerald Isle and became its great Apostle.

Then a very famous son of this Irish Church, Columba, founded a noble monastery at Iona which became a radiant center of Christian light, and the mother of many other like settlements in both Ireland and Scotland. Bede tells the story in the following words (p. 108) : "In the year of our Lord 565, when Justin, the younger, the successor of Justinian, had the government of the Roman Empire, there came into Britain a famous priest and abbat, monk by habit and life, whose name was Columba, to preach the Word of God to the provinces of the Northern Picts, who are separated from the southern parts by steep and rugged mountains ; for the Southern Picts, who dwell on this side of those mountains, had long before, as it is reported, forsaken the errors of idolatry, and embraced the truth, by the preaching of Ninias, a most reverend bishop and holy man of the *British nation,* who had been regularly instructed at Rome, in the faith and mysteries of the truth; whose episcopal see, named after St. Martin the bishop, and famous for a stately church (wherein he and many other saints rest in the body), is still in existence among the English nation. The place belongs to the province of the Bernicians, and is generally called the White House, because he there built a church of stone, which was not usual among the Britons." Wakeman reminds us that "From Ireland came S. Columba in 563, to begin, as it has been well called, the noblest missionary career ever accomplished in Britian, in the Island of Iona off the West coast of Scotland. From Ireland went S. Columban and S. Gall to carry the message of the Gospel to the remote valleys of Burgundy and Switzerland. While Rome was engaged in the intellectual struggles of theological controversy, Ireland was sending missionaries to convert the heathen at the very gates of Italy. In Wales the Celtic Church was throwing off the weakness and recovering from the degradation caused by the long struggle with the English conquerors. Organized like the Church in the East and West under territorial bishops, it too had developed, under S. David, Dubricius, and Teilo, a real and true life of its own, *wholly uninfluenced by Rome*. It had great schools of learning at Bangor Iscoed and elsewhere. As in Cornwall, it produced a vast number of local saints, built churches, and hallowed sites in a way which shows it to have had a strong hold over its people. A Church like this, conscious of its own vigour, would naturally resent a claim of foreign authority which treated it as barbarous, and cling to its own customs as part and parcel of its history and methods however imperfect they might be" (pp. 16–17). (Exactly what happened when Augustine tried to dominate the British bishops.)

Patterson (p. 19) remarks thus concerning Columba's work: "The type of Christianity which he established at Iona was Irish, and in striking *contrast with that of Rome.*" It became an inspiringly active and Heaven-blessed missionary center thirty years before Augustine landed in Britain. The most famous and productive off-shoot of Iona was the monastery at Lindisfarne. These two monasteries became the great centers from which the missionaries went who won permanently the greater part of England for Christ.

Let us now see how these British-Celtic Christians went into the various kingdoms in which the Italian missionaries and teachers had been unable to establish a *permanent* work, as well as into those parts unvisited by the Roman brethren. We shall see also that wherever the representatives of the British-Celtic Church went their missions were permanent. First then let us follow them into

East Anglia

Sigebert or Sigberct had now become King of East Anglia. He had embraced the Christian faith while he was an exile in Gaul, and desired to have all of his subjects share in its benefits. Consequently he asked a Burgundian bishop, called Felix, to come into East Anglia and help. Honorius, Archbishop of Canterbury, having also urged him, he came and set earnestly to work. He was greatly assisted in his undertaking by Fursey, a monk belonging to a noble family of Scots, who came with a little band of laborers from Ireland and so captivated the people by his earnest preaching that the Christian faith at once took a firmer root than it had ever done before among the Anglo-Saxon tribes. Bede thus describes the effectiveness of Fursey's work (p. 132): "Whilst Sigebert still governed the kingdom, there came out of Ireland a holy man called Fursey renowned both for his words and actions, and remarkable for singular virtues, being desirous to live a stranger for our Lord, wherever an opportunity should offer. On coming into the province he was honourably received by the aforesaid king, and performing his usual employment of preaching the Gospel, by the example of his virtue and the efficacy of his discourse converted many unbelievers to Christ, and confirmed in His faith and love those that already believed." Among the chief causes of the steady and even rapid progress of Christianity in this kingdom was a school for training a native clergy. Wakeman (p. 21) speaks of the school in these terms: "There, at Dunwich, on the coast of Suffolk, Felix set his bishop's stool in 631, [It is most suggestive that this godly and effective man is thought of as establishing a 'bishop's stool' of prayer before the throne of God, rather than a bishop's throne of authority among men. More of that spirit among the leaders of the Church will soon be reflected in spiritual vitality and power in the body of the people.—Author.] and founded a school in connection with his cathedral, and a monastery at Burgh castle, from which soon poured forth bands of

Christian teachers, priests, monks, and layman, who quickly established the Church among the numerous villages of the rich East Anglian plain." One of the men of this school, whose name was Thomas, became Bishop of the kingdom in 647. He is, therefore, the first Anglian or Englishman who became a bishop, and the Church in East Anglia then had its full organization from among its own native people both for maintaining itself and for spreading the Gospel of our Lord among other people. And this policy of a native ministry has been thoroughly justified by experience in every age and in every land.

In Northumbria

Paulinus, one of Augustine's companions, was sent into the important province of Northumbria and made a start, but subsequently fled in the face of a heathen reaction. Bede tells us that Edwin, the King, called together his principal friends and counsellors to consider the claims of Christianity, and called on every one to say what he thought of the new doctrine. Bede (pp. 90–92) writes: "To which the chief of his own priests, Coifi, immediately answered, 'O King, consider what this is which is now preached to us; for I verily declare to you, that the religion which we have hitherto professed has, as far as I can learn, no virtue in it. For none of your people has applied himself more diligently to the worship of your gods than I; and yet there are many who have received greater favours from you, and are more preferred than I, and are more prosperous in all their undertakings. Now if the gods were good for anything, they would rather forward me, who have been

more careful to serve them. It remains, therefore that
if upon examination you find those new doctrines,
which are now preached to us, better and more effi-
cacious, we immediately receive them without any
delay.'

"Another of the king's chief men, approving of
these words and exhortations, presently added: 'The
present life of man, O King, seems to me, in comparison of that time which is unknown to us, like to the
swift flight of a sparrow through the room wherein you
sit at supper in winter, with your commanders and
ministers, and good fire in the midst, whilst the storms
of rain and snow prevail abroad; the sparrow, I say,
flying in at one door, and immediately out at another
whilst he is within, is safe from the wintry storm;
but after a short space of fair weather, he immediately
vanishes out of your sight, into the dark winter from
which he had emerged. So this life of man appears for
a short space, but of what went before, or what is to
follow, we are utterly ignorant. If, therefore this new
doctrine contains something more certain, it seems
justly to deserve to be followed. The other elders and
king's councillors, by Divine inspiration, spoke to the
same effect.'

"But Coifi added that he wished more attentively
to hear Paulinus discourse concerning the God whom
he preached; which he having by the king's command
performed, Coifi, hearing his words, cried out, 'I have
long since been sensible that there was nothing in that
which we worshipped; because the more diligently I
sought after truth in that worship, the less I found it.
But now I freely confess that such truth evidently

appears in this preaching as can confer on us the
gifts of life, of salvation, and of eternal happiness.
For which reason I advise, O King, that we instantly
abjure and set fire to those temples and altars which
we have consecrated without reaping any benefit from
them.' In short, the king publicly gave his licence to
Paulinus to preach the Gospel, and renouncing idolatry
declared that he received the faith of Christ; and when
he inquired of the high priest who should first profane
the altars and temples of their idols, with the enclosures that were about them, he answered, 'I; for
who can more properly than myself destroy those
things which I worshipped through ignorance, for an
example to all others, through the wisdom which has
been given me by the true God?' Then immediately,
in contempt of his former superstitions, he desired
the king to furnish him with arms and a stallion; and
mounting the same, he set out to destroy the idols;
for it was not lawful before for the high priest either
to carry arms, or to ride on any but a mare. Having,
therefore, girt a sword about him, with a spear in his
hand, he mounted the king's stallion and proceeded
to the idols. The multitude, beholding it, concluded
he was distracted; but he lost no time, for as soon as
he drew near the temple he profaned the same, casting
into it the spear which he held; and rejoicing in the
knowledge of the worship of the true God, he commanded his companions to destroy the temple, with
all its enclosures, by fire. This place where the idols
were is still shown, not far from York, to the east-
wards, beyond the river Derwent, and is now called
Godmundingham, where the high priest, by the in-

spiration of the true God, profaned and destroyed the altars which he had himself consecrated. King Edwin, therefore, with all the nobility of the nation, and a large number of the common sort, received the faith, and the washing of regeneration in the eleventh year of his reign, which is the year of the Incarnation of our Lord 627, and about one hundred and eighty after the coming of the English into Britain."

It was not surprising that people making a change of faith on such grounds as given by Coifi should as readily lapse into the old faith in the face of opposition and defeat, and especially when deserted by their leader and teacher. Hence when Edwin was slain in battle with Penda, King of Mercia and Cadwalla, King of the Britons, the Northumbrian people gave up their allegiance to Christ. As Bede says (on p. 102) : "The affairs of the Northumbrians being in confusion, by reason of this disaster, without any prospect of safety except in flight, Paulinus, taking with him Queen Ethelberga, whom he had before brought thither, returned into Kent by sea, and was honourably received by the Archbishop Honorius and King Eadbald." After Edwin's death the Kingdom was divided, each part having a separate king. Osric, cousin of Edwin, ruled one, and Eanfrid, son of Ethelbert, Edwin's predecessor, reigned over the other. Both of these young kings repudiated Christianity to appease the fierce old heathen Penda, and Northumbria became wholly heathen again. This, however, did not prevent Penda's making war upon them in order to bring Northumbria into complete subjugation to Mercia. Now many years before, when Edwin defeated and slew Ethelfrid, the three sons of the latter, Eanfrid, Oswald and Oswy, fled to Iona and took refuge in the Christian establishment there, receiving protection and education. Eanfrid, the eldest, was continually occupied with thoughts and schemes for regaining his father's throne and so had little time to examine into the Christian religion. Oswald and Oswy, however, became earnest adherents of Christ, and when they came into the rule of the kingdom they invited the representatives of Iona to send Christian teachers into Northumbria. The first whom they sent was a man without tact. He was replaced by Aidan. Oswald, the king, received him with great favor and aided him in every way in furthering Christianity among his people and among the neighboring kingdoms. As in East Anglia, schools and colleges were established for the training of missionaries who could speak the native tongue, and the Kingdom of Christ went forward in life and power.

Wessex

The kingdom of Wessex was brought to Christianity in this way. Cynegils was king there. Oswald, the Christian king of Northumbria, married a West Saxon princess. He used all of his influence to induce the king of Wessex to become a *Christian also,* being aided by Birinus who had volunteered his services for work among the heathen English and was sent thither by Honorius the Pope. At his baptism, Oswald acted as Godfather to Cynegils. His son, Cenwalsh, or Coinwalch, however, who succeeded him in 643, according to Bede was not favorable to Christianity. But when he was compelled to flee into East Anglia, where he saw the Christian religion at work in the lives of its devotees, he changed his mind and became a supporter of the Christian faith, and established a see at Winchester, appointing as the first bishop, Wini, a Saxon. In the record of the Conversion of Wessex must also appear the name of Agilbert of whom Bede writes (p. 113) : "When Coinwalch was restored to his kingdom, there came into that province out of Ireland, a certain bishop called Agilbert, by nation a Frenchman, but who had then lived a long time in Ireland, for the purpose of reading the Scriptures. This bishop came of his own accord, to serve this king, and preach to him the Word of life." Thus the West Saxons were made Christians, their leader being a native Saxon and when their kingdom obtained supremacy over all the Anglo-Saxon kingdoms, it became the greatest stronghold of Christianity in Britain.

Middle Anglia

The kingdom of Mercia was brought into allegiance to Christ after this fashion: Oswy, converted at Iona, succeeded Oswald as king of Northumbria. He desired to allay strife between his kingdom and Mercia. Accordingly, he married his son to the daughter of Penda, the king of Mercia, who was an inveterate foe of Christianity. Peada, son of Penda and now ruler of the southern portion of Mercia, sought to marry Alchfleda, or Elfleda, Oswy's daughter. Oswy, however, would not agree to this without a guarantee that she should be allowed to continue as a worshipper of

Christ. Peada, from time to time, had frequent opportunity of observing Christianity in Northumbria as he mixed with its people, and he was easily persuaded, not only to allow Alchfleda to worship in the way in which she preferred and in which she had been trained by the bishops and monks; but also he himself was baptized, and welcomed to his kingdom a company of priests from Aidan's College in the year 653. These were Diuma, a Scot, and three Englishmen or Anglians named Adda, Betti and Cedd, who were very successful in their labors. Bede's account of Peada's conversion contains a lot of human interest as the reader will see. It reads thus (pp. 137, 138) : "At this time, the Middle Angles, under their Prince, Peada, the son of King Penda, received the faith and sacraments of the truth. Being an excellent youth, and most worthy of the title and person of a king, he was by his father elevated to the throne of that nation, and came to Oswy, king of the Northumbrians, requesting to have his daughter Elfleda given him to wife; but could not obtain his desires unless he would embrace the faith of Christ, and be baptized, with the nation which he governed. When he heard the preaching of the truth, the promise of the heavenly kingdom, and the hope of resurrection and future immortality, he declared that he would willingly become a Christian, even though he should be refused the virgin; being chiefly prevailed on to receive the faith by King Oswy's son Alfrid, who was his relation and friend, and had married his sister Cyneberga, the daughter of King Penda.

"Accordingly he was baptized by Bishop Finan, with all his earls and soldiers, and their servants, that came along with him, at a noted village belonging to the king, called At-the-Wall. And having received four priests, who for their erudition and good life were deemed proper to instruct and baptize his nation, he returned home with much joy. These priests were Cedd and Adda, and Betti and Diuma; the last of whom was by nation a Scot, the others English. Adda was brother to Utta, whom we have mentioned before, a renowned priest, and abbat of the monastery of Gateshead. The aforesaid priests, arriving in the province with the prince, preached the Word, and were willingly listened to; and many, as well of the nobility as the common sort, renouncing the abominations of idolatry, were baptized daily."

Mercia

When the old heathen king, Penda of Mercia, who kept the northern part of his kingdom, while turning the southern portion called Middle Anglia over to his son Peada, died, then all of that portion of the kingdom of Mercia was another field for labor by the monks. Diuma of Lindisfarne was made bishop of Mercia, 656; and to celebrate this event, Oswy and Peada founded the monastery at Peterborough whose church stands to-day as one of the noblest cathedrals in all England. Bede comments thus on the close of the war between Oswy and Penda in which the latter was slain (pp. 144–145): "King Oswy concluded the aforesaid war in the country of Loidis, in the thirteenth year of his reign, on the 15th of November to the great benefit of both nations; for he both delivered his own people from the hostile depredations of the pagans, and having cut off the wicked King's head, converted the Mercians and the adjacent provinces to the grace of the Christian faith.

"Diuma was made the first bishop of the Mercians, as also of Lindisfarne and the Midland Angles, as has been said above, and he died and was buried among the Midland Angles. The second was Ceollach, who, quitting the episcopal office whilst still alive, returned into Scotland, to which nation he belonged as well as Bishop Diuma. The third was Trumhere, an Englishman, but taught and ordained by the Scots, being abbat in the monastery that is called Ingethlingum, and is the place where King Oswin was killed, as has been said above; for Queen Eanfleda, his kinswoman, in satisfaction for his unjust death, begged of King Oswy that he would give the aforesaid servant of God a place there to build a monastery, because he also was kinsman to the slaughtered king; in which monastery continual prayers should be offered up for the eternal health of the kings, both of him that had been slain, and of him that caused it to be done. The same King Oswy governed the Mercians, as also the people of the other southern provinces, three years after he had slain King Penda; and he likewise subdued the greater part of the Picts to the dominion of the English."

Essex

We now pass to the story of the conversion of Essex. This kingdom had received a company of teachers under Mellitus who was Bishop of London and companion of St. Augustine, but it had relapsed into utter heathenism. And now 37 years after Mellitus fled, Sigebert, King of the East Saxons, who had made many visits to Oswy in Northumbria, and had observed the life and the work of the Christian clergy and people there, became a convert himself and asked the monks of Lindisfarne to send missionaries into his kingdom. In response to this request, two young men whom Aidan had trained were soon at work in different parts of his kingdom, and Cedda was chosen to be the bishop in the year 654. He reëstablished Christian services where St. Paul's Cathedral, London, now stands and met with very great success. Thus was restored the line of bishops of this historic see, one of which, Restitutus, had represented the British Church in the Council of Arles in 314, and which was broken when Theonus was driven out in 586 by the heathen Saxons.

Sussex

There was yet one more kingdom outside of the fold of the Saviour which we call Sussex, or South Saxony. It was separated from the other kingdoms by dense forests, and its inhabitants were devoid of all culture —hardly knowing how to provide themselves with the necessities of life. The people of Kent were their next neighbors, and it seems that the Italian missionaries among the Kentish people were without excuse for not making some effort to introduce the religion of Christ into this kingdom. In the year 681, Bishop

Wilfrid, who was trained at Lindisfarne, but who had lived for some time on the Continent and imbibed some current continental notions and as a result was a stalwart Roman partisan, preached the Gospel to those much neglected people.

Bede (p. 184) is our authority for saying that when Wilfrid came to Sussex he found that "Ethelwalch, King of that nation, had been not long *before,* baptized in the Province of the Mercians by the persuasion of King Wulfhere who was present and was also his God-father" (Celtic influence). He also found that the "Queen whose name was Elba, had been Christened in her own island, the Province of the Wicii." And that there "was among them a certain monk of the Scottish nation whose name was Dicul" and with him were five or six brothers in the small monastery. Thus we see that Sussex was not without witnesses for Christ before Wilfrid came and those witnesses were due to the influence of the British-Celtic Church, and having the support of both the King and Queen in his Christian enterprise the way was made easier for Wilfrid's zeal and dynamic personality to secure excellent results. Strong reinforcement of these facts may be found in Bede (Scudder ed.), pp. 36, 106–108, 113, 132, 137–140, 144–5, 184.

The Part Women Played in the Anglo-Saxon Conversions

It seems only right at this time, to record the remarkable part that women played in the bringing of the Anglo-Saxon kingdoms into the fold of Christ.

Bertha, queen of Kent, was a Christian before any of the Italian missionaries ever came, and through her influence, Ethelbert, her king, and their subjects were led to acknowledge the Cross as the supreme throne. Her daughter, Ethelburga, queen of Northumbria, was instrumental in introducing the religion of Christ there. Alchfleda, wife of Peada, was the entering wedge of Christianity in that land. And it is probable that the wife of Oswald and the daughter of the king of Wessex led her father to embrace Christianity and to lend his influence to its support in his kingdom. And the first Christian king of Sussex obtained his wife from the kingdom of Wessex after the Wessex king had become a Christian. And so, as in all good things, we see the women playing a very important part in the conversion of England to the Christian faith. Bishop Browne in "Lessons from Early English Church History" writes thus charmingly (pp. 83–95): "In speaking of the position of women among the Angles and Saxons, I probably need not refer to the influences of women in the conversion of the kingdoms to Christianity. But it may be as well to point out that this influence descended in one line from one generation to another in a curious way, perhaps not generally known to its full extent. It may seem a far cry to Clovis, the first Christian king of his section of the Franks, but in fact we have to begin there. He had married, in 493, Clothilde, a Christian princess of Burgundy, who tried hard to make him a Christian, but without success. At a crisis in a critical battle, he vowed that if Clothilde's God would help him he would become His worshipper and be baptized; for his own gods had not come to his help and he could no longer believe in their power. In the result, he was baptized. His grandson's daughter, Bertha, it was who 100 years later married Ethelbert of Kent, and had a place of Christian worship for herself at Canterbury before Augustine came. Her daughter, again, Ethelburga, it was who married Edwin, king of Northumbria, and had a place of Christian worship for herself before Edwin and his people were converted by Paulinus. And *her* daughter's daughter, Elflaed, (another name for Alchfleda), it was who married Peada of Mercia and took with her, priests who converted the middle parts of England. Thus in one line, in seven generations beginning with Clothilde, there were four women, through each of whom a nation was converted to Christ. That is a striking record of 160 years of family descent in a straight line.

"The Queens and Princesses of the several kingdoms in England showed to a very remarkable degree the desire for the religious life. From the earliest Christian time we see this feature of their character appearing prominently. Long before they had monastic institutions for the purposes of education in their own kingdoms, they went, or sent their young relatives, to monasteries in Gaul to be instructed. There were three of these establishments, especially, to which English girls were sent. So Bede tells us in writing of Earcongota, granddaughter of Eadbald, king of Kent. This king died in 640, having succeeded his father Ethelbert in 616, and having for a time gone back into paganism, and taken for his wife, in accordance with the pagan practice of his race, his father's young widow,

whom Ethelbert had married after the death of Bertha.
Eadbald's son and successor in Kent, Earconbert,
reigned from 640 to 667. He was a firm Christian, and
he has the honor of being recorded as the first of the
English kings who by his royal authority ordered
all the idols throughout his kingdom to be destroyed,
and the fast of forty days to be observed; a quaint
juxtaposition, in one and the same sentence of Bede,
of putting down idols and setting up the Lenten fast.

"The English Church owes him this great debt,
that it was he who first sent Benedict Biscop to Rome,
and gave him as his companion on the way that other
Northumbrian youth, who fills a more prominent place
in the Church of the North than Benedict himself—
Wilfrid. Earconbert sent his daughter Earcongota to
the monastery of Fara; that is, in one compound word,
Faramoustier, which was for long a famous Benedic-
tine nunnery. This nunnery, near Meaux, was founded
about 617 by Fara, or Burgundo-Fara, sister of St.
Faron of Meaux. It was originally of the Columbian
order, but before the foundress's death it became Bene-
dictine. Bathildis, Queen of Clovis II, herself born in
England, added largely to its endowments. The second
abbess was Saetrudis, the daughter of Herusuith, a
Northumbrian lady, sister of Hilda; and the third,
Ethelburga, was daughter of Anna, king of the East
Angles, and his second wife, who was this same Herusuith. Herusuith herself died at Faramoustier. Thus
the connection with England was very close. One of the
other nunneries mentioned by Bede, as usual places of
education for English girls, was Andeley, twenty miles
from Rouen, founded by Clothilde, the wife of Clovis

I, and ancestress of the Kentish line. It was destroyed about 900 by the idolatrous Normans, and the collegiate church and nunneries which sprang up there in the early middle ages have nothing to do with the old foundation. It is a well-known place, on the right bank of the Seine. But the most frequented of all was Chelles, about four miles from Paris, on the banks of the Marne, a nunnery founded by Bathildis, Queen of Clovis II, who was the second foundress of Faramoustier. It was to Chelles that Hilda had intended to go in her early youth, a good many years before Earcongota; probably about 633, when her uncle Edwin, the King of Northumbria, was killed and his kingdom relapsed into paganism. But the foundation by Bathildis had not then taken place, and Hilda's visit would have been made to the smaller nunnery, as founded by Clothilde, Queen of Clovis II. As refounded by Bathildis it was Columbian for a time, and its sisters wore the Columbian attire, a white robe with a variegated under-garment, no doubt a very effective dress. I do not know whether the Scots—Scottish Scots or Irish Scots—claim that Columbanus, who was himself an Irish Scot, merely dressed his nuns in tartan petticoats, and added the white robe over all. It is curious and interesting to find that 1250 years ago those of our English ancestors who could afford it sent their daughters to Paris to be educated. It may interest some here to learn that the earliest example known of a chalice without handles is from Chelles, and that the date assigned to it is just this time we are speaking of, about the middle of the seventh century, the second foundation dating from 656.

"These were the principal schools for girls of the earliest Anglo-Saxon Christian period. It was not only those who were to become nuns that went there, though that no doubt was the lot of many. Others with no view to what was called the religious life, that is the monastic life, were sent, according to one phrase used of them, to learn the highest virtue and comprehensive or cumulated virtue. This, I suppose, means that their education was essentially religious, and included learning in sundry branches; a wide general education on strictly religious lines. If that is the meaning of the phrase, the education was worth going to France for.

"The passion for religious life increased, and spread rapidly. One of the kings of the East Angles, Anna, who converted the king of the West Saxons to Christianity, and reigned in East Anglia from 635 to 654, had six daughters who were abbesses or nuns. One is very well known, Ethelreda, who persuaded her second husband, Ecgfrid, king of Northumbria, to let her take the veil at Coldingham, and the next year founded the Abbey of Ely on her first husband's property, which abbey she ruled till her death. Another, Sexberga, was Queen of Earconbert, whom we have commemorated. She succeeded Ethelreda as Abbess of Ely. Another was Ethelberga, whom we have seen as abbess of Faramoustier. Another was yet a third abbess of Ely, and two were nuns there. Ethelreda's first nunnery, Coldingham, had as its abbess Ebba, King Ecgfrid's aunt, sister of King Oswy and of St. Oswald. But, indeed, it would take far too much time to go into the evidences of the wide-spread desire among royal ladies in England to rule monasteries.

"St. Hilda's work may be taken as an indication of what women could do and did in those days. She became a Christian at the same time as her near relative, King Edwin of Northumbria. It is a striking fact, often overlooked in the stories of Hilda, that she was brought up as a Pagan. There is a curious little note of Bede's which shows that even in a later generation than hers the remembrance of the practice of paganism was personal. Hilda's nephew, son of her sister Herusuith already mentioned, was king of the East Angles. This nephew, Aldwulf, was a contemporary of Bede, and used to tell that he remembered as a boy, his great-uncle Redwald's compromise between Christianity and paganism. King Redwald had been baptized on a visit to Kent; but when he got home he was after a time seduced from the faith by his wife and certain perverse teachers. And so he had, in one and the same temple, an altar for the Christian sacrifice and a little altar for sacrificing to demons. We fear that a good many of us in these days keep a private altar for that purpose.

"Hilda had gone down into East Anglia, on her way to Chelles,—Cale, as Bede's Latin calls it, one of the many words which make it so difficult to see how mediæval and modern spelling and pronounciation came from the Latin, if the Latin was pronounced with broad vowels. But Bishop Aidan called her back to the north, gave her some land at the mouth of the Wear, and admitted her a nun. She was not the first nun in Northumbria; that primacy being held by Heiu, who also received the veil from Aidan. After a year's experience she succeeded Heiu as Abbess of Hartlepool, where the earliest Christian cemetery in these islands has been found, with the names of the nuns of Hilda's time, and down to about 750, cut in runes and in Anglian letters on the little stone pillows under their heads, adorned with ornamental crosses. She at once reduced this monastery to regular order, as she had been instructed by learned men; for Aidan and other religious men frequently visited and diligently instructed her, having the warmest regard for her innate wisdom and her love for the Divine servitude.

"After some years she founded an abbey at the place we call Whitby. There she established at once the regular discipline. She taught justice, piety, chastity, and other virtues, but especially peace and charity; so that after the manner of the primitive Church no one there was poor, no one rich, but all was common to all. Her prudence was so great that kings and princes sought counsel of her. She made those under her study so carefully the Holy Scriptures and practice so diligently the works of justice, that very many of them were found fit to undertake the service of the altar. Indeed, no less than five of the men trained in the monastery under her superintendence became bishops —Bosa of York, Haeddi of Dorchester, Oftfor of Worcester, John (of Beverley) of Hexham, who ordained Bede, and Wilfrid of York, of Leicester and finally of Hexham. The great synod of Whitby was held in her abbey, one of the most striking events in the history of the English Church; itself brought about by the firmness of the queen and her ladies in their observance of what had then become the Catholic rule for the incidence of Easter, as opposed to the rule observed by the king. And on one other great occasion her abbey was probably used as a meeting-place of the chief persons of the realm. The story of her devoted work through the last six years of her life under continuous and great bodily affliction is well worthy of study and reflection, and—if possible—of imitation.

"I must mention only one other example of the position and influence of women, at a time when we might have supposed that men of arms were more likely counsellors and confidants. When Aldfrid, king of Northumbria, was dying at Driffield in 705, he summoned to his bedside among others Elflaed, now Abbess of Whitby, consecrated to God as an infant by her father, King Oswy, in thanksgiving for his victory over the pagans, and Oedilburga, Abbess of Hackness, whose beautiful monument with its tender expressions of love, is still to be seen in priceless fragments in Hackness Church. To them he gave his last words, which, according to a practice continued to the Confessor's time, were regarded as his last will and testament. After a time one of the greatest of the English synods on record was held on the banks of the Nidd. Berthwald, Archbishop of Canterbury, was there, with the Northern bishops; the princes and chief men were there; and Elflaed was there, ever the consoler and best counsellor of the whole province. The question was the ecclesiastical position of Wilfrid. Aldfrid, in his lifetime, had opposed Wilfrid, who was an uneasy person at close quarters, though delightful at a distance. 'Nightingales,' Fuller said of him, 'sing sweetest far from home.' At a critical point in the debate the

Abbess Elflaed rose. The bishops had spoken their last word against Wilfrid:

" 'How can we' (they had asked conclusively), 'how can any one alter that which Archbishop Theodore of blessed memory, and Ecgfrith the King, and the bishops, decreed?—alter that which later, at Austerfield, in thy most excellent presence, Archbishop, we, and with us almost all the bishops of Britain, with King Aldfrith, decided?'

"When they had thus given their conclusion, Elflaed rose and said:

" 'As the truth is in Christ, I declare the testament of Aldfrith the King in that illness which ended his life. He vowed a vow to God and St. Peter, in these words: "If I live I will carry out the judgments of the Apostolic see respecting Blessed Wilfrid the Bishop, which hitherto I have refused to carry out. But if I die, say ye to my heir, my son, in the name of God, that for the remedy of my soul he carry out the Apostolic decision respecting Wilfrid the Bishop."

" 'Thereupon the prince next in authority to the young king declared that it was the wish of the king and princes to obey the mandates of the Holy See and this testamentary injunction of the late king. The bishops thereupon consulted apart, now with Archbishop Berthwald, now with the most wise virgin Elflaed, and then —they gave in.' "

It must not be overlooked, however, that the final decision in this, as in other cases, rested upon the *authority of the Archbishop and Synod. Their* vote determined the subsequent action. The incident is recited here simply to show the great influence exerted by this consecrated woman in the affairs of the Church. She, by her personal influence, gave direction to the course of the Synod in this particular, even against its own judgment. Failure to remember this has sometimes led to a false interpretation of that action of this Council.

CHAPTER VII

THE CONSOLIDATION OF THE CHRISTIAN FORCES IN THE BRITISH ISLES INTO ONE AUTONOMOUS CHURCH INDEPENDENT OF OUTSIDE AUTHORITY

We also see at this time, the close of the seventh century, that all that remained of the original Italian mission was a portion of the county of Kent, this being subsequently added to by the work of the Italian monk Birinus in Wessex (635–650): that the remainder of the work of Christianizing the Jutes, Angles and Saxons was done by the British-Celtic Church. It was important that the two sets of workers in this country should be brought together, if possible, and so present one united front to the enemies of truth and of the higher life of man. Each party had things of real and needed value to contribute to the other, the British-Celtic furnishing a larger measure of genuine Christian enthusiasm and personal zeal, and the Roman, the power of effective organization and the broadening benefits of wider fellowship with Continental Christianity. And it was also to their great common advantage that there should be union and co-operation rather than division and friction and strife. Fortunately, a great ecclesiastical statesman was raised up for the English Church at this time, whose name was Theodore, and of whom we shall learn more later.

The conversion of these Anglo-Saxon kingdoms to Christianity had many effects upon the people, prominent among which was the cessation of continual warfare upon one another. Now that the times were peaceful to an unwonted degree, the people were more ready to undertake plans for the furtherance of the Church. The two most influential princes at this time were Oswy of Northumbria and Egbert of Kent. Their kingdoms were centers of the rival religious systems. Northumbria's religion was that of British-Celtic Christianity, and Kent's that of the Italian.

These two princes and their kingdoms were on friendly terms, and thought that it would be well if they could get a man from among the native clergy for Archbishop of Canterbury who might unify and coordinate all Christian forces in the country. They chose one Wighard of Kent, but he died of malaria in Rome. When the kings heard of this, thinking that the bishop of Rome knew a larger number of suitable men and had therefore a wider field of choice, as vestries to-day ask clergymen or bishops to assist them in selecting rectors, they asked his aid in the selection of a man to fill their particular need. The ultimate choice fell upon Theodore, who, like the great Apostle Paul, was a native of Tarsus, and was consecrated in 668 at the age of sixty-six years and lived to the good old age of eighty-eight. To avoid a possible misconstruction of Theodore's selection by Vitalian, the pope, it is well to keep it clear in our minds that the kings of Kent and Northumbria in asking the pope's assistance to secure the right man for the archbishopric were *not turning* to him as to one who had the *authority to choose the archbishop*. They had

just exercised that very authority *themselves* in selecting Wighard. They appealed to the pope for aid as to an
elder brother in the family qualified by his knowledge
and experience to help in the matter. Vitalian had selected someone else, who being an older man and feeling
unable to undertake the task, recommended Theodore,
and this same man, Hadrian, who recommended Theodore, also accompanied him into Britain. A similar action was taken when the king of the West Saxons applied to Agilbert, bishop of Paris, to come and be the
bishop of the West Saxons. Agilbert, like Hadrian, declined the position for himself but also, like Hadrian,
recommended another, in this case the priest, Eleutherius, his nephew, saying: "He thought him worthy of
a bishopric. The king and the people received him hon-
orably and entreated Theodore, then archbishop of
Canterbury, to consecrate him as their bishop. He was
accordingly consecrated in the same city and many years
zealously governed the whole bishopric of the West
Saxons by synodical authority." (Bede, p. 114.) Theodore, though born in Asia Minor, when he came to England, grew thoroughly attached to the country and was
devotedly patriotic. Wakeman (p. 34) comments thus
on the new archbishop: "Theodore was a man of orderly
mind, strong will, and untiring energy. He set before
himself two great objects—to establish the authority of
the archbishop of Canterbury over all the bishops of
England, and to organize a legislative body for the English Church. The Church in England was no longer to
remain a vague instrument for making people Christian,
it was to be an organized society with a definite voice
and a definite government."

And conscious of his independence of any outside authority in regard to matters of constitutional regulations he never failed to assert and maintain the same for the English Church whenever they were threatened, although he appeared perfectly willing to take advice from the pope as an elder brother in the Christian family when it seemed not to contravene the rights of the Church of England or of himself as its archbishop. This will be abundantly evident as we go on. For as Patterson (p. 27) declares: "Theodore's reforms had to be carried out in the teeth of Wilfrid's opposition and *in defiance of papal bulls* procured by Wilfrid in his favor."

Under him the Church in the various kingdoms became one. This having been done, it led the way to the consolidation of the Heptarchy into the kingdom of England, but this did not take place until more than three centuries afterwards, when in 1017, Canut became the first undisputed king of all England. We have not time to dwell upon it here, but in this connection it is not amiss to emphasize the fact that the English nation owed its organization, indeed its *existence as a nation* to the inspiration and example of the English Church and to the statesmanlike vision, influence and action of the English bishops and others of her leaders. Stubbs, in his "Constitutional History of England," makes it clear that the English Church *established* the English nation and that, of course, it is consequently absurd to claim that the nation through any king or parliament at any time established or originated the Church. (We use the word "establish" here in its general, not its technical, sense as applied to the English Church.)

Returning to Theodore's ecclesiastical policy, it is

well for us to quote here these words of Lane's "Illustrated Notes on English Church History" (p. 87) : "It is true that all the men whom Theodore appointed, agreed to conform to the Roman use in respect to Easter and the tonsure; but this decision was not arrived at because they accepted the supreme right of the pope as judge, but because they saw that Christianity was more in substance than in rites, and it had always been the desire of the British Church to be in complete accord with the decision of the universal Church. Even Theodore, himself, would have been the last to admit that the pope of Rome had any official or legal jurisdiction in England and he never sent men abroad to be ordained. For having been made archbishop of the Anglo-Saxon Churches and having received the homage of the bishops and the lesser orders from the Scots and Irish and British as well as the Anglo-Saxons, he determined not to allow any foreign bishop to dictate to the Church in Britain, any more than he would sanction one English bishop interfering in the diocese of another English bishop."

We have not time to give many instances of this, but we do desire to recite this one : Wilfrid who, as the Bishop of York, had been insubordinate and disciplined by the archbishop had appealed to Pope Agatho to be reinstated over the entire diocese of York. He had been banished from the country by his king, and Theodore had divided the jurisdiction into four parts. Wilfrid had spent many years in Rome and had imbibed something of the Continental idea in regard to the papacy. He was a man of great ability, but also of strong self-will. He was not disposed to accept a rebuke from either king or archbishop. He would appeal to any power or thing, whether it be to the moon or the stars or the bishop of Rome, if he thought that he could find comfort from such appeal. Wilfrid went to Rome in person and secured, by what means we do not know, whether fair or otherwise, a demand from the pope that he be reinstated in his office and its privileges. If the pope's authority had been acknowledged in England at that time, as some people claim, we should expect that the assembly, the Witan, to which the pope's demand was read, would apologize to Wilfrid for his wrongful banishment and immediately accept the judgment of what they should regard as their supreme spiritual ruler. However, nothing like that happened. The assembly asked these questions: "Who is the pope and what are his decrees? What have they to do with us or we with them? Have we not the right and power to manage our own affairs, and punish at our own discretion all offenders against our laws and customs?" And to emphasize their great indignation for this unjustifiable attempt to introduce a foreign jurisdiction, they burned the papal letters, and the Witan condemned Wilfrid to rigorous imprisonment, from which he was only released by agreeing to stay away from Northumbria. That incident alone is sufficiently clear evidence that there was no such thing as papal supremacy recognized in the land of Britain in the time of Theodore. Wakeman in giving his explanation of Wilfrid's attitude in this controversy shows that Wilfrid himself was not moved to make his appeal to Rome by what we understand to-day as papal supremacy, but by other quite human and likely motives. He writes (p. 37), "It was the opening chapter of a long,

tangled and highly controversial history, which only
ended at the crisis of the Reformation in 1534, but it is
not to be supposed that Wilfrid realized in any way the
importance of the step which he was taking. By appealing to the pope to over-ride and set at naught the action
of the ecclesiastical and civil authorities in England, he
did not in the least intend to maintain, as a matter of
principle, the supremacy of the Roman pontiff over the
domestic affairs of the Church of England, much less to
admit on behalf of the bishops and clergy of the English
Church that they were merely the servants of the pope,
exercising his delegated powers. Such views belong to a
much later stage in the history of the development of
the papacy. To Wilfrid's mind the question was much
more simple. He had been grievously wronged by a vin-
dictive king and an arbitrary metropolitan. To whom
could he turn for justice? His fellow-bishops were all
the nominees of Theodore, and were implicated in his
action. If justice was to be had against Theodore in the
whole wide world, Rome was the only possible tribunal,
and the pope the only possible judge from whence to
obtain it." So his reasoning would naturally run.

The same author (p. 43) thus describes the reconciliation between Theodore and Wilfrid: "The time had
come when he (Theodore) could be generous without
danger to the Church, while the splendid work of Wilfrid in the South, where now even the Jutes on the Isle
of Wight had become Christian, called for recognition.
Negotiations were opened by the archbishop with Wilfrid and Aldfrid, the king, and terms were soon arranged. Nothing was said on one side or the other about
the *decision of the pope. It was simply ignored.* But

arrangements were made by which Wilfrid should, as far as possible, receive back for his lifetime his old diocese. Eata, bishop of Hexham, had just died, and Wilfrid at once resumed possession of that part of his see. In the same way, when Cuthbert died in 687, he also became bishop of Lindisfarne, and thus actually regained the administration of all of his old diocese, except Lindsey, which had now fallen to Mercia, and Lothian, which was in the hands of the Picts. But he regained it only in name, for later in the same year Eadbert was consecrated to Cuthbert's see at Lindisfarne, and John of Beverley to that of Hexham. Perhaps the arrangement was in the nature of a compromise by which Wilfrid was permitted to regain for the moment a diocese coterminous with the kingdom, on condition that he agree to its immediate division according to the archbishop's scheme."

Subsequently, Wilfrid was again banished. Archbishop Bertwald called a conference at Easterfield for considering Wilfrid's case again. It was very largely attended by English bishops and abbots. We are told: "But argument did not tend to bring about peace. The fault of Wilfrid, in the eyes of his fellow-countrymen, lay not so much in his masterful temper and arrogant claim of superiority, as in his want of patriotism. They could not forgive the man who had sought to coerce his own king, and reverse the decisions of the national Witan by the help of a foreign power, however venerable and sacred. It was not that the Northumbrian kings and clergy were wanting in respect or reverence for the see of Rome. They were willing to listen to the counsels of the pope with all due deference. But they could not forgive the English bishop, who, despising *his own national institutions,* sought to bring them under the control of the foreigner."

The results of the whole controversy with Wilfrid are summarized by Wakeman (p. 45–46) in these words: "The episcopate thus formed was duly subordinated to the metropolitan archbishop at Canterbury, not according to the caprice of a despot, but by the *adoption of recognized principles* of ecclesiastical law. The bishops with their primate were summoned in provincial synod to form a legislative body for the local Church in subordination to the laws and decisions of the *ecumenical councils of the Church Universal.* The very troubles consequent on the quarrel between the archbishop and Wilfrid in the end served only to intensify the rule of law, for while all attempts on the part of Wilfrid or the pope to overturn the decisions and alter the policy of the National Church in the matter of its own territorial divisions were steadily repulsed, it was none the less clear that no archbishop or king would ever again attempt to interfere with the diocese of a bishop against his will. Thus by the quarrel itself the true principles of *episcopal authority and national independence* were brought into clearer prominence."

The same spirit and principle are manifested in the address of King Withred of Kent delivered before a solemn assembly of the kingdom. "The Anglo-Saxon Chronicle" (pp. 29–30) makes this note under the year 694: "As soon as he was king, he commanded a great council to be assembled at the place which is called Baccancelde, in which sat Withred, king of the Kentish-men, and Berthwald (or Bertwald) the archbishop of Canterbury, and Tobias, bishop of Rochester, and with them were assembled abbats and abbesses, and many wise men, all to consult about the bettering of God's churches in Kent. Now began the king to speak, and said, 'It is my will that all the ministers and the churches that were given and bequeathed to the glory of God in the days of faithful kings my predecessors, and in the days of my kinsmen, of King Ethelbert and those who followed after him, do so remain to the glory of God, and firmly continue so to all eternity for evermore. For I, Withred, an earthly king, instigated by the King of Heaven, and burning with the zeal of righteousness, have learned from the institutes of our forefathers, that no layman has a right to possess himself of a church, nor of any of the things which belong to a church. And hence strictly and faithfully do we appoint and decree, and in the name of the Almighty God and of all His saints we forbid to all kings our successors, and to ealdormen, and all laymen any lordship whatever over the churches, and over all their possessions, which I, or any elders of olden days, have given as an everlasting inheritance to the glory of Christ and of our lady St. Mary, and of the holy Apostles. And observe, when it shall happen that a bishop, or an abbat, or an abbess, shall depart this life, *let it be made known to the archbishop, and by his counsel and advice, let such an one be chosen as shall be worthy.* And let the archbishop inquire into the life and purity of him who is chosen to such a duty, and in nowise let any one be chosen to such a duty *without the counsel of the archbishop.* It is the duty of kings to appoint earls and ealdormen, shire-reeves and doomsmen, *and of the archbishop to instruct and advise the community of God and bishops and abbats and abbesses, priests and deacons, and to choose and appoint and consecrate and stablish them by good precepts and example,* lest any of God's flock stray and be lost.' "

Whitby and Chad

Before leaving Wilfrid and Theodore it will be interesting to consider two events in which they had part and which by partisans might be made to appear as recognitions of Roman primacy and authority— namely the Council of Whitby and the re-ordination of Chad. First then the Council of Whitby. As has been mentioned before, there had been a long and bitter controversy in Britain concerning the different times of observing Easter, and as to the difference in clerical tonsure and certain minor ceremonial matters. Bede tells us that King Oswy "observed that it behooved those who serve one God to have the same rule of life." And therefore "it was agreed that a synod should be held in the monastery of Straneshalch which signifies 'the Bay of the Lighthouse' where the Abbess Hilda, a woman devoted to God, then presided." The Council was held in the year 664, and while it was a most interesting event it was neither crucial nor epochal in determining real principles. The questions discussed were not fundamental, but of secondary importance, and the discussion itself turned on a trivial point and was decided on grounds both unhistorical and unscriptural. We shall let Bede (p. 152) give the climax of

Wilfrid's argument and the final decision of the king:
"And if that Columba of yours (and, I may say, ours
also, if he was Christ's servant) was a holy man and
powerful in miracles, yet could he be preferred before
the most blessed prince of the Apostles, to whom our
Lord said, 'Thou art Peter, and upon this rock I will
build my Church, and the gates of hell shall not prevail against it, and to thee I will give the keys of the
Kingdom of Heaven?'

"When Wilfrid had spoken thus, the king said, 'Is
it true, Colman, that these words were spoken to Peter
by our Lord?' He answered, 'It is true, O king!' Then
said he, 'Can you show any such power given to your
Columba?' Colman answered, 'No.' Then added the
king, 'Do you both agree that these words were principally directed to Peter, and that the keys of Heaven
were given to him by our Lord?' They both answered,
'We do.' Then the king concluded, 'And I also say
unto you, that he is the door-keeper, whom I will not
contradict, but will, as far as I know and am able, in
all things obey his decrees, lest, when I come to the
gates of the Kingdom of Heaven, there should be none
to open them, he being my adversary who is proved
to have the keys.' The king having said this, all present,
both great and small, gave their assent, and renouncing the more imperfect institution, resolved to conform
to that which they found to be better."

We may also say that the real solid argument used
by Wilfrid was not that British-Celtic Christians should
change their time of observing Easter because it was
the *Roman* custom alone, but because it was the *universal* custom save in these Islands. For Bede (pp.

148–9) quotes Wilfrid as saying: "The Easter which we observe, we saw celebrated by all at Rome, where the blessed Apostles, Peter and Paul, lived, taught, suffered, and were buried; we saw the same done in Italy and in France, when we travelled through those countries for pilgrimage and prayer. We found the same practised in Africa, Asia, Egypt, Greece, and all the world, wherever the Church of Christ is spread abroad, through several nations and tongues, at one and the same time; except only these and their ac-complices in obstinacy, I mean the Picts and the Britons, who foolishly, in these two remote islands of the world, and only in part even of them, oppose all *the rest of the universe.*"

Now if any one were disposed to attach crucial significance to this Council as indicating the establish-ment of papal authority in England he would be com-pelled to change his mind, or at least seriously modify his conclusion, when he remembers the immediate subsequent action of Theodore in setting at naught the papal bull in behalf of Wilfrid and the still greater overshadowing of the Council of Whitby by the larger and vastly more important Council of Cloveshoo in 747.

Then some have seen in the re-ordination of Chad by Theodore a recognition of Roman authority, which seems strangely far-fetched and in ignorance of the real facts in the case. Upon Wilfrid's nomination to the episcopate, he went to Gaul for consecration and remained there nearly a year. And Wakeman (p. 33) states: "But in the meantime the Northumbrians, tired of being so long without a bishop, prevailed upon Oswiu to replace Wilfrid by Chad. Even Chad's humility could not escape from the importunity of both king and people, and early in 666 he was consecrated to be bishop of York by Wini, bishop of the West Saxons, and two Celtic bishops probably from Cornwall or South Wales. Thus the *Roman,* Gallic, and Celtic lines of succession centred on the pupil of Aidan and the future Apostle of the Midlands. Later in the year Wilfrid reappeared at York, but found his see most worthily filled through his own unworthy neglect. With unusual self-control, possibly prompted by compunction, he accepted the inevitable and quietly retired to his monastery at Ripon."

Things went splendidly, Chad leading his people with great earnestness, self-sacrifice and spiritual devotion until Theodore came into his diocese three years later. We now pass to the words of Bede (p. 165) : "Theodore, visiting all parts, ordained bishops in proper places, and with their assistance corrected such things as he found faulty. Among the rest, when he upbraided Bishop Chad that he had not been duly consecrated, the latter with great humility, answered, 'If you know I have not duly received episcopal ordination, I willingly resign the office, for I never thought myself worthy of it; but, though unworthy, in obedience submitted to undertake it.' Theodore, hearing his humble answer, said that he should not resign the bishopric, and he himself completed his ordination after the Catholic manner."

The ground of Theodore's objection to Chad's consecration was not that it was not *valid,* but that it was *irregular* and contrary to the Catholic usage in that he was consecrated for a see for which another, Wilfrid, had been consecrated and to whom the jurisdiction rightly belonged. Manifestly it could not have been on the ground that he had not received Roman consecration for as Wakeman points out, in his consecration the *Roman,* the Gallican, and Celtic lines were joined. Then again Theodore found other bishops and hundreds of priests who had received British-Celtic ordination and no objection was made to them and no demand for re-ordination. When Augustine came and found British bishops and other clergy, neither he nor Gregory gave any intimation of insufficiency of ordination nor made the slightest suggestion of the need of re-ordination in order to enter into full fellowship with the Roman Church. And Bede does not say that Theodore re-ordained Chad, but "completed his ordination after the Catholic manner"—that is, ordaining for a jurisdiction that was his own and not for another's which would make him an intruder and a contradictor of Catholic usage. Such procedure, largely indulged in, would indeed destroy orderly unity and produce veritable chaos. It is of interest to recall here also a canon passed at the Synod of Soissons about 700 to the effect that "wandering bishops," that is bishops without definite jurisdiction, might not ordain priests, but if any priests should have been so ordained and were found to be good priests they should be re-ordained to make their ordination regular according to law, as well as valid according to the essentia of ordination and Apostolic transmission.

It is well-nigh impossible to estimate how large is the debt that the English Church and nation owe to Theodore, and we cannot leave him without some ref-

erence to the service that he rendered through the
Council of Hertford held in 673. It was the first Council
of the whole English Church and was attended by *all*
the English bishops in person or by proxy with the
exception of one then under condemnation. Stubbs
describes it as "the first constitutional measure of the
English race." It may be thought a far cry from Hertford to the first national Parliament in the time of
Edward I, but it can hardly be doubted that the unification of the Church led to the unification of the nation.
Englishmen were members of the one Church before
they belonged to the one nation. Bede gives us a list
of canons passed by the Council, which consisted for
the most part of ancient decrees concerning the government and its organization as applied to the needs of
the English Church. Its main significance, however,
lay in its constitutional and national character.

In this time, as in the early days, the English Church
was distinguished for its adherence to the old historic
faith and for its missionary zeal. As illustrating this,
we recall that the Synod of Hatfield in 680 emphatically declared its firm adherence to the decrees of the
five General Councils that had been held up to that time,
namely: Nicea, 325; Constantinople, 381; Ephesus, 431;
Chalcedon, 451; and Constantinople, 553. These Councils, together with the decrees of the sixth General
Council held at Constantinople 680, are still the authority for the faith of the Church in Britain, so furnishing
another line of continuity of the Church in these Islands
with the universal Church in other lands and in olden
times. And in that generation also, from schools such as
Glastonbury and Lindisfarne, men were sent forth to

convert the Teutons who had colonized what we now call Germany. Bede gives a very interesting account of the missionary activities of Wilbrord, Swidbert, and others with them in Frisland (pp. 237–246). And Patterson (p. 39) writes: "The early Church of England produced many types of saintship; her activities were manifold. While Bede was living his quiet and uneventful scholar's life at Jarrow, other Englishmen were engaged in missionary work, carrying the Gospel to the heathen races of Frisia and Germany. Of these the most famous were S. Willibrord of Northumbria, who took up Wilfrid's work in Frisia, and after a long life of missionary work died in 739, and Boniface, the Apostle of Germany. Boniface, born in Devon about 680, was consecrated bishop by Pope Gregory in 723, and laboured in Frisia, Thuringia, and Bavaria. In 743 he fixed his archiepiscopal see at Mainz, and for many years he worked among the German tribes, assisted by other English missionaries. He crowned his splendid missionary life with a martyr's death in Frisia, 755." It is well worth while to quote at this point from "Augustine and His Companions" by Bishop Browne (pp. 71–72): "I may as well, having said so much on considerations rising directly out of the consecration of the first bishop and archbishop of the English, say a few words on the earliest synodical enactment respecting appeals. In or about 747, the Englishman who had been the Apostle of Germany, that is, Boniface, the archbishop of Mainz, wrote to Cuthbert his friend, the archbishop of Canterbury, that at a German synod they had resolved that if any bishop found in his diocese matters which he was unable to correct and amend, he should bring them before the archbishop in full synod with a view to their being corrected. And this in the same manner as the Roman Church bound with an oath those whom it ordained, that if they were unable to correct priests or people they should take the matter always to the Apostolic see and the Vicar of St. Peter for amendment; for thus all bishops were—in the opinion of Boniface— bound to act towards their metropolitan, and he towards the Roman pontiff. It is a difficult question whether this letter preceded the English Council of Cloveshoo or followed it. In either case, the fact remains, that the Council of Cloveshoo enacted the *first* part, directing bishops to bring matters which were too difficult for them to the archbishops in full synod to be corrected. *There they stopped.* The archbishop was the authority for the final appeal. They did *not* enact the second part, directing the metropolitan to bring matters which were too difficult for him to the Apostolic see and the Vicar of St. Peter. The significance of this cannot be overrated. Boniface did all he could to bring the English Church to take the view he had persuaded the German Church to take, and *he failed entirely."*

And as evidence of the sincerity of the faith and the purity of their lives, even queens and kings gave up their thrones in order to enter monasteries and devote their whole lives to religion and its works. One of these was Ina, King of Wessex. After he had renounced his kingdom, he and his wife made a journey to the city of Rome and there abode for many years. While there, they established a school where Anglo-

Saxon children might come and be taught the civilization of the Continent and become acquainted with the ways of foreign countries. The endowment of this school by Ina, it is thought by some, furnished the foundation of what is called Peter's pence or "Rome-shot" paid by England to Rome. For in subsequent years the Roman clergy diverted the funds from the support of the school to the support of the papal see, and so claiming it in after years, as the tribute from England to the papacy.

We pass next to an incident in the time of Alfred the Great, which showed that at the end of the ninth century and in the beginning of the tenth, the English Church was still holding itself as free from the domination of any other, but always ready to learn from her sister churches. It is said that for the encouragement of the Church, Alfred sent embassies to the great bishops of Rome and Jerusalem, even as he sent embassies for the development of trade and commerce to large cities and ports of other countries. He sent ships to India with alms for the poor Christian missions, which the Apostles St. Bartholomew and St. Thomas are said to have established there. So we see that just as in Alfred's reign was laid the foundation of British naval and commercial enterprise, and fellowship with other nations, so also we see intercommunion and on *equal terms* between the English Church and other Apostolic Churches in Rome, Jerusalem and India.

Now in the time of Offa, King of Mercia, the income of Ina's school in Rome was increased (Patterson suggests that Offa's annual payments to the pope for his ratification of the temporary archiepiscopate of Lichfield may have been the origin of Peter's pence), as also in Alfred's time, by Saxon contributions of a penny from each family, and appropriated by the Roman clergy to the papal see and called Peter's pence or "Rome-shot," which was a plain piece of misappropriation of funds which we ordinarily call robbery, and then "adding sin to sin," they made that dishonest practice, with its accompanying false claim, the ground for other attempted usurpations of power, and the precedent for further papal taxation.

Again, King Edwy of Mercia married Elgiva within the prohibited decrees of matrimony. Dunstan rebuked him. And when an earl of the kingdom committed a like offense, Dunstan excommunicated him. The earl appealed to Rome. Rome in her accustomed habit in those days of currying favor with royalty and trying to win her way by whatever means she could, upheld the earl and ordered Dunstan to restore him to the communion. Dunstan refused. The marriage was abandoned. The pope failed, and Edwy, the king, seeing how little the prelates of the English Church cared for the pope's judgment, gave up his prohibited marriage also, and in barefooted penitence begged the pardon of Dunstan, the abbot. This gives us a clear idea of how the Roman claim to jurisdiction was regarded at this date. Dunstan was soon afterwards made the archbishop of Canterbury.

It is now necessary to give a few facts in the secular history of England as the frame for the picture of events in its ecclesiastical history. Edgar became King of England upon the death of Edwy, 959. Edgar died in 975 and his son Ethelred succeeded him to the throne.

In 991, Northmen from Denmark began invasions of England. To get rid of them, Ethelred gave them a large sum of money. Seeing how easily they could obtain wealth, they came again and the taxes imposed upon the people to pay them off was called Dane's money or Danegeld. In 1002, the king had all the Danes in England massacred. This brought very swift revenge in the form of another invasion under Swegen. King Ethelred had married Emma, daughter of Duke Richard of Normandy, and fearing the Danes, with his wife and children, he went to her father on the Continent. Swegen was declared king, but Edmund Ironside, Ethelred's son, claimed and fought for the throne. Swegen died in 1014 and the Danes in England elected his son, Canut, king, between whom and Edmund many battles were fought. The final result of the contest was the division of territory, and upon Edmund's death a short time after, Canut became the first king of all England whose title was not disputed. Canut married Emma, the widow of Ethelred, from which union sprang two sons, Harold and Harthnacanut, who succeeded their father—Harold in the North and Harthnacanut in the South.

Upon the death of Harthnacanut, Edward, son of Emma by Ethelred, who had been living in Normandy, returned to England and claimed his father's throne. Harold was driven out and Edward became king and was known as Edward the Confessor, the same who built Westminster Abbey 1061 and lies buried there. He brought with him many Norman bishops and other clergy, the most important of whom was Robert, bishop of London, who was afterwards made archbishop of

Canterbury. The introduction of these foreign prelates, whose number was so much augmented under William the Conqueror, was a most unfortunate circumstance for the realm and for the Church. They brought ideas strange to the Church in England, and were not loyal to the best interests of the kingdom or the Church. And we shall see later, that to them was due more than to any other cause the insinuating influence that the papacy gained in England in the coming centuries.

Edward the Confessor had declared that his brother-in-law, Harold, son of Godwine, an English earl, should succeed him, but he had also promised that Emma's nephew, his own cousin, William, the Duke of Normandy, should be king of England. Upon his death, therefore, arose a conflict between Harold and William. The natives, both in Church and State, sided with Harold the Saxon. He was elected in all representative assemblies of the land, and was crowned in Westminster Abbey. Harold prepared to meet William, as he knew of his coming invasion. Harold's men, however, were mostly farmers, unprepared for war, and as William waited for time to discipline his forces thoroughly, Harold's forces became tired of waiting and returned to their farms, where they were greatly needed. When William came, Harold was unprepared and in the Battle of Hastings in 1066, Harold was slain and William the Conqueror then became king. In our next chapter we shall trace the life of the English Church from the time of the Norman Conquest to the Reformation.

CHAPTER VIII

THE EFFECT OF THE NORMAN CONQUEST ON ENGLISH CHURCH HISTORY

This is what might be called the Dark Period in English Church history—a time when mediæval superstitions and corruptions of the primitive faith and worship of the Church crept in through foreign influence. During this period, encroachment on both the political and ecclesiastical rights of Englishmen was more pronounced than in any previous time, and also there was frequent friction between the Crown and the Church, the king and the archbishop of Canterbury playing against each other any outside influence that could further the personal interest of one or the other.

It is really impossible to understand rightly the relations between the papacy and the English at this time without giving attentive and thoughtful consideration to the ambitions, jealousies and personal animosities of the leading characters in Church and State. Without the knowledge of and without giving due weight to this political, and personal background we cannot properly evaluate the papal claims and their reception, adverse or otherwise, in England. Great and sacred were the traditions and prestige of the Church of England; greater still, however, in the minds of many, influenced by the decretals forged in the interests of the papacy, were the papal traditions and prestige. As Mr. Wakeman (p. 117) writes: "The Norman Conquest had brought the two into closer contact. The struggle between the Church and the Crown welded them into the closest of alliances. England sought from the papacy the moral support of the most powerful of western institutions, the political assistance of the most ambitious among all the western sovereigns. Against a king who ruled half France as well as England, there was no ally so able to help as one who could appeal to European monarchs, both as their political equal and their spiritual father. The papacy, on the other hand, sought to extend the bounds of its dominion, to establish direct enforceable rights over a country which had hitherto been less under its control than any other part of western Christendom, to use the wealth of England to assist it in the death struggle which it was waging with the empire. The popes were willing to help the Church of England to keep herself independent of the authority of the Crown, provided they were permitted to establish their own tyranny in the place of the ousted king. Shylock did not more ruthlessly exact his pound of flesh from his Christian debtor than did the popes, the acknowledgment of their authority by England as the price of their assistance. Throughout the last centuries of the Middle Ages the Church of England found herself ever shifting uneasily from one horn of the dilemma to the other, in the vain hope of preserving her liberties intact. Threatened by the tyranny of a strong or wicked king, she called to her aid the power of a masterful and greedy pope. Ruined by papal exactions, abused by papal misgovernment, she turned in her need to implore the protection of a powerful and ambitious king. That she succeeded in keeping a good deal of independence in the appointment of her clergy, the enactment of her laws, and the administration of her affairs, must be ascribed mainly to the fact that danger from a common tyranny bound Church and baronage and people together in a common alliance." And again (pp. 119–20) the same author tells us: "They [the popes] sought by all the means at their disposal to gain both money and political power. They became more and more immersed in political schemes. They degraded their spiritual prerogative by using it to further their ambition. They allied themselves with princes, and betrayed to them the interests of the people and even of the clergy. In England this altered policy took a double form. From the end of the twelfth century to the Reformation the consistent aim of the papacy was to gain as much direct authority over England as possible, and to use that authority when gained, for the purpose of obtaining money. In the history of the dealings of the papacy with the English Church in the Middle Ages we find, accordingly, a strange mixture of moral government, political tyranny, and gross rapacity, and each motive must be duly allowed its true weight if we would rightly estimate the relations between the two powers." And again Mr. Wakeman throws further light on the situation in these words (p. 129) : "When the popes sent legates, demanded taxes, controlled appointments, collected money in the thirteenth century, it was often difficult to say whether they did it by virtue of their ecclesiastical or their feudal position, and it often happened that the *feudal lord* succeeded in establishing rights which would have been *strenuously denied to the ecclesiastical head*. During the minority of the king, Pope Honorius III and Archbishop Stephen Langton co-operated with Pembroke and Hubert de Burgh to secure the safety of the throne and the liberties of the nation. But in 1227 Henry III declared himself of age, and Gregory IX succeeded to the papal chair. From that moment all went amiss. The young king, fretful in temper, impatient of control, ever nourishing splendid designs, incapable of carrying one of them into effect, was the sport of favourites and the tool of foreigners. Religion and gratitude combined with pride to throw him into the hands of the pope to save himself from the barons who would control him."

Bishop Boyd-Carpenter analyzes and interprets the situation in an interesting manner. He tells us (p. 44) : "The Bishop of Rome was looked upon as the patriarch of the West. This, however, did not mean that all lands to the West were under his authority; for, to take an example, island Churches were independent. Those bishops of Rome, however, who were filled with a missionary spirit felt themselves responsible for whatever Christian work was needed in the Western world, even in regions of the West which were not strictly under their jurisdiction. It will thus be seen that it was only by slow degrees that the authority of the bishop of Rome spread. It was not at first pressed as a right. It was rather an influence which gained power over men's minds in an unconscious way through the prestige which the name of Rome, as the capital of the world and an Apostolic see, carried with it."

Then writing of a later period the Bishop says (p. 107): "The clergy, as I told you, often suffered from the tyranny of the bishops. As long as the bishops could exercise an uncontrolled authority, their clergy were at their mercy. If, therefore, it could be shown that the oppressed and dissatisfied clergy had a right to appeal to the pope, then the clergy would no longer be wholly at the mercy of the bishop. How could this be proved? *Church history,* as shown in the decrees of Councils, afforded no ground for any such claim on behalf of the pope. The bishop of Rome had indeed always enjoyed a dignified prestige, derived from the importance of the city which had once been the metropolis of the world; but pre-eminence of supremacy had never been accorded to him. Bishops stood on an equality as regards office; a certain controlling power was given to the archbishops or metropolitans, and of these there were many; any intrusion into the affairs of any province by the metropolitan of another province was strenuously resisted. There was no precedent or decree which would justify the claims of the bishop of Rome to interfere outside his own province or jurisdiction. But if evidence does not exist where it is thought it ought to exist, then it may be invented. The now celebrated Dreyfus case is an illustration in point. Evidence which was deemed necessary was deliberately forged. The writer of the Isidorian decretals did the same thing in his day. He desired to re-establish the claims of the pope to exercise wide authority, and he proceeded to forge the evidence. If evidence to establish the supreme power of the pope was not to be found in existing chronicles or letters, he forthwith inserted it. Such were the famous decretals which for centuries kept man in bondage. The study of these perverted the mind of Becket; the dread of them paralyzed the growing spirit of liberty; the belief in them so worked upon the minds of men that nations and churches surrendered their independence. For centuries they were looked upon as genuine; for years, after they were doubted and discredited, they were hotly defended in Rome; and though in the present day they are abandoned as spurious by all competent scholars, they are sometimes surreptitiously introduced in controversies by unscrupulous or ignorant men."

Friction between the bishop and other clergy, regular and secular, as well as friction between the Crown and the Church, was seized upon and utilized as the pope's opportunity; and he always made the most of it for strengthening and extending papal claims. The papacy, too, in these times was very designing, presumptuous, audacious and in great power. Two of the most able, astute and ambitious men that have ever occupied the Roman see, were popes in this period, namely, Gregory VII or Hildebrande, and Innocent III. But it is a characteristic of all of them, particularly of this period, which we are sorry to be compelled to believe and in all fairness to state, that they were ready, always, to stoop to any sort of double-dealing and trickery to advance their own personal ambitions, and to further the influence of the papacy. It will be seen at the same time, that whenever the issue of independence was made, the Church and the realm of England resisted the encroachments of Rome. It is also clear that while the Roman influence was much felt in England, as in all other European countries in these times of which we now speak, the English Church and people never accepted in an authoritative way or through any authoritative body, either the leadership or domination of the Roman Church, and furthermore the English Church never acknowledged the control and was never an acknowledged part of the Roman organization. Even so pro-Roman a writer as Father Knox writes (p. 171): "In this way it happened that by the time of the Reformation the Church in Western Europe, although primarily conscious of itself as one, none the less was familiar with the idea that the ecclesiastical organization of each country possessed *a certain independent character of its own,* and *could on occasion take independent action either against the temporal ruler of the country or against the papacy."* And Bishop Gore states: "But in fact the Church of England from Augustine to Parker was something much more than two Western provinces. *It was a recognized National Church."* ("The Anglo-Catholic Movement of Today," p. 38.) All through these centuries the English Church stood sturdily for her own national independence as a Church complete in herself, even as the Episcopal Church in the United States to-day is a national independent unit of the Anglican communion.

Beginning with the sixth century it will be remembered that the British bishops declined to make the British Church a part of the Roman organization, and refused to acknowledge any of Rome's pretended authority over them in answer to Augustine's overtures.

Next we quote these words of Bishop Browne ("Augustine and His Companions," p. 151), telling of the change in Gregory's plan without any reference to Rome for the establishment of the archbishopric in London after Augustine's death, instead of continuing it in Canterbury: "This only throws up into more prominence the fact that there is no hint of consulting Rome. If Mellitus had succeeded Augustine, it might have been said that the order of Gregory was being obeyed. As it was, the spiritual head of the Church of the English acted on his own responsibility and set up another metropolitan to succeed him, with no more ceremony than the consecration of a bishop. That, if it is a fact, is a very great fact for us, in view of the later *interferences* with our liberty."

We also recall these words from the International Encyclopedia: "Theodore had not long succeeded in effecting this confederation before he began to act almost as an English pope. In Wilfrid, Archbishop of York, he met a prelate of consummate talents and determination who would not allow the claims of anyone to supremacy over him. When Theodore undertook, without his consent, although supported by King Egfrid, to carve new dioceses out of his jurisdiction he at once appealed to Rome. This is the *first* of *such appeals* from England of which we have any record. He obtained from the pope an order to Theodore for the ratification of these diocesan lines, with the threat of deprivation or excommunication for any clergymen or laymen who might disobey the mandate. The King, however, imprisoned Wilfrid and allowed Theodore to go on, unchecked, in his scheme of organization for which he seems to have had uncommon genius." Bishop

Gore in "The Anglo-Catholic Movement of Today," p. 31 writes: "So the dogma of the papal supremacy and infallibility as something substantially belonging to the Catholic tradition as held from the first, is plainly contrary to the facts of history. Thus the Roman development of Catholicity is a development which has narrowed its scope and meaning by its constant accentuation of authority and by its centralization. In these tendencies, it does not represent the New Testament spirit or the spirit of the early Church: it has made the Roman communion impossible for many, and many of the best men who would have been at home in the undivided Church; and *it is responsible in very large measure for the divisions of Christendom.*"

Later on, in the sixteenth and seventeenth centuries, the English Church was also influenced in a measure by the Lutheran, Calvinistic and other Christian bodies. In the great Commonwealth of Christianity, we are all members, one of another, and exercise influence, one upon another. The extreme Reformers of the sixteenth century, it will be recalled, were as insistent that their influence and way of thinking should be paramount in the Church of England as the Roman papacy was for the introduction of its polity, policies and customs that were deemed by the English Church unscriptural and uncatholic.

Our grand old Mother has ever stood immovable by either, maintaining valiantly her own independence and preserving her faith, polity, and worship against unscriptural and uncatholic addition on the one hand or similar diminution on the other. And thus she constitutes an inspiring and noble spectacle, strongly planted on solid foundations of Apostolic faith, order and worship, unafraid amidst the storms of controversy and the assaults of her enemies—both political and ecclesiastical. It might be well to quote here these words of Mr. Freeman. In his "History of the Norman Conquest," he says, "The English crime in the eyes of Rome—the crime, to punish which, William the Conqueror's crusade was approved and blessed by the pope —was *the independence still retained in the Island, Church* and nation. A land where the Church and nation were but different names for the same community; a land where priests and prelates were subject to the law like other men; a land where the king and his Witan or Parliament gave and took away the staff of the bishop was a land which, in the eyes of Rome was more dangerous than a land of Jews and Saracens." William, as we know, had no true foundation for his claim to the throne of England. He, therefore, sought the moral prestige of the pope's support. The pope was willing to give it if sufficient recompense were in the offing. Patterson relates the matter in this way (p. 57): "William's right to the English throne was really nil; for it was with the Witan that the right to elect a king lay, and no promise of Edward the Confessor or oath of Harold could possibly defraud the Witan of their right or foreclose the question of the succession in William's favour. There was a third ground which William skilfully used to win support for his invasion. To the papacy he represented his plan of conquest as a crusade; the English nation and Church he denounced to Pope Alexander as adherents of the schismatic Stigand, and *as people who had never paid proper deference to the see of Rome.*" And Wakeman informs us that the pope in blessing William's ambitions charged him "to bring *the stubborn and independent Island into* subjection." What the English Church did in the sixteenth century therefore, in declaring all claims of the pope to jurisdiction in England to be false and without justification, was just the same thing that she was declaring in all these previous centuries, with the exception that in the sixteenth century the declaration was more emphatic and carried to further practical extent, as the accumulated needs and the larger and more acute situation of the time required.

Now we recall that previous to the coming of William the Conqueror, the way had been prepared for Norman influence in England by the marriage of King Ethelred with Emma, the daughter of Richard, Duke of Normandy; by Ethelred's sojourn in Normandy for several years and by their son, Edward the Confessor, who was trained chiefly in Normandy. Patterson remarks that "with the *reign* of *Edward the Confessor* the Norman Conquest began. The Court of the Norman Duke was to Edward what the Court of Louis XIV was in a later age to Charles II." We must remember, too, that Emma, a Norman lady, was the wife of two of England's kings, having married Canut after the death of Ethelred, and was the mother of two other kings of England, and therefore her influence in the realm, including both Church and nation, was very extensive and continued through a long time. Through her and her royal husbands and sons, many Normans were brought over to fill the English sees, even the archbishopric of Canterbury, as well as the position of deans, and prebendaries in the cathedrals and rectorships of many important parishes. We can now readily understand how the religious ideas prevailing on the Continent, where these men had received their training, should be transferred in a measure, at least, to the land where they were put in the positions of teachers and ecclesiastical rulers. We have already pointed out how it was that William and Harold became rival claimants to the throne of England. Because the natives of both Church and nation sided with Harold the Saxon, William felt no gratitude toward the English Church, and desired to replace as quickly as possible its leaders who had stood firmly by their English king, with men from Normandy who would be willing staunchly to maintain William's ways and who would bring with them religious ideas to which the Norman family had been accustomed. These foreigners were promoted to lucrative and influential offices in the English Church and to positions of honor and power in the realm. English nobles were able to hold their own more effectively, and for a longer time than the English prelates. But the earldoms and abbacies and bishoprics were given to Normans in such measure and so fast that at the end of William's reign only a few English *earls* held estates, and only *one English bishop* retained his see, Wulfstan of Worchester.

This was the kind of change that took place following the Norman Conquest. And consequently it requires only a little imagination to see the effect that such a change would have upon the English Church in the maintenance of her ecclesiastical policy and polity and her faith and worship. To our own observations on this point we add the following comments of Bishop Boyd-

Carpenter (pp. 72–73): "The Norman Conquest brought with it foreign habits and customs which effected considerable changes. Life in England was no longer the same, and the changes altered the complexion of the Church of England. We must try to understand the character of these influences.

"Now the bishops in England exercised considerable power; they were leading men amongst the people; their position, their wealth, and their learning gave them authority and influence. William resolved that the bishoprics should be filled as little as possible by Englishmen, and as much as possible by his friends, the Normans. Naturally the first to suffer was Stigand, the Archbishop of Canterbury, who had taken a leading part in supporting Harold, and was consequently distrusted by William the Norman. Unfortunately, too, Stigand was in a difficult position for he had been appointed to the archbishopric of Canterbury while Archbishop Robert was yet alive. This and some other matters gave to William what he wanted, a pretext for deposing Stigand."

Then to return to the effect of these foreign abbots, and priests and bishops being brought into positions of influence and authority in the English Church. We know, of course, that one of the chief tenets that the French Church held and taught was papal supremacy. These men had been accustomed to that thought throughout their lives, and therefore, when they were established in the Church of England, they brought these notions and predilections with them. But they came into a land where such things were strange and where the people were not willing to follow them. As an illustration of this, we recall that after the Conquest, Gregory the Seventh, or Hildebrande, sent legates to England to demand William's homage for his kingdom. Although William was quite willing to have the backing of the pope when he made his invasion of England, and was willing to acquiesce in a measure to some of the pope's demands, yet when established upon the throne, and having felt the national pulse, he had no intention of making himself a vassal of the pope, or rendering any sort of homage to him and, therefore, he thus replied to Hildebrande: "Homage to thee I have not chosen, nor do I choose to do. I never made a promise to that effect, *neither do I find that it was ever performed by my predecessors to thine.*"

William expressed his relationship to the papacy in very emphatic terms whenever occasion arose. For example, when an abbot in one of the monasteries of England complained to the pope in regard to a certain matter, the king said, "I have great respect for the pope's legate in things concerning religion, but if any one in my dominions tries to raise a complaint against me, I will have him hanged on the highest tree of the forest." Patterson, commenting on one of the principles of William in dealing with the papacy, says (p. 72): "The principle, in Eadmer's words, was this: 'He would not allow any one in all his dominions to accept the man who was appointed pontiff of Rome as the representative of the Apostle, save at his own bidding, or any way to receive his letters, unless they had been first shown to himself.' This maxim of policy was probably laid down at the time of Gregory's struggle with the Emperor's anti-pope. It clearly enabled William to put *severe* restrictions on the papal power, and was the germ of the later Praemunire legislation."

And subsequently, when William had Odo, Bishop of Bayeaux, imprisoned for unjust oppression of the English, the pope demanded his release and the king paid no heed to the pope's communication and kept Odo in prison throughout his whole reign.

It is significant also that Hildebrande cited English bishops to appear before him at Rome, but neither the bishops nor the king regarded his summons, and Hildebrande allowed the matter to drop. As an outstanding example of this we recall the case of Lanfranc, then archbishop of Canterbury. We use Patterson's words to relate the story (pp. 71–72) : "The relations between the pope and archbishop became even more strained as years went on. There is a letter extant in which Gregory upbraided Lanfranc for his neglect to appear at Rome, and threatened him with suspension from his episcopal office if he did not appear before the papal Curia within a specified time. There is nothing to show that Lanfranc was in the least degree moved by the papal threat." So that we see that while there were deplorable results of William's bringing to England Norman bishops, clergy and nobles, yet we see clearly also even from his own actions and words, that the things they attempted to introduce were distinctly novel at that time, and also that the subsequent encroachments of the papacy with their attendant mediæval superstitions, false doctrines and practices, were extraneous to the English Church, were indeed as carbuncles on the body. It is plain, therefore, when the English Church through her properly constituted authority in Convocation, supported by Parliament and the king, threw these extraneous things off—cut these carbuncles away from her body—she was not only thoroughly justified, but even was required so to do by wisdom, self-preservation, and her duty to bear witness to the primitive purity of the Gospel which she had received.

There was one action of William the Conqueror, however, that was the source of much trouble in the future, though the act itself seemed to be perfectly right at the time. The troublesome consequences came from the susceptibility of the act to the vitiating and distorting influence emanating from the unscrupulous methods of the papacy in that day. The act to which we refer is that by which civil and ecclesiastical offenses were separated and the offenders tried in different courts. From this, there arose the claim by the papacy that ecclesiastical persons, as ecclesiastical offenses, were not to be tried in civil courts, but only in ecclesiastical courts, and that the highest appellate jurisdiction for ecclesiastical persons and offenses was Rome. This, of course, gave to the papacy a tremendous prestige and power. Men like Anselm and Lanfranc, as archbishops of Canterbury, trained in France and Italy with the Continental ideas firmly in their minds, would use such a method or procedure for greatly enhancing the authority and power of the papacy, except, of course, when it ran contrary to their own personal ambitions and will, as was sometimes the case. For example: Anselm, as archbishop of Canterbury, deposed another bishop for what he regarded as contumacy. The bishop appealed to Rome. The pope sent a communication to Anselm, requiring the reinstatement of the offending bishop, but Anselm paid no other attention to the pope's bull than to throw it into the fire and see it crumble to ashes. And in Lanfranc's time, there was a heated and long-continued controversy between the sees of York and Canterbury, as to which should be regarded as the head of the English Church. This question, had the pope's right to appellate jurisdiction been acknowledged in the English Church, indisputably would have been definitely decided by the pope. But after much discussion and strife, it was finally settled by a synod of the English Church held at Windsor 1072 in favor of Canterbury.

It was at this time that Gregory VII, or Hildebrande, set up the claim to be universal bishop and excommunicated Constantinople and all the Eastern Churches. It will be recalled that another Gregory, known as Gregory the Great, had declared that "anyone who assumed the title of universal bishop or claimed any authority over other bishops outside of his own province, was Anti-Christ." Gregory's reply to Augustine's question as to his attitude toward the bishops in Gaul is also pertinent here. We let Bede speak for us: "But you, of your own authority, shall not have power to judge the bishops of France, but by persuading, soothing, and showing good works for them to imitate; you shall reform the minds of wicked men to the pursuit of holiness; for it is written in the Law, 'When thou comest into the standing corn of thy neighbours, then thou mayest pluck the ears with thine hand; but thou shalt not move a sickle unto thy neighbours' standing corn.' For thou mayest not apply the sickle of judgment in that harvest which seems to have been committed to another; but by the effect of good works thou shalt clear the Lord's wheat of the chaff of their vices, and convert them into the body of the Church, as it were, by eating. But whatsoever is to be done by authority, must be transacted with the aforesaid bishop of Arles, lest that should be omitted, which the ancient institution of the fathers has appointed." It is interesting to ask again, how the modern papalists can reconcile this and other like matters with their theory of papal infallibility. If Gregory the First, one of the purest and noblest men that ever occupied the see of Rome, was correct in declaring that the man who claimed supremacy over other bishops was of the spirit of Anti-Christ, then what shall be said concerning this other Gregory and all of his successors who have maintained this similar haughty, audacious Petrine claim, insupportable both Scripturally and historically? Hildebrande ordered that all English married clergy should desert their wives and remain single. This papal bull was regarded as null and void, and was not heeded in the English Church.

Perhaps it is well to say something here concerning Anselm, the abbot of Bec in Normandy, who was made archbishop of Canterbury in 1093. He was a native of Italy and received his early training in papal lands and of course held the Continental idea in regard to the Roman Church and her practices. When he came to England as archbishop, there were, as was often the case, two rival popes. William Rufus, son of William the Conqueror, was then king of England and Urban II was the pope that was recognized in Italy. Clement III was the rival pope who reigned at St. Angelo. France and Normandy admitted Urban's claim. And as the Abbey of Bec was in Normandy, Anselm had declared before his consecration that he considered Urban to be the true pope. Rufus said, "According to my father's laws, no one may acknowledge a pope in England without my sanction, and I have not acknowledged Urban." The question was referred to an assembly of prelates and barons. They said to Anselm, "Give up this Urban, cast off this yoke of bondage, *act in freedom as becomes an archbishop of Canterbury.*" But he refused. He was adjudged an outlaw, and condemned as disloyal to the king and the laws of the realm; and the bishops renounced their obedience to him. In the meantime, Rufus had sent a commission to Rome to find out who was regarded as the true pope in the city of Rome. The members of this commission having brought word that Urban was the one accepted as pope there, Rufus allowed Anselm to receive his pall from the altar in Canterbury Cathedral where it had been placed by the pope's legate. On another occasion, Anselm, in a controversy with his king, appealed to Rome for advice. The king replied that he should not attempt to introduce papal jurisdiction into England by appealing to the see of Rome against his king. All of this shows that these encroachments were regarded as something *new,* and as that which did not belong to the real life and character of the Church or the realm of England. And as Wakemen says (p. 225) : "Marsiglio of Padua in his 'Defensor Pacis,' written at the end of the thirteenth century, refused to admit that S. Peter had any superiority at all over the other Apostles, or was proved ever to have been bishop of Rome, much less to have endowed the popes with a prerogative of government as his successors. But the majority of the opponents of the papacy were not prepared to go so far. While admitting in principle the spiritual headship of the pope as the *normal guarantee and evidence of the unity of the Church,* they maintained that his power as such visible Head was of a *constitutional* and not of an *autocratic* character. William of Occam contended that the pope even in the discharge of his spiritual functions was subject to the general voice of Christendom."

We recall also that the pope demanded the restitution of Anselm's temporalities of which he was deprived because of what was considered as contumacy toward his king; but William Rufus, in reply to the demand of the pope, expelled the pope's messengers from his country. When William Rufus was succeeded by Henry the First, the controversy between Anselm and the king was renewed. Anselm refused to be reinvested with his authority as archbishop of Canterbury and appealed to the pope, Paschal the Second. The pope refused to give his consent and Henry then declared that the opinion of the pope and the decision of the Roman Council were alike indifferent to him. "I will not lose the *customs* of my *predecessors,*" he said, "nor endure in my kingdom one who is not my subject."

About this time, the archbishop of Vienna came to England and claimed authority over its bishops in the name of the pope. This distinct infringement on the rights of England was strenuously resisted, and by none more than by Anselm, who was very jealous of his own personal dignity. Consequently, the legate had to depart immediately from the country. Such an attitude seems consistent with Anselm's convictions as held and expressed at the time the archbishopric was offered him by William Rufus. At first he declined it. Then all the clerics at the sick king's bedside at the time clamored for his acceptance, and pressing the pastoral staff in Anselm's hand hurried him to the nearest Church. Anselm then said to them: "Ah, my friends, do you know what you are doing? The plough of the Church in England is borne by two strong oxen, the king and the archbishop of Canterbury; one of these oxen, Lanfranc, is dead; will you yoke me, an old and feeble sheep, with a fierce, untamed bull?" The control of the Church is seen here to be *inside* and not outside of the realm—in the archbishop and the king, and not in the pope. And when on his recovery from his illness Rufus insisted upon Anselm's acceptance of the appointment, he agreed to do so on certain conditions, one of which was that "the King must accept him" (that is, the archbishop not the pope or any other person) "as his special counsellor in things religious."

Anselm's appeals to Rome were usually, if not always, in behalf of his own dignity and prerogatives and as against the authority of the king, for *clerical* rather than papal, supremacy in the Church as opposed to royal or any other form of lay supremacy in things spiritual. Although he could resist and did resist the pope and his authority when it suited his personal interests or enhanced his personal dignity, still practically his influence was distinctly toward papal encroachments in both the Church and the realm of England. However, there were so many currents and cross currents flow-

ing here and there in the life of the people of England
in these confused times that it is not always easy to
discern the controlling influence or the pre-eminently
dominant force in a given day or event. For example,
Wakeman writes (pp. 102–3) : "The first great struggle
between Church and State in England since the days of
Wilfrid had ended in the victory of the Church, largely
because the champion of the Church was Anselm. It
was a victory of *character over law,* or moral ascendancy over material force. Both William and Henry had
the letter of the law on their side. On that of Anselm
were the rights of conscience. Both William and Henry
had the power of the nation behind them to enforce
their will. With Anselm there was but the strength of
the martyr's weakness. It is true that the archbishop could
not have maintained the struggle at all had he not had
the power of Rome at his back. Yet the pope dared give
him little open support, *and the adherence of the barons
and the clergy in England* to his side did far more to
influence the royal policy than all the remonstrances
of Rome. Englishmen quickly saw that the struggle
between Anselm and Rufus was but part of the eternal
struggle between right and wrong. They realised gradually that the question between Anselm and Henry was
part of the far wider question of a united Christendom
or an insular Church. They felt dimly that bound up
with the resistance of the archbishop was the sacred cause
of their own liberty. Anselm was fighting for the liberties of England no less than for his own conscience
or the claims of the pope. The Church was the one
power in England not yet reduced under the iron heel
of the Norman kings. The clergy were the one body

which still dared to dispute their will. To them fell the noble task of handing on the torch of liberty amid the gloom of a tyrannical age. The all-mastering despotism of the Crown was the special danger to England in the eleventh and twelfth centuries. It was the Church which in that time of crisis rescued England from slavery. Had there been no Anselm, Henry I would have issued no charter of liberties. Had there been no Becket, Stephen Langton would have failed to inspire the barons to wrest the Great Charter from the reluctant hands of John."

On the other hand, however, as has been said by one of the English historians, "he assailed the prerogatives of English kings; and they did right to maintain them. Anselm was entirely unjustified in his desire to set up the authority of an unacknowledged pontiff over that of his lawful sovereign, and in presuming that the declarations of a synod of Rome could override the ancient laws and customs of England. When the position he assumed—to maintain which he neglected the greater duties of his primacy and spent long years abroad—is considered apart from his private and personal virtues, it will be seen that no man did more to establish precedents which compromised the independence of the English Church and nation, and to encourage the encroachments of the papacy."

It must not be forgotten, however, that in spite of the number of the foreign clergy and the positions of authority that they occupied, the great body of the Church, whenever given a chance to express its opinion, showed the spirit of independence of any outside jurisdiction. Along this line Wakeman (p. 90) says: "Willing as were William and Lanfranc to bring the higher ideals and superior organization of the Roman Church to mould and discipline the Church of England, they were by no means the humble slaves of the Hildebrandine papacy. Rome was to be an example of a more disciplined life, the pattern of a better administration, the teacher of a higher morality, not the source of authoritative law, still less the dictator of action, or the supreme judge of conscience. She was to persuade opinion, not to enforce obedience. *The right of the papacy to command, the duty of kings to obey, were claims to which William I never thought of listening for a moment."*

As an illustration of presumptuous encroachment on the rights of the English Church we recall the appointment of John of Crema in 1125, as papal legate. Although in priest's orders only, yet he claimed to take precedence over the archbishop of Canterbury. William of Corbeil, archbishop at the time, was not a strong character, and yielded in the premises and to save himself further indignity, went to Rome and secured the appointment of himself as legate. Wakeman (p. 104) makes the following comment on the incident: "By the appointment of John of Crema in 1125, and afterwards of Henry of Winchester in 1139, to govern the Church of England by virtue of the office of legate, the popes were in fact making a claim that all metropolitical, if not episcopal, power was derived from them, and was exercised by delegation from them. Such a claim was no more likely to be admitted by the Church of England in the twelfth century than by the Church of Spain at the Council of Trent, but neither side wished to push matters to an extremity."

The Constitutions of Clarendon

In the next generation, however, came the Constitutions of Clarendon passed in January 1164 in an assembly near Salisbury, numbers eight and twelve of which are: "(8) Appeals were to go from the archdeacon to the bishop, and from the bishop to the archbishop. If the archbishop failed to do justice, the cause was to be settled in the archbishop's court by the precept of the king, and not to go further without the king's leave. (12) The rents of archbishoprics, bishoprics, abbacies, and priories were to go to the king during vacancy. The vacancies were to be filled by election by the principal clergy in the king's chapel, with the consent of the king and his council." Patterson adds this note of his own to number eight: "This was, of course, aimed against appeals to the pope." Boyd-Carpenter (p. 105) writing of these very times states: "It must never be forgotten that the English Church claimed to be national, and was jealous of foreign interference." Patterson says that the most prominent fact in the life of the Church and State in the reign of Henry III was "the increased influence and *encroachments* of the papacy in Church and State," which elsewhere he calls "unwarrantable usurpations." That is the key to the situation in all these years—papal claims in England not resting on rights, but being in their nature "unwarrantable usurpations."

The Church in England was willing to show honor

and spiritual deference to the Church in Rome because of its historic prestige and its central place in Christendom, and because of effects produced by forged documents believed in those days to be genuine, but where matters of right and constitutional liberties were concerned she not only refused acknowledgment of any rightful authority of the pope, but resisted to the limit allowed by circumstance, e. g., character of archbishop, king and pope.

It is of interest here to note that shortly after Thomas of York died, Thurstan was made archbishop of York. He did not wish to acknowledge the supremacy of Canterbury. Ralph, the archbishop of Canterbury, then refused to consecrate him. Thurstan went to France and was consecrated by Calixtus II, one of the two rival popes then governing the Church of Rome. This angered the king of England and the English prelates, and as a result, Thurstan was for a time, banished from England, the ground of his banishment being that his conduct constituted *a breach of the rights* of the *Church of England, by his having been consecrated by a foreign* Church.

CHAPTER IX

An action of the papacy that greatly increased its influence and power in England was the decree freeing monastic orders from the jurisdiction of the bishops and making them directly responsible to Rome. This, of course, weakened the parochial clergy and gave the members of the monastic orders opportunity to do very largely as they pleased, being without control by the local authorities of the Church. At the same time, it gave Roman authority much additional weight, and the Roman influence a further impetus in England, as in other countries. This can be readily appreciated when we remember that these orders were made up of hundreds, even thousands, of men going about preaching as Rome would have them preach. As one historian says: "We can now comprehend the manifold ways in which the popes sought to extend their influence here (that is, in England), yet it must be borne in mind that it was *English* benefices and *members of the English Church* over which the monasteries obtained such unwarrantable and illegal control."

Through the influence of Thomas Becket and the manner of his death, the papal influence again was increased in England. Though an Englishman, Becket

had been educated in France, and was thoroughly imbued with the Continental conception of Christianity,
and when he came to be archbishop of Canterbury, he
brought the Continental preconceptions and prejudices
with him. A very sharp controversy arose between
Henry the Second and Becket as to the relative power
of the Church and the Crown, more particularly, the
rights of the papacy and of the king. We recall that
the controversy between these men culminated in the
murder of Becket in Canterbury Cathedral. The consequences of that crime were very disastrous to the kingdom and the Church of England. Becket was not a particularly good man. He was headstrong, irascible and a
contumacious citizen, but because he was murdered,
and that in the Cathedral itself, and while claiming that
he was dying in defense of the Church, he has been
canonized as a saint, and respect paid to him and his
memory to a degree all out of proportion to what is
right and proper. In 1173 he was canonized by the pope,
but we can but agree with Patterson, who says: "In
spite of this canonization he has no true claim to saintship. His conduct was in many ways heroic; yet he died
a martyr not to the verities of the faith but to the
privileges of the clergy: we cannot help feeling that he
was devoid of true statesmanship and many of the
higher Christian virtues." Because of the sympathy and
horror arising from his death, the king thought it wise
to capitulate and to give to the pope a greater degree
of influence in his realm, in order to re-establish himself in the good opinion of the world. "On his return to
England in 1174, he did public penance: he made a
pilgrimage to the murdered Primate's tomb at Canter-

bury, and was publicly scourged by the assembled monks: we can imagine the pleasure with which Thomas would have regarded such a humiliation of the temporal power. In the next few centuries the cult of Thomas Becket became the most fashionable cult in England: many churches were dedicated to him: innumerable cures were said to have been wrought at his tomb or even by the invocation of his name: pilgrims flocked to his resting-place, and the magnificence of his shrine, far-famed for its gold and jewels, became one of the chief wonders of England" (Patterson, p. 109).

At this time there was in the papacy a very bold and able man under the name of Innocent III. He claimed both temporal and spiritual jurisdiction over *all* the world. He ordered the monks of Canterbury to elect Stephen Langton as their archbishop. This they did, but the king, John, had already nominated the bishop of Norwich for that position, and he refused to receive Langton. Innocent then prohibited the English clergy from performing spiritual duties until John should receive Langton. Some of the clergy paid heed to the decree of Innocent, but a vast number who knew the story of papal aggression, paid no attention to his message or his denunciation, and all the bishops and clergy who obeyed the pope were expelled from the country and their benefices taken away, showing how much the papal documents were regarded in England at that time. The action of the pope would have come to naught utterly had not King John increased his tyrannies and exactions to such an amazing extent. His oppression was so unjust and so great that the people were forced to seek help and get relief wherever they could. They preferred to see Innocent triumph over John to having John's tyrannous yoke made ever heavier and more unbearable to them. The pope now had a large standing army, and he combined with Philip Augustus of France to invade England, drive John out, take the throne and give it to Philip. John knew that the English barons were against him as were the people also, because of his harsh tyranny and his known wickedness. He was terrified, and accepted the terms of submission offered by the pope and Philip rather than face the forces of the two combined, unsupported by his own people. One of the terms of submission was that he should receive the crown of England from the pope.

One historian says that when the people heard this, they were filled with indignation and shame and cried out: "Our king has become the pope's man. The king has degraded himself to the level of a serf!" And another has written: "But he went further—he surrendered his crown to the papacy. Henceforth England was to be a papal fief. John and his successors, kings of England, were to pay the pope one thousand marks yearly as tribute. Thus the prophecy of the hermit Peter was fulfilled in a way that Peter had never contemplated. The surrender was a disgraceful transaction—disgraceful not, perhaps, to Innocent, who only used his opportunities, but certainly to John, from whom the suggestion and initiative came.

"Innocent treated England henceforth as a part of the patrimony of St. Peter. The submission may in the immediate future have saved the English crown for John and his son. It certainly increased for the time the papal power; but the ultimate results were disastrous even to the papacy, since it was the political power exercised by the pope during the succeeding reign, and the fiscal exactions flowing from his sovereignty, which created the strong anti-papal feeling that finally led at the Reformation to the complete expulsion of his power from England."

Now, Langton was, as we have seen, an Englishman who stood as a champion of the English Church and people, against both the king and the pope. When John received his absolution for what the pope considered his crime, Langton administered to him an oath that the laws of Edward the Confessor would be renewed. These laws stipulated the privileges of the prelates and barons. The barons declared themselves ready to die for these liberties. In the meantime, however, the papal legate had been traversing the country, filling up the vacant places in the Church with friends of John and the pope, and in defiance of the voice and rights of the people and the prerogatives of the bishops. Langton would not submit to this and inhibited the legate from making further appointments. The clergy and the barons under Langton and Robert Fitz-Walter formed what is called "The Army of God and Holy Church" against the king and the pope's legate. John seeing this movement within his own kingdom, determined to make another abject submission to the papacy and to bring to bear whatever forces he could to save himself in his own country from the results of the wrath of his own people.

When Langton presented to the king the people's demand for their traditional liberties both in Church and State, John feeling himself strong in the might of papal support, repudiated his promise to ratify the ancient English laws of Church and realm. The barons and the prelates, under the leadership of Stephen Langton, then took the field in defense of their rights. The result was that John was compelled to sign the Magna Charta on the field of Runnymede in 1215. The opening and closing sentences of this great foundation of Anglo-Saxon liberty are these: "That the Church of England shall be free and hold her rights entire and her liberties inviolate." That is the opening sentence and after the various specifications of the rights that pertain to all the subjects of the land, the Charter concludes with the reassertion of its opening principle, "that the Church of England shall be free, that all men have and hold inviolate the aforesaid liberties, truly and peacefully, freely and equally, fully and wholly in all things and in all places for ever." After quoting these words of the Charter, Mr. Patterson makes this comment: "The liberty of the Church no doubt meant freedom from excessive taxation, such as John had extorted from them against their will in 1207, the right of canonical election to vacant sees and abbeys, and all the acknowledged privileges of the ecclesiastical courts. It did not mean freedom from the pope." We have read such before, but we are not satisfied to accept Patterson's dogmatic statement. There was need in the Church for freedom from both the crown and the papacy. Why restrict the emphatic declaration of that freedom in either direction? And why deny the application of its expression to either pope or king? Certainly *the pope himself* felt that it was applicable in his direction and used all his power to nullify the

Charter, and so protect his own interests as he saw them. As one historian observes, "this Charter was signed by King John, June 15, 1215, and is still the standard of appeal in all judicial and secular matters. English Churchmen have, therefore, the right to maintain that it shall be also the standard by which the Church's liberties are to be tested." When the Great Charter was made known to Innocent at Rome, he declared it to be "a mischievous document and to be *in contempt of the Holy See,* and therefore null and void," but the English bishops and nobles stood firm and that document stands now as it has stood through the intervening centuries, "as the foundation of the rights and liberties of Englishmen even to this day."

Stephen Langton was a true and noble statesman, and a brave prelate who was able to resist the encroachments of the see of Rome and to stand as a great mountain peak of protest against the usurpations of that see, and for the rights of the English Church and people. A well-known historian has written thus of him: "He was one of the great nursing-fathers of English liberty. But he was soon disowned by his spiritual superior, Pope Innocent III. This great pope either knew nothing about English politics—which is unlikely, as Rome was then the centre of all international knowledge—or else cared nothing for English liberty. John had surrendered to Innocent his kingdom, and Innocent in his turn was ready to do all he could to maintain his submissive vassal and his own grasp over England. Innocent willingly annulled the Charter and released John from his solemn oath; the papacy thus readily, as ever throughout the Middle Ages, helping to undermine the sense of truth and honour in public obligations." In the latter part of his life, the orders of Friars overspread England. It has been supposed that this was one of the plans of Innocent to bring the Church and people of England more under the influence of the Roman see. In 1219 the Dominicans, or Black Friars, so called because they dressed in black, came to Britain. In 1224, the Franciscans, or Grey Friars, so called because they dressed in grey, made their appearance. These were preaching orders whose members went about in all parts of the country preaching, and living upon what was given them in their preaching itinerary. These orders have sometimes been called the "Pope's Militia," because it was so generally thought that they were commissioned by him to introduce and fasten papal ideas and practices in the English Church.

It was now come to pass that in the reign of Henry III, king and pope combined to oppress the people—devour them as wolf and shepherd-robber. Their combined exactions of the clergy and of the nobility of the land were terrible and the effects upon the people burdensome and disastrous. They seemed to form a conspiracy to denationalize the English Church and realm. The unscrupulous pope and the iniquitous king exercised such tyranny, and hurt the Church and nation to such an extent, that the archbishop of Canterbury, Edmund Rich by name, was impelled to withstand both, and not feeling strong enough to stand the strain, resigned his see and died of a broken heart. Then came a strong man in the person of Robert Grosseteste of Lincoln. By his influence Richard Wych was appointed bishop of Chichester. The king had desired to have another fill this position and appealed to the pope against the appointment of Wych. This appeal came before the Council at Lyons in 1250, where the pope then lived. Grosseteste was present and preached a sermon before Innocent IV and the Roman clergy, denouncing them as the authors of all the troubles that afflicted the English Church, saying, "The foundation and the origin of all this is the greed of Rome, because it commits the care of the flock to ravening wolves." Much more of a like nature found place in this discourse, and we may say it was the first definite protest on the part of the English Church and its representatives against the great and growing worldliness of the papacy, and henceforth the bishops of Rome had often to submit to open reproach. The pope had commanded Grosseteste to institute a mere child over the monastery at Lincoln, but he refused, stating that he would resist and oppose the orders contained in the pope's letters because they deprived Christian souls of the ministry of their pastors and were altogether contrary to the Catholic faith. Had Grosseteste lived, his efforts would perhaps have ended in the complete overthrowing of the papal yoke by the national party, and things might have taken place in the thirteenth century that were delayed through many causes until the sixteenth century.

Grosseteste died in 1253. He was a scholar of wide and profound learning, a man of true piety and deep Christian earnestness and possessed of heroic courage. He was also a stalwart champion of the rights of the English in Church and State, a fearless prophet speaking forth ringing words of truth and light, calling both high and low to repentance, and a noble bishop with a true sense of responsibility and a loving heart for his flock. In short he stands forth as one of the grandest figures of the thirteenth century. And yet at his death the pope showed the very beautiful charity and Christian graciousness of asking "every true son of the Roman Church to rejoice with him now that his enemy was dead"! It will be further illuminating to add these words from Patterson (p. 130) : "In 1250 Grosseteste, the great bishop of Lincoln, read a memorandum before the pope and cardinals denouncing in fierce terms ecclesiastical abuses and tracing them to their origin in the Roman court itself, especially to the system of provisions. He told them plainly that the work of a parish priest, with all its duties of preaching, teaching, and administering charity, could not be performed by the hirelings of an absentee rector, especially when these hirelings did not receive sufficient to support life. In 1253 Grosseteste boldly refused obedience to a papal letter in which he was bidden to provide Innocent IV's nephew, Frederic de Lavagna, with a canonry of Lincoln. To the papal envoy he wrote an outspoken refusal. 'The letter is not in harmony with Apostolic holiness, but is utterly at variance therefrom. . . . It cannot be, therefore, that the Apostolic see, to which has been given by our Lord power for edification, and not for destruction, should issue a command so hateful . . . nor can any one who is faithful to the said holy see obey commands such as this, even though they should emanate from the highest orders of angels . . . but must of necessity resist them with his whole strength. . . . Out of filial obedience I decline to obey—I resist,

I rebel.' When the purport of this letter was reported to Innocent, he is said in his wrath to have shouted out: 'Who is this old dotard that dares to judge our deeds?' and he then proceeded to threaten that he would make Grosseteste an example and warning to the whole world, and that 'our vassal, nay, our slave,' the king of England, would be made to imprison him. He was only dissuaded from any rash step by the cardinals, who pointed out that the letter was founded on truth, and that Grosseteste himself was more Catholic, more saintly and learned than they."

About this time, exactly in 1256, during the papacy of Alexander IV, a demand was made for "first-fruits," annates, that is that every prelate and clergyman in the English Church should pay to the pope his first year's income. So great was the popular hatred against foreigners at this time, that when an alien had been installed in St. Paul's Cathedral, London, three young men, in the broad day-light, in the presence of a large assembly murdered him, and not one of the bystanders even attempted to capture the assassins. The chroniclers on every page denounce "the yawning gulf of papal needs," "the greed and avarice of the Romans." In 1231 a secret society was formed of "men ready to die rather than tolerate the Romans beneficed in England." Outrages followed at which the Justiciar himself, Hubert de Burgh, was thought to connive. Foreign ecclesiastics were attacked by masked men. The barns of absentee Romans were pillaged. The papal collector became the best-hated man in England.

A single story will illustrate the general feeling. Master Martin was supposed to have brought from

Rome blank parchments with the papal seals affixed, so that he could write on them whatever he wished. His extortions were so severe that the baronage, in 1245, sent a messenger ordering him to leave England immediately. Martin went to the king, but the king was irritated, and told Martin that he could with difficulty restrain the barons from tearing him in pieces. Martin, in alarm, asked for a safe-conduct out of the kingdom. The king, without his usual urbanity, answered, "The devil take you and give you a safe-conduct through hell." Martin was, however, given an attendant to escort him to Dover. On their journey they came across a group of people gathered by a wood. Martin in terror said to his attendant: "Alas! what I feared has happened—see, they are going to attack us. Ah! my friend Robert, have you son, grandson, kinsman, or friend for whom you desire ecclesiastical promotion? I am ready to obtain all you demand." Robert politely declined, but telling Martin to wait, he said that he would find out the purpose for which the men were assembled, and, if necessary, would show them the king's warrant. Having approached the group, he found that the men were engaged in the harmless occupation of negotiating a sale of timber; but returning to Martin quickly, he told them that the men were with difficulty prevented from tearing him in pieces, and urged him to hurry, and in the event of his escape never again come near the country.

The influence and authority of the popes, as we see again, was never accepted by the Church of England, but always resisted, although kings, and nobles mostly consisting of foreigners, sometimes and for their own personal advantage, aided and abetted the pope in his efforts to extend his usurped authority. At this point it is pertinent to recall these words of Bishop Boyd-Carpenter: "It is in this epoch that we are now to trace the history of the Church. It will be seen that though in an intermittent way Churchmen reflected the growing national and patriotic feeling, they were largely blind to the movements of their time, and their blindness was due to their devotion to what they believed were the interests and rights of the Church. The papal influence was always exerted to divide and rule. Friction between Church and king was the pope's opportunity. The leaders of the Church did not always see that the true independence of their Church might be jeopardized by the patronizing aid of Rome. They failed to perceive the unwisdom of refusing to bear their share of national burdens in an age when all round them their countrymen were awakening to the duty of patriotic service." ("History of the Church of England," p. 133.) In writing of the situation in England in the time of Henry VIII, Wakeman refers *back* to these days of which we are writing in these terms (p. 203) : "No one who knew anything of the past history of England could shut his eyes to the fact that until the coming of the Normans no such administrative rights as those claimed by the popes had ever been exercised. During the past three centuries they had gradually been successfully asserted, but *never admitted without protest*. When they had been freely exercised it was by arrangement with the crown, not by virtue of any inherent prerogative of the papacy. It was no light matter to despise the counsels or disregard the wishes of the Apostolic see. They came with all the moral prestige of the greatest spiritual institution in the Christian commonwealth. But it is one thing to acknowledge the *weight of moral authority, it is another to admit the force of indefeasible right.*" However, the influence in the moral and spiritual spheres of the papacy due to the position that Rome occupied in the Western world and particularly to the effect of the forged decretals falsely exalting the papacy, might have been retained if the popes had been godly men and not princes of avarice and immorality, and "principal causes of abuse and injustice."

In Edward the First's reign, the opposition on the part of the English Church and realm to the encroachments of the Roman pontiff was more organized in character than it had previously been. During his reign, the first complete representative parliament was convened, sitting in the year 1295, *in the Chapter House of Westminter Abbey,* and being composed of the barons and prelates by virtue of their order, with representatives from among the clergy in each Cathedral, two to represent the clergy of each diocese, as well as two knights from each shire, two citizens from each city, and two burgesses from each borough. This parliament so representative of all elements of the nation, both the Church and the State, sitting at Carlisle in 1307, protested against the multitudinous forms of papal exactions and refused to allow the papal legate to leave England with the money that he had collected. This statute is sometimes said to contain the first anti-papal act of Parliament, but, as Bishop Boyd-Carpenter points out, this is only partially true as "several earlier acts must be reckoned as anti-Roman in as much as they are designed to protect the liberties of England against the tyrannical claims of Rome" (p. 138). Whether this was the first anti-papal act of Parliament or not, certain it is, that it was not the last by any means, as we shall see.

In the reign of Edward III, statutes were passed against further exactions of the papacy, the principle being that the people were willing to enable their king to conduct glorious wars abroad, but they were not willing to contribute to enrich foreign princes. And foreign clergy were expelled from the country, and the ships which brought them to England were confiscated, and *any who brought papal letters into the land were condemned to forfeit all their possessions*. The act of Parliament called the "First Statute," or "The Statute of Provisions," declared that papal provisions made for benefices by which the "first-fruits" were sent to Rome were illegal, and forbade, under penalties, the execution of orders in this respect. Some of the words of this statute are "kings and all other patrons are to present unto benefices of their own or their ancestors' foundations, *and not the pope of Rome*." It further asserted that the holy Church of England was founded by the ancestors of the king and his barons to teach the law of God and Holy Church and then enacted that elections to bishoprics should be free, subject to the royal, not papal, license and assent and further, that if candidates provided by the pope tried to assert their supposed rights they were to be kept in prison until they paid a fine at the king's discretion, and promised not to prosecute their case in the Roman court.

This step in the vindication of the national character of the Church was soon followed by the passage of the Act of Praemunire in 1353, which declared that all who should sue for redress in any foreign court should be put out of the protection of the law in England and forfeit all their goods to the State. In 1365 this statute was re-enacted and strengthened with special reference to the papal court. In 1366 Parliament finally repudiated the payment of the annual tribute to the pope, agreed to be paid by John, which had been for many years in arrears. In 1390 the Statute of Provisors was re-enacted with additional safeguards. In 1391 the scope of the Mortmain Act was enlarged. In 1394 the Statute of Praemunire was again re-enacted and made more stringent. Patterson's comment on these acts is full of interest. He says: "These important Acts of Provisors and Praemunire were henceforth, though imperfectly, observed, the *great bulwarks of the national Church against the encroachments of Rome*. It was in vain that Martin V (1417–1431) beat against the bars of the cage, and threatened Archbishop Chichelle with excommunication if he did not secure the repeal of the obnoxious statutes." We see, then, how strong was the movement at this time for the complete overthrow of papal influence in England, but the Hundred Years' War, having commenced some twenty years earlier, prevented the movement from reaching an early culmination. Most likely, however, even this would not have prevented it, had there not been so many foreign prelates and other clergy, and alien nobles in the country.

John Wycliffe—Morning Star of the Reformation

At this time, we meet a very wonderful personality, called the "Morning Star of the Reformation," John Wycliffe, born about the year 1320. Wycliffe, a clergyman of the Church of England—some of his ancestors having filled the same office—was deeply moved by the immoralities that he saw among the monks and the foreign clergy, and also was set against the papal encroachments.

He composed a great many theses against the doctrines and practices of the Roman Church, which were immediately received with hearty approval by a large circle, some of whom were selected and trained to propagate his teachings throughout the country—these being called "poor priests and preachers." It is said that they numbered in a short time as many as three thousand. Besides pointing to the two rival "infallible" (?) popes who spent much of their time and thought in fighting and anathematizing each other and each other's followers, and the scandalous lives and unscrupulous acts of many of them, he published a pamphlet which opened the eyes of men to the manifold enormities of the papal system, and in which he attacked not only the teaching and character of the popes, but *challenged the whole theory of papal power,* denied the claims of the papacy as unscriptural, and declared the pope to be Anti-Christ.

There was a wide-reaching movement of thought supporting his ideas, manifested not only in his so-called "poor priests" or "poor preachers," but in the general literature of the time as represented in Langland's "Vision of Piers the Plowman" and Chaucer's poems. For example, Chaucer gives us this picture of a begging friar.

> "In every house he gan to pore and pine,
> And begged mele and chese or elles corne.
> His felaw had a staff tippid with horne,
> A pair of tables alle of ivory,
> A pointell polished full fetously;
> And wrote alwey the namis as he stode
> Of all the fold that gave him any gode,
> Askauncis, as if he wolde for them pray."

He gives us further a picture of the Pardoner who brought in his wallet pardons "from Rome, all hot" :—

> "And in a glas he had a pigges bones
> And with these reliques when that he fand
> A poort person dwelling upon land,
> He gat him more money in a day
> Then that the parson got in months twaie."

The galling tyranny, both spiritual and political, of the papal system was being felt and the heart of the Church and the nation was rising in condemnation of it and intent on freeing itself from it, notwithstanding some clerical and royal opposition at times, of which we shall write later. He also translated the Scriptures into the common tongue and proclaimed it the duty of men to read them for their knowledge of Christianity rather than to look to conciliar decrees and traditions of any Church. It has been written that "The vilest epithets have been launched against him, but every true Englishman will number him among the foremost upholders of our national independence, and as a leader and a pioneer of those brave men who helped by right living and conduct to strengthen the hearts of their countrymen until they were able to overthrow entirely an intolerable and alien oppression."

In what has been written thus far, we mean no reflection upon the present generation of Roman Catholics whose good works are abundantly manifest in many spheres, nor do we deny the claim of their Church to be a recognized part of the Catholic Church—although a part, we believe, not without serious error in doctrine and form of organization, if Holy Scripture and primitive use are of any value in guiding us—but have merely intended to be loyal to the facts of history and make clear to our readers the established truth, from which it is manifest that the pope had no properly constituted or authorized jurisdiction in England and legally never had before this date, nor since. Now a striking confirmation of this is seen in 1399, when Richard II was deposed, it being charged against him that he had asked the pope to confirm his actions. Whereupon, Parliament declared that "the kingdom of England, and the rights of its crown have always been so free, that neither the pope nor any other outside the kingdom might interfere therewith." And Bishop Boyd-Carpenter, speaking of the last Act of Praemunire passed in 1393, says: "This last Act of Praemunire was one of the strongest measures passed against Rome, and it is said by Bishop Stubbs to furnish the clue to the events which connect the Constitutions of Clarendon with the Reformation. It is well to remember statutes such as these, for they constitute a clear and changeless witness to the claim that the *Church of England, however much and often its rights have been infringed, has ever been regarded in the Constitution of this country as a national Church."*

During the reign of Henry VI, the pope endeavored to procure the repeal of these anti-papal acts of Parliament, but the House of Commons made petition to the crown that "England's ecclesiastical liberty might be maintained and that the encroachments of the pope be not tolerated." We emphasize the "House of Commons" as the party making this petition because it represented in those days the great body of the lay people of the Church of England, the Church and the nation being practically one at that time. Pope Martin then issued bulls suspending Archbishop Chichelle and excommunicating all English bishops. As soon as these documents reached England, they were seized by the Lord Protector and destroyed—this happening in the year 1426.

Here we wish to repeat again that whatever influence or authority was exercised over the English Church and nation by the papacy, was a *usurpation* which came through the influence of foreign prelates and nobles, through the audacity, terrorism, political trickery, military power and fear and such like things of unscrupulous popes often of scandalous lives, aided and abetted by designing, ambitious and wicked kings, sometimes of foreign extraction and training. The spirit of England, however, was against these things and the complete repudiation of these presumptuous pretensions was delayed only by the circumstances of which we have already spoken—The Hundred Years' War with France, and the War of the Roses. Therefore it is true as Mr. Lane has well said, "When they threw off the papal yoke, they must not be considered to have lost their nationality, but to have *regained* it, and for the same reason, the English Church which was the nation organized for spiritual purposes did not lose its identity by repudiating the pope's supremacy, but was restored *thereby* to its original position as a part of *the universal Church of Christ, relying only upon its Apostolic origin, and the purity of its faith as it had done in the days before the Norman Conquest, when as yet the papacy had not asserted a claim to jurisdiction over Catholic Christendom.* The facts of history we have referred to have long been known to students, but negligently kept out of the reach of the 'millions.' " ("Illustrated Notes," p. 241.) It is interesting to quote also these words from the historian, J. R. Green (Vol. II, p. 151): "Parliament had hardly risen into life when it became the organ of the national jealousy, whether of papal jurisdiction without the realm or a separate life, or a separate jurisdiction of the clergy within it. The movement was long delayed by religious reactions and civil wars." And Cardinal Manning of the Roman Church said that "The English Reformation was a success after many failures." That is, the movement was constantly in process from the beginning of the time when there was need of it, but had been stopped first by one thing and then another, and was a continuous effort, which came to final successful culmination in the sixteenth century.

The claim that the pope had no rightful jurisdiction over the English Church was amply re-echoed in the Councils of Pisa and Constance. Before the Council of Pisa in A. D. 1409, two rival popes presented their claims. The Council recognized neither, and elected a new pope, but those whom the Council condemned declined to accept its decision, so three rival popes were in the field, each claiming absolute infallibility and spending his time chiefly in excommunicating the adherents of the other two! The Council of Constance in 1414–1418 deposed all three of these popes, and Martin V was elected, giving clear evidence of the absurdity of the claim of the infallibility of the pope, and clear evidence also of the judgment of the Church, that a council is of higher authority than any bishop, whatever might be his see. The Council of Constance passed a decree to that effect—that popes are inferior and subject to General Councils; and this decree was put into effect by the Council of Basle, meeting from 1431–1449 when it *acted* upon the principle, pronouncing the sentence of contumacy against Pope Eugenius IV for not appearing in answer to its citation. And when he resisted their decree, the Council deposed him from the papacy and elected another in his place. It is quite clear, therefore, that England was not alone in her determination to resist papal aggrandizement and encroachment. The above Councils were fairly representative of Western Christendom.

It is quite interesting to recall here the following words of Father Knox whose pronounced pro-Roman tendency has already been noted, and the writing of which is evidence of the overwhelming power of historical fact in the premises, though running contrary to the writer's ecclesiastical bias: "We have seen that the claim that Catholic unity depends on visible communion with the See of Peter involves the somewhat difficult assumption that the Eastern Church has since the year 1054 been outside the fold of the one true Church. In view of the fact that that Church has preserved the Catholic life and the Catholic religion intact for so many centuries in the face of almost continual persecution, it is difficult not to regard the claim with some suspicion. We have seen further that there is in fact a fatal objection to the claim to make visible communion with the Holy See in all cases the one test of Catholic unity. For the centre of Catholic unity has itself been divided during the period of the Schism in the West, when two rival claimants to the See of Peter, the rival popes of Rome and Avignon, each claimed to be the one true successor of St. Peter and excommunicated all who supported the claims of their opponent. Thus it has to be admitted that there was a period of some forty years when it was impossible to solve the question of unity with the Catholic Church by the test of unity with the Holy See; for there were two Holy Sees not in communion with one another. Thus our suspicions of a theory of Christian unity which excludes the Eastern Church from the Body of Christ are amply confirmed." ("The Catholic Movement in the Church of England," p. 194.)

Apropos of this general subject of the papacy and its claims, it is a pleasure to quote these words of the Rt. Rev. Dr. Frank Wilson: " 'The Catholic Encyclopedia' (Vol. XII, p. 262, under the article 'Pope') says that 'the permanence of that office is essential to the very being of the Church.' Yet there were considerable periods of time which elapsed between the elections of successive popes—the interval between Clement

IV and Gregory X being more than three years. The question is—where was the Church during those three years? If the office is 'essential to the very being of the Church,' did the Church cease to be, during those years when its essential element was wanting? If, on the other hand, it could survive three years in the absence of its own essence, why not a hundred years or a thousand years or for the rest of the earth's natural life?

"In the same article (pp. 266–267) the Encyclopedia also stated that the extraordinary powers of the pope are 'immediate in character' and not delegated to him by the Church. They are powers which belong only to the pope. Granting, then, for the sake of argument, that Christ's words indicate a supremacy for St. Peter over the other Apostles (which is contradicted by a large majority of the early Church Fathers) ; granting that St. Peter was actually bishop of Rome (a claim never advanced before the year 170) ; granting that this supremacy was meant to be transmitted to his successors in office (which is merely surmise) ; and granting that Roman bishops are capable of receiving such inherited powers (which is a gratuitous assumption)— the further question arises as to how these strictly personal powers can be transmitted when a new pope cannot even be elected until his predecessor in the office is dead? With no one left on earth in possession of papal powers, who is equipped to transmit them to the newly elected incumbent? Not the Church, for the Church never had them; not the cardinals, for they are incapable of receiving them; not the previous bishop of Rome, for he is dead. It can only be by a new creative act of Divine grace; in which case it is not the privilege of Peter at all, but an entirely new privilege in each succeeding pope. So the papacy itself vitiates the fundamental principle of apostolic succession—namely, that one can transmit only that which he himself possesses." ("The Divine Commission," pp. 72, 73.)

Before closing this period in the life of the Church, we desire to mention Henry VII of the Tudor dynasty. His claim to the throne was an uncertain one, and he desired, of course, to have all the support possible to secure. Therefore, he went as far as he could to obtain the help of the papacy by allowing the pope a long reign in the English Church. The culmination of foreign usurpation occurred when Cardinal Kempe was appointed by the pope to the see of Canterbury, and then made extraordinary legate of the pope. This is regarded as a great overshadowing, for the time, of the national character and rights of the English Church. Once, and only once, before the eve of the Norman Conquest had any papal legates been sent to England and that was in the reign of Offa in 786, at the time of the temporary exaltation of Lichfield into a metropolitan see. It may have seemed more or less harmless at the time, but it was the beginning of an unauthorized encroachment that developed in later years into serious usurpation and interference with the rights of the English Church. During that period, the papal chair was filled by men of immorality and viciousness, murderers like the Borgias, adulterers like the Medici and infidels like Leo X. Their avarice and ambition led them to degrade the Church, her ministry and her sacraments for payments in money to their agents and collectors. Naturally they lost not only spiritual leadership, but spiritual life itself, yes even the power to recognize and sympathize with spiritual ideals and moral earnestness. Hence by way of illustration, "to Savonarola, Pope Alexander VI could offer nothing but the stake." And the king connived at such things in order that he might have the support of the papacy to make his claim to the throne a little more secure. But now that the realm had peace, the people began to think more of their rights and liberties as Englishmen and as English Churchmen. Wycliffe's teaching was revived and he found successors in Colet, Thomas More, Grocyn and such like.

A review of this Dark Period in the history of the Church of England then reveals clearly these facts— that from the time of the Norman Conquest to the middle of the sixteenth century the influence of the Roman Church insinuatingly, but gradually, grew, and the pope exercised some authority in its affairs, the result of influence gained by the introduction of foreign prelates, deans and clergy, nobles and friars, and based upon forged documents on the one side and ignorance and superstitious dread on the other. The influence however was constantly resisted.

Resistance by English Ecclesiastics to Papal Orders

As strange as it may seem it is sometimes said that there was practically no resistance by ecclesiatics to the papal authority in England before the Reformation, one teacher of Ecclesiastical History going so far as to say that he "knew of only three such resistances to papal orders and was sure that there were not more than five." This seems to be a good place therefore to cite some definite instances of resistance to papal claims and orders from the time of the refusal of the British bishops to accept Augustine's authority or fall in line with Gregory's scheme and acknowledge his jurisdiction, to the days of the Reformation some of which have already been mentioned in previous pages.

The next ecclesiastical resistance to the papal will is seen in the attitude of the great Theodore relative to the appeal of Wilfrid to the pope. Wilfrid had spent much time abroad neglecting his duties at home and the archbishop decided to divide the great diocese of Northumbria over which Wilfrid had presided, into four parts, and he consecrated bishops for Bernicia, Lindisfarne, and Lindsey, leaving to Wilfrid at York only the larger part of Deira. Wilfrid was indignant and appealed to Pope Agatho. Agatho issued a bull restoring Wilfrid, but Theodore refused to carry out the directions, and paid no serious attention to the pope's judgment in re. Then later, 680, he appeared before the king and Witan armed with a papal bull. His reception there was condemnation and banishment. But Wilfrid was a fighter and he "came back" again and Patterson says: "Theodore's reforms had to be carried out in the teeth of Wilfrid's opposition and *in defiance of papal bulls.*" When Athelheard, Archbishop of Canterbury, died in 805 and Wulfred was appointed to succeed him, the clergy of the English Church protested against his going to Rome for the consecration and to receive the pall. The pope gave in and Wulfred did not go to Rome, but the pope sent him the pall.

Then Dunstan an English abbot excommunicated an earl for contracting what was regarded as an unlawful marriage—a marriage within the prohibited degrees of relationships. The noble appealed to Rome. The pope ordered Dunstan to restore him to communion. Dunstan refused to obey the papal order. The marriage was abandoned. The king himself having contracted a similar marriage and seeing how little effect the pope's judgment had in the English Church at that time gave up his marriage also and sought absolution at the hands of Dunstan. Dunstan shortly afterwards was made archbishop of Canterbury. Then when Lanfranc was archbishop, he was commanded by the pope to appear at Rome and he refused. Patterson tells us (p. 7): "There is a letter extant in which Gregory upbraided Lanfranc for his neglect to appear at Rome, and threatened him with suspension from his episcopal office if he did not appear before the papal Curia within a specified time. There is nothing to show that Lanfranc was in the least moved by the papal threat." Jenkins, on page 101, says: "His independent spirit led him to resist the frequent importunities of Gregory to do homage to him in Rome, the king with true Norman chivalry, supporting the archbishop in his refusal."

William, Archbishop of York, about 1146 was deposed by Eugenius III, made resistance, finally triumphed and in due course was canonized. And Rev. Robert Ritchie in "Rights and Pretensions of the Roman See" (p. 163) tells us: "When the pope, in his weakness, temporized, and failed Becket, he rebuked him in terms inconsistent with papalism." He then adds: "It seems to me clear that Becket's idea was of the *ecclesiastical* as distinguished from the *papal* Supremacy. He applies to his own action the text so often claimed by popes: 'See, I have set thee over the nations and over the kingdoms, to root out and to pull down, and to destroy and to throw down, to build and to plant.' We remember too that during the reign of Henry III on one occasion some papal exactions were laid before the synod of Westminster, and 'the Synod,' one historian tells us, 'laughed' and the king said a very good thing: 'When the rest of Christendom shall have consented to this measure, we will consult with our prelates whether it be right to follow their example.' It was strongly suggested that there might be a secession from Rome. As time went on the irritation increased. Papal envoys were ill-treated and papal bulls trampled on."

Then historical students are aware of the fact that Anselm, Archbishop of Canterbury, was commanded by the pope to restore a bishop whom the archbishop had deposed, and that the only attention that Anselm paid to the papal bull was to cast it into the fire, and the deposed bishop was not restored.

Perhaps the reader is already familiar with the attitude of the pope toward the Magna Charta and Archbishop Stephen Langton. The pope described the Magna Charta as a "mischievous document" and declared it "null and void." He ex-communicated the barons who had signed it and ordered Langton to publish the bull of ex-communication which the archbishop refused to do. He ordered him to appear at Rome. This he also declined to do, and remained loyal and unafraid as the champion of the Great Charter. Let us add these words of Boyd-Carpenter: "In the midst of this misery and oppression the archbishop, Stephen Langton, stood

firm, like a rock in the time of flood. He refused to
be the agent of injustice. He refused to publish the
sentence of excommunication against the barons of
England. He was threatened. The pope ordered his
suspension but he was unmoved. A more sacred cause
than that of king or pope was entrusted to his care and
he abode by his trust." Of course, we remember
that Wycliffe was a clergyman of the Church of England and his whole movement was of a clerical nature
and based upon and expressed strong ecclesiastical resistance not only to the teaching and practice of the
papacy, but to the very institution itself. And the primacy of Edmund Rich, Archbishop of Canterbury,
Patterson (p. 140) says, "is more memorable for
his opposition to the alien and unconstitutional party
. . . for the relative independence of his attitude towards the pope; *on more than one occasion he ignored
the papal jurisdiction.*" And again he writes: "The opposition to the foreign influences of the pope and the
favourites gradually gathered head under the leaders
of the Church, such as Edmund Rich (d. 1240) and
Robert Grosseteste (d. 1253), and the leaders of the
barons, such as Gloucester and, greatest of all, Simon
de Montfort."

At this point belongs also the recollection of the
earnest protest of the Berkshire Rectors against the
demands of the papal legates in 1240. This most
probably inspired, as it was followed by, the protest of
the nobility of England at the Council of Lyons 1245
in the presence of the pope.

Again Patterson (p. 130) says: "In 1250 Grosseteste,
the great Bishop of Lincoln, read a memorandum be-

fore the pope and cardinals denouncing in fierce terms ecclesiastical abuses and tracing them to their origin in the Roman Court itself, especially to the system of provisions. . . . In 1253 Grosseteste *boldly refused obedience to a papal letter* in which he was bidden to provide Innocent IV's nephew, Frederic de LaVagna, with a canonry of Lincoln." The following are the words of Grosseteste himself: "I decline to obey, I resist, I rebel!" Boyd-Carpenter on p. 125 writes: "The pope was furious. It is said, though this is not probable, that he excommunicated Grosseteste; but if this were so, it does not seem to have had much effect and Grosseteste continued his protests. He appealed to *all who were in power to maintain the independence of the Church of England.* The papal impositions had grown through the patience or the great folly of the English people; but they united in defending the Church in her freedom. With his last breath Grosseteste protested, declaring that the action of the pope was the action of an Anti-Christ for it imperilled men's souls." Again Patterson says of him (p. 143) : "Whether we regard him as an advancer of learning and encourager of the friars or as the *nationalist leader against papal encroachments,* or as the close ally of the progressive party of the State, or as the great bishop, we must admit that he was one of the grandest figures of the thirteenth century." About the year 1225 the pope was making greater and more pressing demands for money from England. When the demand was read to the English Assembly it was greeted with derisive laughter, and the request that a number of English benefices—that is incomes from endowments to support the services of parish priests and bishops of dioceses—be given was refused. In 1296 Pope Boniface VIII issued his famous bull "Clericis Laicos," forbidding the clergy under pain of excommunication to pay taxes to princes. At first Archbishop Winchelsey and the clergy generally obeyed the bull, but when the king, Edward, and others in authority in England strenuously objected, the *archbishop and clergy disregarded the papal bull* and left the pope to save his face by explaining away the bull as best he could.

It will also be remembered that William of Occam contended that the pope, even in discharge of his spiritual functions, was subject to the general voice of Christendom. The *whole realm* is seen to rebel against the papacy in number VIII of the Constitutions of Clarendon, Wakeman, p. 109: "Appeals were to go from the archdeacon to the bishop and from the bishop to the archbishop. If the archbishop failed to do justice, the cause was to be settled in the archbishop's court by the precept of the king, and not to go further without the king's leave," which, of course, carries far greater weight than the refusal of any individual ecclesiastic to obey any particular order of the pope.

Boyd-Carpenter, p. 155, writes thus of the celebrated Hugh of London: "He had a firm and discriminating course. Evil doing in princes was to him still evil doing, and he had so acted toward King Richard that the lion-hearted king declared, 'If the rest of the bishops were such as he, no king or prince would dare to lift up his neck against them.' He showed equal courage in proclaiming the rights of the English Church against the encroachments of the pope. When the pope ordered the suspension of Geoffrey, Archbishop of York, Hugh of Lincoln said: 'I would rather be suspended myself than suspend the archbishop,' and did not obey the papal order."

Mr. Jenkins tells us that the conflict between Archbishop Baldwin and Pope Urban centered about a dispute between the regular and secular clergy, and in Mr. Jenkins's own words, p. 136, "Here the great cause of warfare between the secular and regular clergy reveals itself in all its force and magnitude, and we see the first pre-Reformation effort to free the Church of the crushing weight of the monastic orders and of the absolute subjection of the ordinary and national jurisdiction to that of an *illegitimate and foreign power*. However injurious the rule of Baldwin must have seemed to the monks, to the parochial clergy he must have appeared a real deliverer; while to the *popes,* whose devoted clients the monastic orders had been from the first, he was as dangerous a reformer as he was to the monks. The foundations of a new cathedral had been actually laid—a building five hundred feet in length—and this in spite of the protestations of the monks. They were suspended and deprived of their rents and, finally, even of their villes. Urban *ordered the restitution of all their property,* and *denounced as accursed the work of the archbishop; notwithstanding which the building was continued, and the controversy carried on with almost increased bitterness.* Meantime, Urban died and Gregory, 'who patronized the archbishop,' succeeded him. Baldwin again triumphs."

In regard to Archbishop Warham, Mr. Jenkins

writes (pp. 236, 237) : "We may remember with pleasure the often neglected fact that Warham was the president of that Convocation which abrogated the papal authority in England, and was in a certain sense the first primate of the Reformation. The gradual removal of the papal legislation was easy after the great principle of the independence of the English Church was re-established for as the rule of the canons affirms, 'Non firmatur tractu temporis quod de jure ab initio non subsisti' and 'Quae contra jus fiunt, debent utique pro infectis haberi.' The Court of Arches from which the Canon of St. Radigund threatened to carry up his appeal to Rome had now recovered its *natural rights,* and the freedom of the archbishops and of the Church of England began before the primacy of the 'incomparabilis heros' of Erasmus had closed."

It is clearly seen, therefore, that there are considerably "more than three or even *five* English ecclesiastics" who resisted papal orders. And futhermore, from the Councils of Hertford and Cloveshoo, and the Constitutions of Clarendon, and so on, it is perfectly clear that the Church as well as the State resisted the encroachments of the papacy. But, of course, we cannot forget that there was not as much necessity for separate action by the Church as there would be in a country like ours. For, previous to the Reformation, the personnel of the State and the Church in England was the same and both the Witan and Parliament contained bishops and other clerical members, and this aspect will be discussed more fully a little later on. The papal authority exercised to whatever degree, was never legal and never recognized as such, either by Church or realm, but was audacious usurpation, pure and simple, without right or warrant in morals, reason, Scripture, conciliar decree or Catholic usage.

As seen above, there is ample evidence and distinguished and weighty authority for the statement that the Church of England regarded herself as a national Church free in herself, and that nowhere in its Constitution is found any suggestion that the Church of Rome or any other foreign power had either the inherent right or delegated authority to control its affairs, but we do find much in its deliberately expressed attitude and actions to the contrary. Yet at the same time there is abundant evidence that there was in England great respect for what was then believed to be the "See of St. Peter," and much deference was shown to the papacy as the most venerable institution of Western Christendom, and on account of these things the popes exercised both influence and power over the English Church in the mediaeval period. These two attitudes, if properly understood, are seen to be not contradictory, but quite compatible. For what is often spoken of as the spiritual headship or spiritual primacy of Rome so far as England is concerned was essentially a matter of honor, reverence and influence and not one of inherent right or constitutional authority as the see of Canterbury to-day is the titular head of the Anglican Communion, and we here in America have great respect for and delight to pay preferential honors to Canterbury, but recognize no authority on the part of the archbishop to interfere with our affairs, although he may be called in a sense the spiritual head of the Anglican Communion. In the less enlightened and less critical time of the Middle Ages encroachments and usurpations were easily built upon such foundations, which could not be even seriously entertained in these days.

Was the English Church Ever "Papalissima" or Even Papal?

This seems to be a good place to consider a statement made by Mr. W. M. Patterson in reference to this subject. On p. 176 he writes: "There was a theory popular some little time ago, and backed by the authority of great names, which maintained that the Church of England during the Middle Ages was, relatively speaking, a national anti-papal Church. But this theory in the light of fuller investigation must be altogether discarded. The mediæval Church of England was papalissima." Now we have already described some incidents in the history of the English Church, using words of Mr. Patterson himself, which would indicate that the English Church was not wholly papal, still less, "papalissima," but rather it *was national*. And he himself constantly speaks of the assumed powers of the pope as "encroachments," and *"unwarrantable* usurpations." Our English dictionaries define "encroachment" as "entrance upon the *rights* and *domain* of *another,"* "intrusion *without right* or permission," "trespass, infringement," etc. His own terms show therefore that the things that made the Church appear as papal were not of its real life and nature, but rather excrescences on the body. We have also cited above Bishop Gore's judgment that the English Church "from

Augustine to Parker was a recognized *national Church*."

We now wish to set over against these words of Patterson the statements of another highly esteemed historian of the Church of England, Mr. H. O. Wakeman. On p. 220 of his history of the Church he writes: "It has often been asserted that Henry VIII, in his breach with Rome, abolished the papal Church in England, and established a new Church, partly royal, partly Protestant. Such a theory will not bear historical investigation for a moment. *There never was in any true sense of the word, a papal Church in England;* but for nine hundred years there had been planted in England the Catholic Church of Christ, over which, during the last four hundred years, the popes had gradually acquired certain administrative rights which were now abolished." And again he says on p. 223: "There is no need to multiply instances. It would not be seriously contended by any well-informed writer at the present day that the *popes ever acquired any permanent rights of government over the English Church or nation.*"

And of the papal claims of an administrative nature, Wakeman says: (pp. 223–4) "These included rights of appointing bishops, appointing and sending legates, holding visitations and synods, granting of the pall to metropolitans, hearing cases on appeal, taxing the clergy, appointing to benefices by provision, granting dispensations and privileges, granting and refusing bulls for the consecration of bishops, etc. Most of these were not exercised at all before the Norman Conquest. The only one which was exercised with regularity from the time of Augustine to the Reformation was that of granting the pall. The majority of the others became gradually established in the twelfth, thirteenth, and fourteenth centuries, especially during the reigns of Stephen and Henry III, when the papacy was strong and the crown weak. Some of them, such as the right to send legates and hold synods apart from the permission of the crown, were never established at all, while others, such as the right of granting dispensations and hearing appeals, were freely exercised from the twelfth century. Against all of them except that of sending the pall *protests* were made from time to time either by the king or by parliament or both, and some of those protests were embodied in formal legislation. William I, according to Eadmer, distinctly claimed the right of deciding between rival popes and of refusing to admit papal letters, and subsequent kings enforced it. The Constitutions of Clarendon under Henry II, the remonstrances of Parliament against papal taxation, and the statutes of Provisors and Praemunire in the fourteenth century, are more conspicuous examples of such legislation. These claims, therefore, never formed part of the *law or custom of the Constitution in England,* and their successful exercise depended upon the connivance of the king."

Then again as to the spiritual nature of claims of the popes, the same author tells us (p. 225) : "Marsiglio of Padua in his *'Defensor Pacis,'* written at the end of the thirteenth century, refused to admit that St. Peter had any superiority at all over the other Apostles, or was proved ever to have been bishop of Rome, much less to have endowed the popes with a prerogative of government as his successors. But the majority of the opponents of the papacy were not prepared to go so far. While admitting in principle the spiritual headship of the pope as the normal guarantee and evidence of the unity of the Church, they maintained that his power as such visible Head was of a *constitutional* and not of an autocratic character. *William of Occam* contended that the pope even in the discharge of his spiritual functions *was subject to the general voice of Christendom."* . . . "This constitutional view of the papal spiritual headship seems to have been the one recognized in England before the Norman Conquest. Northumbria ignored the papal decision in Wilfrid's case, and Dunstan refused to absolve an offender when commanded to do so by the pope. Even in the later Middle Ages it was by no means forgotten. English lawyers were found to maintain that papal law was not binding in England, even on questions of faith and morals, *unless it had been accepted by the national authorities."* And on this point Bishop Boyd-Carpenter is very clear and emphatic throughout his excellent book on the history of the Church of England. He tells us that "Throughout the fourteenth century measures of national protection against papal aggression became necessary and popular." And he further says that these great acts of the nation were like the movement of troops taking up one strong position after another for the great battle. "The conflict which ensues," he writes, "is against papal claims and papal *teaching."* And steps were taken in these years "which vindicated the *national character* of the Church." From these statements as well as from other considerations, it appears that there is more evidence to support Mr. Wakeman's position than that of Mr. Patterson.

Besides it appears to us that a serious and fatal fallacy underlies Mr. Patterson's reasoning. He seems much influenced by an apparent misconstruction of the true meaning and real force of the Statutes of Provisors and Praemunire and all other acts, both of the Witan in the early days of England and of the Parliament just before the Reformation. His words are (p. 176) : "The attempts by Acts of Praemunire and Provisors to limit the papal power were acts, not of the English Church, but of the English State."

This seems specious, but like much speciousness, it is superficial and misleading. Mr. Patterson seems in these considerations to forget two things. First, that the Witan, or national assembly of the early days, and the Parliament of the Middle Ages were composed *of members of the Church of England and contained clerical and episcopal members as well as lay.* Indeed, they were the great representative bodies of the Church as well as of the State, and constituted the *legislative enacting power of the Church.* Parliament in those days most likely registered and expressed more accurately the real sentiment and feeling of the Church at large than did the clerical assemblies or the bench of bishops, just as we think that the House of Clerical and Lay Deputies in the Episcopal Church in the United States would more truly reflect the opinion and feeling of the great body of the Church than could the House of Bishops alone. We need, as the Church wisely requires, the concurrence of all three orders, bishops presbyters and laymen, to express the complete judgment of the Church, but in our opinion if one House should be put against the other, of the two, the House of Deputies would more accurately represent the thoughts and feelings of the whole body.

And we must by no means have in our minds an analogy between the English Parliament of the Middle Ages and the American Congress in our day in their relation to the Church. Congress speaks for the State alone, and our General Convention for our Church. But Parliament, even now with the complex religious situation in England and with its own mixed religious membership, speaks in some measure for the Church as in the case of the recent rejection of the revised Prayer Book; and in the Middle Ages, it was the Church's chief voice in her relation to other institutions, and the voice of Parliament was final in such matters. In regard to the actual ability of Parliament to represent the mind of the Church at large, there are members of the Church of England to-day, thoughtful men too, who have publicly stated that they believe that the recent vote of the Commons on the proposed Prayer Book does faithfully register the attitude of the *general body* of English Churchmen. If this is even in the *least possible now,* how vastly greater was not only the possibility, but the probability, if not the certainty, that the Parliament in the thirteenth and fourteenth and fifteenth centuries, when every member of it was a member of the English Church, should represent the real convictions and desires of the constituency of the Church!

Then too it must be remembered that parliament was much freer to act than the bishops and other clergy. Its members were less under the fear, and less subject to the awe-inspiring spell of the papacy, as well as being out of the reach of papal patronage. Bishop Boyd-Carpenter speaking of conditions in the Church of England at the end of the thirteenth and beginning of the fourteenth century says that "with patronage largely under control of the pope the clergy became more and more Romanized." It is not difficult to understand this process, for even in our free and democratic America, clergymen are often afraid to be frank with their bishops if their opinions are contrary to the episcopal judgment and policy, fearing to fall under the ban of their displeasure and to be the victims of their unfavorable influence, and so suffer the loss of such official patronage as the bishops may possess. Quite interesting as well as pertinent are these words of Wakeman (p. 14): "English Churchmen, both clergy and laity, began to realise that the administrative supremacy of the popes cost them dear. They summoned to their aid the spirit of patriotism to combat the spirit of obedience. They appealed once more to the old national feeling to resist encroachments by a foreigner on behalf of foreign interests. When the popes settled at Avignon, and became the avowed partisans of a rival and often hostile power this feeling naturally increased. As scandals developed in the papacy, and the schism succeeded to the capitivity, it grew stronger. The *national assembly of Parliament* became its mouthpiece, and during the course of the fourteenth and fifteenth centuries statute after statute was passed with the object of checking the interference of the pope *in English ecclesiastical affairs.*"

Another consideration that enters largely into this question is the personal equation of pope, bishop and king. When, for instance, as in the time of Edward II, the king was weak and vacillating and the episcopate deficient in moral rectitude and strength, and the pope ambitious and aggressive, the influence and power of the papacy would increase. On the other hand when the king was a strong man and the episcopate under the leadership of the archbishop was high-minded, patriotic and fearless, as in the days of Langton, the papal encroachments were resisted and the bulls of the popes often set aside and their wishes denied, and the national character of the Church asserted.

What does all this mean? The one straight-going thread that runs through all this diverse network seems to be this: The rights—the inalienable rights—of a true national branch of the Catholic Church were always existent and never abrogated, though trampled on by a power built up on false pretenses, forged documents, ignorance of history, and oftentimes also, evil principles and unscrupulous personalities—a power expressed not in constitutional ways, but in *unjustifiable encroachments and unwarranted usurpations*. Very appropriate are these expressions of Bishop Boyd-Carpenter and worthy of repetition here (p. 153): "This last Act of Praemunire was one of the strongest measures passed against Rome, and it is said by Bishop Stubbs to furnish the clue to the events which connect the Constitutions of Clarendon with the Reformation. It is well to remember statutes such as these, for they constitute a clear and changeless witness to the claim that the

Church of England, however much and often its rights have been infringed, has ever been regarded in the Constitution of this country as a National Church."

Some Particular Features

There are certain features in the relationship of England to the papacy, the imperfect understanding and the inadequate presentation of which have caused some confusion of thought. For instance, the frequent, but *not universal,* reception of the pall by the archbishop of Canterbury from Rome, papal legates in England, pilgrimages of some English kings to Rome and the case of Lichfield. It seems wise and helpful, therefore, to say something special about these features and inasmuch as the matter of the pall is stressed more than the others we give more extended notice to it.

The Pall

Frequent reference is made to the receiving of the pall from the pope by the archbishop of Canterbury, and it is often cited as evidence of papal supremacy in England, one teacher of Church history going so far as to say: "Without exception the archbishops of Canterbury from Augustine to Cranmer received the pall from the pope, usually going to Rome to get it." And it is sometimes stated that the archbishop of Canterbury previous to the Reformation could not exercise his office until he had received the pall. We shall see that these statements quite overshoot the mark and that the significance of the pall is not altogether what is claimed for it.

First, historians tell us that for four hundred years it was not used at all. Then Patterson (pp. 8–9) says: "The pall was a vestment conferred originally by the emperor, then by the pope *with the emperor's consent on distinguished* prelates who were *not always metropolitans*. In course of time it became an important instrument for building up the papal power, for after a while the popes insisted that—

(a) They alone could give the pall;

(b) That no one could exercise metropolitan powers until he had received it.

And by this means the popes secured the submission of all metropolitans. In form the pall became gradually fixed to the shape that can be seen in pictures of the archbishops. It is a band of white wool passing over both shoulders, with pendants in front and behind, marked in each case by four purple crosses." And Wakeman, speaking of its origin "as a mark of honor" bestowed by emperors on high officers of Church and State, adds on p. 14: *"After the destruction of the Western Empire* it became customary for the popes to make the grant in Western Europe instead of the emperors, and the pall gradually became looked upon more and more as a distinctly ecclesiastical vestment."

That it was even in the time of Gregory the Great regarded chiefly, not as a technical badge of authority, but as "an advantage or honor" and recognition of merit to stir its recipients "vigorously to apply themselves to the care of their spiritual work," is clear from Gregory's letter to Augustine which reads in part as follows: "To his most reverend and holy brother and fellow bishop, Augustine; Gregory, the servant of the servants of God. Though it be certain, that the unspeakable rewards of the eternal kingdom are reserved for those who labour for Almighty God, yet it is requisite that we bestow on them the advantage of *honours,* to the end that they may by this recompense be enabled the more vigorously to apply themselves to the care of their spiritual work. And because that the new Church of the English is, through the goodness of the Lord, and your labours, brought to the grace of God, we grant you the use of the pall in the same, only for the performing of the solemn service of the mass; so that you in several places ordain twelve bishops, who shall be subject to your jurisdiction, so that the bishop of London shall, for the future, be *always consecrated by his own synod,* and that he receive the *honour of the pall* from this holy and Apostolical see, which I, by the grace of God, now serve."

We observe that Bede seems to regard the bestowal of the pall (before and in his day it was usually "sent" and not bestowed in person) as an event quite worthy of notation and places it usually, if not always, in the caption of the chapter in which the record occurs. While he is very careful and specific in his mention of the pall being sent to Augustine and Justus he makes no mention of its having been sent or otherwise given to either Laurentius or Mellitus. It is really inconceivable that Bede would give such outstanding notice to the pall being received by Augustine and then by Justus and Paulinus and ignore its reception by Laurentius and Mellitus if they had received it. And Pope Boniface in sending the pall to Justus wrote him (Bede, p. 78): "We have also, my brother, encouraged by zeal for what is good, sent you by the bearer of these, the pall, which we have only given leave to use in the celebration of the sacred mysteries." Bede also omits any mention of the pall being given to Archbishop Bertwald (692) and Tatwine (731).

The Anglo-Saxon Chronicle also makes the same omissions and several others besides in the times subsequent to the close of Bede's history. To be specific, we recall that The Chronicle gives dates of the consecration of these men as archbishops of Canterbury without any mention of their receiving the pall: Laurentius, Mellitus (619), Bertwald (693), Cuthbert (741), Bregowin (759), Athelard (790), Athelred (870), Dunstan (961), Living (1013), Siward (1044), and others. And yet in contrast, The Chronicle always sets down the year when the pall was received in cases of its reception. It sometimes gives even the exact day as e. g., Elpric received his pall from Pope John "on 2nd before the Ides of November 1026." And Anselm received his "at Canterbury at Pentecost in 1095."

Again we learn from both Bede and the Anglo-Saxon Chronicle that in many cases archbishops were consecrated, and proceeded to fulfill the functions of their office both spiritual and administrative for a year or two before receiving the pall, indicating that the pall was not absolutely necessary to holding the office or discharging its duties. As instances of this we recall from The Chronicle that Lambert was consecrated archbishop in 762 and received his pall in 764; Eanbald was consecrated "on the 19th before the Kalends of September" in 796 and received the pall on the 6th before Ides of September" in 797, in the meantime, of course, actively performing their functions. Again Wulfred consecrated in 803, received the pall in 804, and Wulfhelm consecrated 925, received his pall at Rome 927—a lapse of 2 years—as also was the case of both Lanfranc consecrated 1070 and received the pall 1072, and Anselm consecrated 1093, and received the pall in 1095. Patterson makes this comment on Anselm's case which of course, applies with equal force or more to the others (p. 78) : "It was clear to Anselm that in the face of royal hatred he could effect no reforms. So at the beginning of 1095 he asked William for leave to visit the pope and fetch his pall. It is clear that at this time the *possession of the pall was not in England considered absolutely necessary for the exercise of metropolitan authority;* for Anselm had already consecrated a bishop, and had proposed to hold an ecclesiastical council." And Wakeman (p. 216), writing of later times—the sixteenth century—says: "It was true that the grant of the pall was in itself *only a mark of honour,* was unknown in the first four centuries of the history of the Church, and had in reality no doctrinal or constitutional significance whatever."

From these facts and considerations, therefore, it appears that too much stress has been laid upon it, and too much significance attached to this custom of applying for or receiving the pall generally, but "not universally or without exception," followed from the days of Augustine to the time of Cranmer.

Papal Envoys and Legates

Another matter sometimes confusing the thoughts of men in regard to the national, independent character of the Church of England is the act of the popes in sending legates to England, at first for special reasons, and then later the popes seeking to make their appointment a regular thing and to have them regarded as residential. It was just another form of papal encroachment on the rights of England, both Church and State, commencing more or less inoffensively, and passing on to a high degree of exceedingly objectionable usurpation.

The only visit to England of papal legates before the eve of the Norman Conquest was that of the delegates sent most probably by request of King Offa in 786. Mr. Wakeman writes: "By the appointment of John of Crema in 1125, and afterwards of Henry of Winchester in 1139, to govern the Church of England by virtue of the office of legate, the popes were in fact making a claim that all metropolitical, if not episcopal, power was derived from them, and was exercised by delegation from them. Such a claim was no more likely to be admitted by the Church of England in the twelfth century than by the Church of Spain at the Council of Trent, but neither side wished to push matters to an extremity." Again the same author (p. 224), writing from the viewpoint overlooking all the years of English history, tells us that some of the claims of the mediæval papacy "such as the *right to send delegates* and hold synods apart from the permission of the crown were *never established at all.*" And we know that in many instances the legates were not allowed to land in the country and at times were harshly dealt with, their mission repudiated and they themselves driven out of the country.

The weak archbishop of Canterbury, William of Corbeil, aided the development of this intrusion by asking for himself the appointment as legate, an opportunity for aggrandizing the office quickly seized by the pope, and so became the first *legatus natus,* which had a tendency to make the power of the archbishop derivative rather than inherent in his own office. And in the reign of Henry III the exercise of the legatine power was still increased, was made more continuous and reached out into political as well as spiritual affairs, and the activities of the legate became another expression of papal usurpation.

Royal Pilgrimages to Rome

Some have taken the fact that certain kings of England made pilgrimages to Rome as evidence of England's recognizing the papal supremacy. But a knowledge of the facts in each case will make it clear that in most instances it was a personal and not an official matter, and that the pilgrimage was made out of personal reverence for the Holy City and not as an expression of official allegiance to the papacy as an institution. It is illuminating on this point to recall the resistance of the kings to the pope, from Egfrid of Northumbria in the case of Wilfrid on down the centuries, recalling such high lights as William the Conqueror, William Rufus, Henry II in stout defiance, and such national action under the leadership of the king as seen in the twelfth of the Constitutions of Clarendon (Wakeman, p. 109): "The rents of archbishoprics, bishoprics, abbacies, and priories were to go to the king during vacancy. The vacancies were to be filled by election by the principal clergy in the king's chapel, with the consent of the king and his council." And again Wakeman says of the pope's claims of a temporal nature based on the forged donation of Constantine (p. 223): "These claims were uniformly repudiated by both the king and the nation whenever the king was a strong ruler and the nation able to express its wishes." And Patterson (p. 224) writes: "Under this title Henry VIII claimed first, all those powers over the Church which *the kings of England had exercised or claimed since the Conquest,* e. g., the *supreme appellate jurisdiction, and the right to refuse admission of papal bulls.*" The "title" referred to here is the title of Supreme Head of the Church and Wakeman says: "The *right of the papacy to command,* the duty of kings to obey, was a claim to which William the First *never thought of listening for a moment."* We see, therefore, that the royal pilgrimages to Rome were matters of personal taste and feeling, and not any register of official allegiance to the pope, and the whole history of the resistance on the part of the kings of England to the encroachments of the papacy is abundant evidence that their going to Rome on these visits was a pious and interesting journey to them, and not to make obeisance to the pope. And we know how the action of King John created deep and wide resentment on the part of England. Wakeman (p. 293) tells us: *"Mary Tudor was the first Roman Catholic sovereign of England.* She accepted to the full, the universal headship of the pope over the Church as a religious dogma." Let students of English history ponder carefully that statement.

The Lichfield Case

Offa, King of Mercia in the latter part of the eighth century, was ambitious for the prestige of his kingdom and desired to have a metropolitan see and archbishop within its borders. He accordingly asked for the pope's influence to divide the Province of Canterbury and to elevate Lichfield to an archiepiscopal center. This was done temporarily. Some have pointed to it as an illustration of papal supremacy in England at that time. It will be interesting and useful then to relate the facts and conditions of the transaction. And for this purpose we use the words first of Patterson (p. 42) : "At the legatine synod of Chelsea, 787, which was attended by the bishops of the provinces of Canterbury, and also by Offa and his Witan, Lichfield was raised to metropolitan dignity, and more than half of the sees dependent on Canterbury transferred to the new archbishop of Lichfield. It is to be noted that the creation of this new metropolitan see was not effected simply by the pope, *but by an English synod*." And Boyd-Carpenter writes (p. 48) : "But the internal rights of the Church in England were so far recognized that at the Council of Chelsea the archbishop of Canterbury gave up a portion of his province, and Highert, Bishop of Lichfield, became archbishop and metropolitan, with six bishops under him. Thus England became possessed for the time of three metropolitans. This did not last long but the incident serves to show us the different forces which were at work. It shows us, too, how Rome exercised influence in English affairs. There was no doubt great reverence for the patriarchal see of the West, but no *legally defined authority was insisted on or formally acknowledged at this time.* The canons I have spoken of, and the making of Lichfield into an archbishopric, were the *acts of a synod or council of* the English Church. In 803, at Cloveshoo, an English synod (the second held there) with the approbation of Pope Leo decided to abolish the archbishopric of Lichfield and to restore the ancient dignity of Canterbury. The Church of England might be open to *influence,* but her *independence* was unchallenged." Then Wakeman (p. 57) says: "Leo gave his consent to a return to the old state of things, and *at a council held* at Cloveshoo in 803 the archbishopric of Lichfield was formally abolished and the province reunited to that of Canterbury. It is worth noticing that, although care was taken to procure the approval of the pope to the contemplated changes, the authority by which the archbishopric was actually *established* and *afterwards abolished* was not that of the pope or a papal bull, but of the *national synods of the English Church.*"

It is seen from these authorities that while the pope used his influence to further Offa's wish, for which Patterson tells us he was well paid, still *the action* was taken by the authority of the *National Synod.* That was true both of the elevation of Lichfield to be an archbishopric in 786, and its reduction to its former state of a diocese in 803.

CHAPTER X

THE REFORMATION BEGINS OPENLY

The period of history upon which we now enter has been greatly misunderstood, and its facts in relation to the Church of England grossly misrepresented, and oftentimes supplanted by false statements. Before entering upon its consideration, let us express the hope that sufficient information respecting the old British, Anglo-Saxon and mediæval epochs of the history of the Church and the people in the British Isles has been given to show that papal encroachments upon the rights of the Church and the realm alike were obtained by usurpations, never legally acknowledged and always accompanied by strong objections and protestations on the part of Englishmen against such papal aggrandizement and usurpations. And Prof. Geo. P. Fisher writing of conditions in England in the middle of the fourteenth century says:—"In England there *had long been a growing spirit of resistance,* which was naturally quickened now that the papacy had become the instrument of France." This popular feeling against foreigners and foreign interference that began with the time that the encroachments began, and that took more definite shape in the reign of Edward I, continuously grew until the English Parliament in conjunction with the Convocation, the Assembly of the Church of Eng-

land, passed a statute declaring once and for all that
the usurped jurisdiction over the English Church and
realm, and the false claims thereto made by the popes,
had always been illegal, and could no longer be tolerated. This movement, arrested by the Hundred Years'
War with France and the civil War of the Roses, resumed its progress in the quieter time of King Henry
VII, continued through the reigns of Henry VIII
and Edward VI, then was checked and set back by
the reaction under Mary and finally came to its successful culmination in the reign of Queen Elizabeth.

The action of King John in laying down his crown
and receiving it again from the pope had been a bitter
memory to Englishmen of every generation since the
humiliating deed took place. When the people heard
what the wicked John had done, they tingled with a
sense of shame and, as we have previously stated, cried
out: "The King has become the pope's man. He has degraded himself to the level of a serf." This same sort
of thing happened again in the reign of Henry II after
his quarrel with Becket, and Becket's murder. It will
do no harm to repeat here what we said in a former
chapter, namely: When the English people, with this
sense of shame still burning within their breasts, and
with the sense of their national importance growing,
threw off the papal yoke, they did not lose their nationality, but only regained it. "For the same reason,"
writes the historian, "the English Church, which was
the nation organized for spiritual purposes, did not
lose its identity by repudiating the papal supremacy, but
was restored thereby to its original independent position as a branch of the universal Church of Christ,

relying upon its Apostolic order and the purity of its faith, as it had done in the days before the Norman Conquest, when as yet the popes had not asserted a claim to jurisdiction over Catholic Christendom." The parallel thus drawn between the papal claim over realm and Church is very apt and convincing. The claim of the popes to the right to assert their authority over the kings by their legates was as emphatic in some instances as the claim of jurisdiction over the Church in giving palls to the archbishop of Canterbury through papal representatives. Green, Vol. I, p. 235, tells us, for example: "That while Innocent was dreaming of a vast Christian Empire with the pope at its head to enforce justice and relying on his under-kings, John believed that the pope's protection would enable him to rule as tyrannically as he would." Again and more pointedly Green writes, Vol. I, p. 237: "The position of Gualo, as representative of the papal over-lord of the realm, was of the highest importance, and his action showed the real attitude of Rome towards English freedom." And once again (p. 481): "He (Urban V) demanded with threats the payment of the annual sum of a thousand marks promised by King John in the acknowledgment of the suzerainty of the see of Rome. The *insult* roused the temper of the realm. The king laid the demand before parliament, and both houses replied that 'Neither King John nor any other king could put himself, his kingdom nor his people under subjection save with their accord and assent.'" Innocent, as we have seen, annulled the Great Charter in August and at the close of the year excommunicated the barons. We have seen also that neither bishops nor barons paid heed to the pope's denunciation. Now it should seem perfectly clear to every one that as the rejection of the claim of the popes by the realm, though in cases *previously allowed,* did not create a new nation, so neither did the repudiation of the false and usurping claim to have illegal and uncatholic jurisdiction over the Church create a new Church. The reasoning is as sound and irresistible in one case as in the other, and the facts constituting the basis of the reasoning are as clearly authentic and historical in one as in the other. Nor was the Church of England alone in asserting its right to repudiate the supremacy of the pope. For we remember, for example, the action of the Councils of Pisa, Constance and Basle in the previous century by which certain rival popes were set aside and others elected, and that at the Council of Constance a decree was passed stating the principle of the supremacy of the General Council over the pope, in which latter Council the English Church was represented by Hallam, bishop of Salisbury, and also the bishops of Bath and Hereford.

We know that along with the false jurisdiction of the papacy there grew doctrinal abuses as taught in words and expressed in the practices and worship of the Church. This, we saw, came chiefly by reason of the introduction of foreign bishops and clergy and by the invasion, so to speak, of England by the army of monks and friars commissioned by the pope. We can readily understand, as has been pointed out before, why such a result was inevitable under the conditions just stated. This is especially apparent when we recall that often the English kings were wicked, licentious men, and the popes sometimes men of most scandalous lives—murderers, adulterers and infidels. The evil and avarice of these men led them to degrade the Church and her Sacraments in return for money and for political support in dealing with other princes. Of course, under such conditions, with such motives and purposes in mind and heart, they were not careful of the morals of those whom they promoted to positions of honor, particularly in the Church. The less scrupulous and conscientious they were, the better they fitted into their plans and the more effective they were in the fulfillment of their unholy methods and purposes. Consequently, when the people of the nation and the Church determined to correct these evils, they no more destroyed their identity and became new creatures than the pruning of a dead branch from a tree makes a new tree, or the washing of one's face makes a new man, or the healing of one's sores causes death. It is as though a Masonic jurisdiction fell under the influence of a powerful man or set of men and adopted some customs strange to the principles of the Order, and then when relieved of the influence of such man or men, it entered again into its old ways. We cannot say that a new Order was then and thereby created. Not even a new jurisdiction had been formed, but the old was simply restored to its primitive purity and old-time allegiance. Hardwick, in his "Reformation" (p. 166 ff.), makes this very clear when he tells us, "that the impulses by which this country (England) was aroused to vindicate its independence of all foreign jurisdiction, to assert the ancient faith and to recast the liturgy and other forms of public worship, are resolvable into three descriptions: First, the feelings of distrust, and ultimately of resentment, which had been awakened and exasperated by the follies, schisms and usurpations of the papacy, a class of feeling frequently appearing in transactions of the older English parliaments. Secondly, the higher standard of intelligence and piety prevailing in the English universities, especially in that class of students who imbibed the literary tastes, and with them, the reformatory spirit, propagated by Erasmus. Thirdly, the direct influence which had been exerted by the circulation in England of Lutheran tracts, and other publications tending to produce analogous results." The extended knowledge of antiquity had widened the horizon of theological students and impelled the scholars and the clergy to more sedulous investigations of the Bible and the ancient Fathers. Mr. Hardwick also tells us, "Such pursuits, however, had not seriously weakened their attachment to the service books or ritual institutions of the English Church. *The reformers based their work upon the principle that English institutions, and consequently English Churches, do not owe allegiance as a matter of divine right to any foreign potentate whatever.*" This is confirmed by Green's testimony (Vol. II, p. 196), given in these words: "In form nothing had been changed. The outer constitution of the Church remained utterly unaltered. The English bishop freed from papal control, freed from the check of monastic independence, seemed greater and more imposing than ever. The priest still clung to rectory and church." A very striking example of this is afforded in the history of Peterborough Cathedral of which a certain historian writes: "It was founded in the seventh century in memory of Peada's conversion and when its rank was changed from an abbey to a Cathedral (which was done in Henry VIII's time), there was no alteration whatever in the building, its endowment or the personnel of the clergy. The abbot was made the bishop, the prior became the dean and things went on just as before. The service was said from the same service books for the same congregation, and therefore there was not only no transfer from one set of persons to another with different vision, but the continuance of the same person in the same place only under reorganized and revised rules. This indicates that the great body of the English Church, clergy, monks and laymen alike, were heartily in favor of the changes that were being made to cleanse and purify the national Church from worn out rules of personal life as well as from unauthorized and uncatholic dogma. And we cannot help perceiving that this formation of new sees was not an endowment out of papal monasteries, but the tardy development of Saxon monasteries into the episcopal foundations, which they would have become long before, had not foreign influence retarded the growth of the native English episcopate." Lane, "Illustrated Notes (Modern)", p. 56.

We now turn to consider some of the far reaching things that happened at this time. The fall of Constantinople to the Turks in 1453 drove many Christian Greek scholars westward. The Renaissance had already begun in Italy, and men had commenced the study of the Latin classics and the Latin Fathers of the Church. The revival of interest in Greek included both the classics and the ancient Greek Fathers. Men of England like

More, Colet, Linacre and Grocyn, all men of the Church of England, saw the need of reform within the Church and loudly declaimed against ecclesiastical scandals. These were joined and greatly assisted by the famous scholar Erasmus, Professor in Cambridge University. Colet's continual advice to those who heard him was, "Keep to the Bible and the Apostles' Creed and let the divines, if they like, dispute about the rest." From this time forth, the watchword of the Reformers and the reforms of the Church of England was "Scripture and the Primitive Fathers" as against mediæval traditions. Let us not forget that Colet was dean of St. Paul's Cathedral, London. Erasmus, whose point of view was practically the same as that of Colet, was professor of Greek in Cambridge University under the control of the Church of England, and Thomas More, a layman, a lawyer and a member of Parliament.

Let us add here the following brief sketch and estimate of Colet. "John Colet was the son of an ex-Lord Mayor of London, born in 1467; he had visited Italy to study Greek in 1495 at the time when the scandals of the Borgia régime were at their height—Alexander Borgia was pope—and Colet may, perhaps, have listened, though we have no evidence on this point, to the fiery denunciations of the age by the prophet Savonarola. On his return to Oxford he delivered public lectures (1496–7) on the Pauline Epistles. These lectures opened a new era in the history of Biblical exposition. Hitherto, the Bible had been regarded as a storehouse of detached texts, and the plain meaning of Scripture had been twisted and distorted by allegorical and other fantastic methods of interpretation. Colet tried to visualize the man St. Paul as he worked and lived, and the special circumstances of the churches to which he wrote. In his eyes the purity of primitive Christianity had been defiled by the accretions of scholastic philosophy and by the mediæval Church. For Duns Scotus and St. Thomas Aquinas he had no good words; in his eyes it was far better to keep to the early Fathers, to the Bible, and the Apostles' Creed. His great aim was to get back to St. Paul and to Christ Himself. As Erasmus wrote, 'Colet's aim is to bring back the Christianity of the Apostles, and clear away the thorns and briars with which it is overgrown.' "

In 1505 Colet was made dean of St. Paul's, and he continued in London the work begun at Oxford. Five years later he founded St. Paul's School—the first fruits in England of the New Learning—"to increase knowledge and worshipping of God and our Lord Jesus Christ, and good Christian life and manners in the children." Colet's whole being was consumed with zeal for the reform of the Church. The traffic in, and the worshipping of relics, as can be seen from Erasmus' account of his visit with Colet to Becket's shrine, filled him with disgust.

What was happening in the Church, therefore, was a movement represented by both the clerical and lay orders of the English Church. Neither was it a new-born movement, but one started several centuries before, and greatly furthered by Wycliffe, who we recall, of course, was a clergyman of the Church of England, but was interrupted in its onward movement by foreign and civil wars.

The general demand for reform in the Church was

now so great that even Cardinal Wolsey took it up and
prepared to press it with vigor. He had suppressed many
monasteries and nunneries. With the money gotten
from the property of these suppressed monasteries and
nunneries, he proposed to establish schools and colleges
under the influence of the Church. In accordance with
this plan, he established Christ Church College at Oxford and the public grammar school at Ipswich. He
also purposed to increase the number of English bishops
which had not been done during the papal interference,
the popes desiring all revenue possible for themselves
and their particular plans. He also endeavored to persuade France to throw off the papal yoke, taking the
position that each national Church had a right to local
self-government and that any jurisdiction claimed from
without was nothing more than usurpation.

When Sir Thomas More succeeded Wolsey, as
Chancellor, he made these plans for reform the subject of his early official utterances. They were changes
desired for generations by England and that were
bound to come in the very nature of things. It could
not have been stopped now any more than the French
Revolution could have been stopped in the last half
of the eighteenth century. The forces had accumulated
in both cases. No suppression in either was possible.
Expression was a fundamental necessity of the situation.

In this connection, we recall these words of the
historian Green, "The movement [the same to which we
have just referred] was long arrested by religious reaction and civil war. But the fresh sense of national
unity as the monarchy gathered all power into its single

hand, would have itself revived the contest even without the spur of the divorce of Henry VIII from Catherine of Aragon."

Thus it is clear, that it is not only a gross historical error, but evidence of the shallowest kind of thinking or evidence of no thinking at all, to say or to suppose that a movement so mighty as the English Reformation, with its roots so deep in the past and in the fundamental rights and things of men, could have been produced by the domestic infelicities or the lusts of a wicked, licentious and self-willed king. The divorce of Henry from Catherine was an incident, but a mere incident, that made easier the carrying out of the plans of the Reformers and accelerated their movement. Had there been no Henry or a Henry with no divorce, the movement would have gone forward with absolute certainty, but no doubt with more difficulty, if the monarch had opposed every phase of it. In this connection let us reproduce these words of W. M. Patterson (p. 208): "Now the occasion of the revolution which resulted in the repudiation of all papal authority over England was the attempt of Henry VIII to divorce his wife, Catherine of Aragon. But this was not *the cause* of the Reformation. If that had been all, on the death of Catherine, or at any rate on the death of Henry, the old relationship between Rome and England would have been restored. If Henry VIII had not quarrelled with the pope over the matter of the divorce, the Reformation would have come all the same, though in point of time it would have been later, and the circumstances would have been different. For the Reformation in England and elsewhere was the result of converging forces; the ground had long been prepared and mined. Henry VIII only led his subjects on to the final rush at the papal citadel."

In support of this, we remember that Church reform was in full progress in 1523. The divorce was not obtained until 1533, nor even thought of until 1527. And the chief steps by which the Church of England was regaining national independence had been taken if not at the suggestion of Convocation, the Clerical Assembly, certainly with its consent, before that event and independent of it. Of course, it is understood that the Convocations were then made up only of bishops and other clergy, and Parliament was the Church's real House of Laymen and just as truly a part of the Church. There had been no objection of serious nature in the House of Lords, wherein the bishops sat, to the statues directed against papal authority and jurisdiction, either before or after the divorce. And Parliament was but a representative cross section of the Church—indeed its "mouthpiece," as one historian puts it. The plain fact is that Englishmen had long been wishing, even yearning, to be rid of all foreign jurisdiction in State and Church. Quoting Mr. Green again: "Parliament had hardly risen into life when it became the organ of national jealousy whether of any papal jurisdiction without the realm or of the separate life and separate jurisdiction of the clergy within the realm." It is important at this point to emphasize that each stage in the Reform movement in England received every legal sanction, and was effected by legally constituted authority in Church and State and was done in constitutional manner and by constitutional means.

In 1529, the Convocation and the Seven Years' Parliament were convened and all the measures of reform relating to the Church were first passed by the Church's representative assemblies—convocations of York and Canterbury—and then submitted to parliament and the king for ratification. The convocation never surrendered its power or authority to suggest or initiate changes in the ceremonies and rites of the Church, and of course never allowed princes to administer God's Word and Sacraments.

It will be interesting at this point to review what some of our historians teach us about the organization and operation of convocation. Wakeman (p. 132) describes its origin under Edward I in these terms: "In the establishment of safeguards of national liberty against the king might be found, too, the surest defence against the pope. Almost to a man the clergy, with the exception of the foreigners, threw in their lot with the barons in the great constitutional struggle which marks the end of the reign of Henry III. They triumphed with Simon de Montfort at Lewes. They formed no inconsiderable part of his parliament of 1265. They suffered after the fall of the stout earl of Evesham. With the accession of Edward I, in 1272, they had their reward. By his enlightened statesmanship, parliament was organized to be first the champion, then the guardian and eventually the dictator of English liberties, and in the chief house of parliament, as representing the Church, sat the bishops and the more important of the abbots. Under his superintendence, the provincial synods of Canterbury and York assumed a full representative character, and in the form of the convocations of the clergy obtained in 1283 the sole right of taxing the clerical estate. Had he been able to carry out his will, representatives of the clergy would also have sat in the House of Commons; but the clergy themselves, afraid for their independence, persistently refused to be dragged into such dangerous relations with the king, and were content to leave their parliamentary interests in the hands of the bishops and abbots of the upper house."

Then Wakeman tells us something about the functioning of the convocations in the formative period. For example, in regard to the adoption of the Prayer Book of 1549 he says: "On the other hand, the council, writing to Bonner in the king's name in July 1549, distinctly assert that the Book was set forth 'by the learned men of this, our realm, in *their synods and convocations provincial.'* This assertion taken by itself would not be of much weight, as the history of the forty-two articles shows that the Council were not above telling a downright untruth on such a matter if it was to their advantage. But Bonner was bishop of London at the time, and as such was a prominent member of both parliament and convocation, and it is incredible that the council should have gone out of its way to tell a deliberate untruth to a man who could instantly refute it of his own knowledge." And Patterson writes (249–250) :—"In November 1547 both convocation and parliament met. The Clergy in the Lower House of Convocation presented to the bishops some interesting petitions. They urged that a revision of the canon law should be once more authorized by parliament; they petitioned that representatives of the minor clergy should, in accordance with the ancient writ, be admitted to the Lower House of Parliament, and that the work of the committee on Church services should be presented to them. In this last petition they probably referred to Cranmer's two schemes, which are still extant, for a reformed Breviary. These petitions had no *immediate* result. But on the 2nd December, 1547, convocation came unanimously to the important decision that Communion should be administered to the laity in both kinds; this resolution rendered necessary the issue of a new Communion office, to which convocation in anticipation gave its approval. Convocation also resolved that the marriage of the clergy ought to be legalized." . . . "In accordance with the resolution of convocation, and to satisfy the Act of Parliament, a new order of Communion was published by proclamation on 8th March, 1548. Cranmer had felt his way by a series of interrogatories addressed to the bishops; he was anxious to carry with him as far as possible the bishops of the Old Learning." . . . "Parliament met for its second session on 27th November, 1548. An Act was passed for legalizing the marriage of priests in accordance with the resolution previously voted by convocation." Patterson also asserts (p. 259): "On the other hand, we have a definite statement from Edward in a letter to his sister Mary that the book *received the assent of the clergy* in their *several synods and convocations.*"

A fuller statement of these matters is given in Procter and Frere's "A New History of the Book of Common Prayer" (pp. 50–51): "The King wrote to Bonner on July 23, 1549, asserting that the Book is 'set forth not only by the common agreement and full assent of the nobility and commons of the late session of the late parliament but also by the like assent of the bishops in the same parliament and of all the other learned men of this realm in their synods and convocations provincial.'

"In a further letter to the Lady Mary he speaks of 'one full and whole consent both of our clergy in their several synods and convocations, and also of the Noblemen and Commons in the late session of our parliament.'

"It is hardly possible to have better evidence than two such letters as these written by the king, and to persons who had every opportunity of denying the accuracy of the statement if it could be denied. Such further evidence as is forthcoming adds nothing to the strength of these."

So we see the grounds for Bishop Gore's assertion: "We need not of course glorify the authority which made the Prayer Book, or whitewash the Reformers where accurate history has darkened the colours. But the Prayer Book comes to us with the legitimate authority of the National Church and consecrated by the use of a long succession of saintly men and women, and we have no justification for refusing to make the best of it." ("The Anglo-Catholic Movement To-day," p. 40.) One or two illustrations of that general statement may be of interest.

In 1531 the convocation, speaking in the name of the National Church, suggested that the obedience of England, to whatever extent it may have existed, should be withdrawn from the see of Rome. This had nothing whatever to do with the divorce of Henry, but was prompted by papal action in other respects. We shall let Mr. Lane state the case for us ("Illustrated Notes, Modern," p. 30) : "The papal Curia would not appoint to a bishopric unless the nominee paid to the pope the whole of his first year's income in advance, together with large sums for bulls of consecration and admission to the see. The clergy had just been punished under Praemunire for accepting Wolsey as papal legate and they naturally argued that an illegal authority could not demand tribute. So they petitioned the king to ordain in this present parliament that these annates or first fruits should no longer be paid, but that if the pope should proceed to enforce payment, by interdict or otherwise, then the obedience of the king and his people should be altogether withdrawn from the pope. Parliament assented to the petition of convocation by passing a statute in accordance with its terms, and the king agreed to it." And so it was throughout. The convocation, the parliament and the king moved together in reform and in the repudiation of papal authority in England. On March 31, 1534, the convocation of Canterbury declared "that the bishop of Rome had no greater jurisdiction conferred on him by God over this country than any other foreign bishop." The convocation of York made a similar declaration in the May following. The clergy and the monks in both provinces, almost without exception, signed the document, and parliament and the king accepted it. And thus by the three elements in the realm, Church and parliament and king, the papal jurisdiction in England was terminated forever. And Professor

Geo. P. Fisher says: "The measures by which the Anglican hierarchy was separated from Rome flowed from the concurrent action of convocation and parliament."

It has been said: "The Seven Years' Parliament did not pass a single statute nor clause of a statute which had for its object the annihilation of the old religious body of the land and the formation of a new religious body. All changes received the prior assent of the old National Church by its own representative assembly of convocation which sat concurrently with parliament throughout. The declared object of parliament was the *restoration* of rights and privileges anciently held, but afterwards usurped. The effort on the part of the Church at this time was simply to satisfy the cravings of her own children." Hardwick in speaking of papal interference, tells us in his "Reformation" (p. 178) that Henry was inclined to pay more deference to the English convocations than to the English Parliament, regarding the inquiry as ecclesiastical or spiritual, and therefore was anxious to secure the co-operation, not only of the Church legislature, but of all other institutions which were thought to represent that branch of the body politic called the "Spirituality." Actuated by such feelings he consulted both the Southern and Northern convocations, the universities, the cathedral chapters, and the conventual establishments, all of which, with only a few dissenting voices, answered that "The Roman pontiff was not authorized by Holy Scripture in putting forth his claim to jurisdiction within the realm of England."

CHAPTER XI

It is well for us to keep in mind the difference between the religious movement on the Continent and that which took place in England. The changes on the Continent constituted a revolution. That is, it was a tearing up by the roots and the severing of connection with the historic past, throwing over institutions that had been in the Church from Apostolic times, such as the threefold ministry of bishops, priests and deacons, and the liturgical form of worship. It was accompanied also by civil wars and revolution. In England the movement was a reformation, a purifying of the old Church by her own bishops, clergy and laymen without severing its connection with any of the great historic landmarks of Christianity, and the establishing of closer connection between themselves and the early primitive faith and order and worship of the Church, at the same time rejecting the mediæval excrescences, doctrinal and liturgical, and those pertaining to the polity of the Church. This was done, consciously and deliberately done, because they overshadowed or contradicted the truth as taught, the worship as practised and ecclesiastical polity as seen at work in the Apostolic and primitive days of Christianity. In the words of

224

another: "She (the Church of England) did not do so (reject these mediævalisms) merely because they (i. e., mediæval errors and tyrannies) were old, but she did so rather because they were *not old enough*"—that is, did not go back to the teaching and ways of the Apostles and their successors in the early Church. This was the meaning of Bishop Ridley who, when pressed by his persecutors under Mary's Roman Catholic reaction, said: "I prefer the *antiquity* of the primitive to the *novelty* of the Church of Rome." The thing accomplished, therefore, was a *restoration*. And whatever was done, was done in conformity with the constitution of Church and country, and their ancient customs.

The same thing is true in regard to the changes made in the Liturgy of the Church in the sixteenth century. As has been said by another, "There need not be any mistake respecting the intentions which guided the convocations in their liturgical reforms: for the statutes of parliament which forbade the publication of papal bulls in England disclaimed any intention to depart from the congregation of Christ's flock in anything concerning the true Catholic faith of the Church. To maintain the pure doctrine of the Gospels and fellowship with all true adherents of Apostolic faith, had ever been the aim and object of Englishmen." They had not always been able, however, to prevent the introduction of errors and abuses first from one side and then from another. And in their efforts to shake them off, they had not always been free from recklessness, going at times rather farther than was wise, due to the excitement of the days and to the natural tendencies of men; but throughout all changes, they were Providentially enabled to preserve inviolate the fundamental principles of the Catholic order and Apostolic faith and truth. At this time, in order to assure the people of this intention, they included in their fundamental statement the assertion that the Bible and the three Creeds—the Apostles', the Nicene, and the Athanasian —should constitute the only true basis of faith, and the first four Catholic Councils should be the only authority for Church discipline, thus going back at a bound to the decision of Theodore's Synod at Hatfield in 680, and so establishing a clear connecting line of Church allegiance and of Catholic faith between the Church of the seventh and earlier centuries and the Church of the sixteenth. Seebohm (p. 197), as well as do many other historians of the Reformation, points to this distinction between what took place on the Continent and what took place in England, declaring: "In the end, England was forced from the yoke of the ecclesiastical empire of Rome by constitutional means without the revolutions and civil wars which followed in Germany," which might also be said to apply to all the other Continental countries of Western Europe as well as to Germany. It is a pleasure to quote here these historically sound and illuminating words of Mr. Patterson (p. 289): "All questions of identity or continuity are determined by the relative importance of the constant and the varying elements. For identity is always compatible with a certain amount of difference. If the acceptance of the jurisdiction and supremacy of the Roman Bishop and of the theory of Transubstantiation is the all-important criterion of a 'church,' then *cadit quaestio*. But no Protestant would dream of such an admission. The claims of the pope were rejected absolutely *as an un-warrantable usurpation*. Transubstantiation was rejected as repugnant to Scripture. On the other hand, the Church of England retained her Apostolic framework of government, and remained a missionary Church to the English people, duly administering the Sacraments and preaching the Word of God. She rejected the mediæval accretions which had disfigured the beauty of her form, but she no more lost her identity by so doing than (to use a famous comparison) a man loses his identity by washing smudges from his face.

"The Elizabethan settlement was both Catholic and Protestant. It was Catholic because it was based on the Bible and *the usages of the primitive Church*. The reformers rightly maintained that mediæval accretions could not be Catholic because they were unknown to the primitive Church. The settlement was Protestant, not only because it rejected the papal claims, but also because it rejected those doctrines and points of Church order which were characteristically mediæval. Thus Transubstantiation, private masses for the dead, the whole theory and practice of indulgences, the withholding of the cup from the laity, compulsory confession, compulsory celibacy of the clergy, the doctrine of purgatory, were rejected. A purer faith and practice were laid down." Along with the above well go these words: "It was the happiness of the Church of England that, in all the changes which befell her, she had both a love of truth and an instinct that the past must count for something in her life. She accepted the free energies of the Reformation period; she repudiated the tyrannies of mediævalism, but she did not do so merely because they were old, *she did so rather because they were not old enough.* She saw that they were tyrannies of ignorance rather than of knowledge, and she brought to bear upon the problem the spirit of liberty, which claims the right to ask what is true, and which refuses to accept things merely because they have been. She gave the chief place to truth, but she certainly gave the second place to what was venerable—to all that *was consecrated by ancient usage and sacred association.*" . . . "Thus the Church of England finally refused to identify herself with Rome, protesting against her uncatholic claims, and distinguished herself from other protesting Churches by the reverent care with which she sought to preserve continuity with the past."

Bishop Boyd-Carpenter calls attention to the excellent illustration of this contained in Dean Swift's "Tale of a Tub" (pp. 211–213).

Then we read in the Britannica Encyclopedia these statements: "Though its doctrine was reformed in the sixteenth century and the spiritual supremacy of the pope was repudiated, the continuity of its organic life was not interrupted, and historically as well as legally, it is the *same Church* as that established before the Reformation." And also: "Legally and historically continuous with the Church of the most ancient times, the Church of England has always had a *national* character. In mediæval acts of parliament it was called by the same name as at present, and *never* was *identical with the Church of Rome,* which was usually described as the court (curia) of Rome. In the sixteenth century, by a series of measures passed by the *three* estates of the realm its vassalage to Rome was broken off, since which time the Roman Court has maintained a hostile attitude toward it."

Bishop Creighton, speaking of resistance of papal claims in later years, says, "The movement against the papacy had been of long standing in England. The *English Church* had never submitted *unreservedly* to papal control. Papal *encroachments* had been guarded against, especially in the reign of Edward the First and Edward the Third, by stringent laws."

J. H. Blunt writes: "During a period of more than twelve hundred years the Church of England has preserved its identity, and during that time England has advanced from a group of small and divided kingdoms into a vast empire, on which the sun never sets, in every quarter of the globe; and love for their country demands from Englishmen a love for their Church. . . . The truth is that there *never was a Roman Church* (properly or legally so styled) *in England;* that no new Church was made and endowed at the Reformation, but only that the old Church was, as the word implies, *reformed* . . . misstatements can be disposed of, and disposed of only by an appeal to history. . . . The author himself neither holds nor would accept any preferment in the Church, so that he cannot on that ground be accused of personal or interested motives. His only desire is *that the truth be known.*"

In this connection we call attention also to this trenchant statement of Bishop Collins, an ecclesiastical historian of considerable note before he was made bishop and who makes a strong appeal for fairness in the statement of facts: "It ought hardly to be necessary to say anything about the ignorant assertion that at the Reformation a Roman Catholic Church was abolished and a Protestant Church set up in its stead. Still, old falsehoods die hard, especially when, like this, they have been repeated and repeated until they have become commonplaces. And as this assertion has been made, and still is, by those who ought to know better a word must be said about it. If, then, the old Church ceased to exist and a new one was made, let our opponents say *when* this was done, and let them produce something in the nature of evidence of the fact. Needless to say, they have no evidence whatever to produce; they do not agree, and never have, as to when it took place. Meanwhile, we affirm that there is no Church in Christendom which has so *unbroken a history as we have.*"

It almost seems like carrying coals to Newcastle to add anything to such quotations, yet it may be just as well to recall a few other authorities, further reinforcing the testimony as to the national independent character of the Church in Britain. Wakeman, for example (p. 93), writing of the close of the eleventh century and throughout the twelfth century, says: "For five hundred years the connection between the Church of England and the Church of Rome had been but slight. Archbishops had received palls from the pope. Peter's pence had been paid with commendable regularity. The more devout of English Churchmen and English kings had made their pilgrimages to Rome, *since the evil days when the invasion of the infidel deprived Christendom of the possession of the tomb of her Lord at Jerusalem.* But no serious attempt had been made by *the popes, since the days of Wilfrid, to impose their own will,* unasked, upon the English Church or to interfere with her own management of her own business. *Her bishops and archbishops were appointed by the king and the Witan. Her laws were either made by synods of bishops and accepted and enforced by the king or made by the king and Witan and accepted by the bishops. They were interpreted by courts held under the joint presidency of the bishop and the earldormen.* The ecclesiastical struggles which agitated the Continent hardly affected the English Church at all."

In commenting upon the early days of the sixteenth century Wakeman makes the following very positive statement about "no papal church ever in England": "It has often been asserted that Henry VIII in his breach with Rome abolished the papal Church in England, and established a new Church, partly royal, partly Protestant. Such a theory will not bear historical investigation for a moment. There *never was,* in any true sense of the word, *a papal Church in England;* but for nine hundred years there had been planted in England the Catholic Church of Christ, over which, during the last four hundred years, the popes had gradually acquired certain administrative rights which were now abolished."

In discussing papal supremacy under the three heads of "temporal nature," "administrative nature," and "spiritual nature," Mr. Wakeman comes to the following conclusions: as to the first, "It would not be seriously contended by any well informed reader of the present day that the popes ever acquired any *permanent rights of government* over the English Church or nation." His conclusion as to the claim of supremacy of an administrative nature, made by virtue of the claim of popes to be the head of the visible Church by Divine appointment, is this: "These claims, therefore, never formed a part of the *law* or *custom,* or the *Constitution in England,* and their successful exercise depended upon the connivance of the king." As to the third claim, Mr. Wakeman writes: "Northumbria ignored the papal decision in Wilfrid's case and Dunstan refused to absolve an offender when he was commanded to do so by the pope. English lawyers were found to maintain that papal law was not binding in England, even on questions of faith and morals, *unless it had been accepted by the national authorities."*

This seems to be an appropriate place to insert this quotation from "The Anglo-Saxon Chronicle" (p. 186): "And Thurstan, archbishop of York, journeyed thither, and because he received consecration from the pope, *against right, and to the prejudice of the see of Canterbury,* and against the king's will, Henry wholly forbade his return to England; and being thus deprived of his archbishopric, he proceeded with the pope towards Rome. This year also Baldwin, earl of Flanders, died of the wound which he had received in Normandy, and was succeeded by Charles, the son of his aunt and of Canute, king of Denmark."

Bishop Boyd-Carpenter points out that the Church of England might be open to influence—that is, from the outside—but her independence was unchallenged. And on p. 105, in writing of the twelfth century, he says: "It must never be forgotten that the English Church claimed to be national, and was jealous of foreign intervention," and again on p. 115, "England was no appanage of Rome; *she had a free, independent, national Church, possessed of its own laws, customs, and rights.* The men who were to make this clear to the world were shortly to come." On p. 125, he says concerning the continuance of the protests against the papacy uttered by Grosseteste: "He appealed to all who were in power to maintain the independence of the Church of England. The *papal impositions had grown through the patience or the great folly of the English people,* but they now united in defending the Church and her freedom. With his last breath Grosseteste protested, declaring that the action of the pope was the action of an Anti-Christ, for it imperilled men's souls'."

These are only samples of the many quotations that may be adduced from Bishop Boyd-Carpenter's work. And Mr. Jenkins, in his "History of Canterbury" (p. 98), speaks of the work of Lanfranc as a "signal proof of the continuity of the teaching of our Church, and of its independence of those Italian influences which were *grafted upon* it at a later period, but which never *assimilated themselves* to the mind of the nation." Again Mr. Jenkins says: "His independent spirit led him to resist the frequent importunities of Gregory to do homage to him in Rome, the king with the true Norman chivalry supporting the archbishop in his refusal." Once again: "It is memorable that while to Theodore, a Greek, the formation and consolidation of the primacy may be chiefly attributed, to Lanfrance, an Italian, and to his *vigorous independent policy,* we owe the preservation of that *national character which up to the very dawn of the Reformation distinguished our Church.*"

Bishop Grafton in his "Lineage of the American Catholic Church" on pp. 70, 72, 195, and 196, says: "The legal opinion of Blackstone is clear and decided. The ancient British Church, by whomsoever planted, was a stranger to Rome and all its pretended authority. This is proved by the fact that the bishops of the British Church were not chosen by the pope, but she selected and consecrated them; nor were they required to take their jurisdiction from Rome. The pope could neither appoint nor remove a bishop at his own discretion, as he now claims the right to do. The archbishop of the Britons was of their own choice. He was not obliged to receive from Rome the pall, which was in early times a gift of honor when conferred. Down to the time of Gregory it was considered nothing more than an honorary and complimentary badge. All executive, legislative, and administrative powers were not, as to-day, centered in the papacy. The idea of subjection to any other bishop or Church than the one of Britain would have seemed quite absurd to the British Christians. The name of Holy Jerusalem or of Great Rome might be spoken of with high honor but that was all. Anything more would have been foreign to their whole mode of thought. That this was so comes out very emphatically when Augustine demanded the submission of the British bishops to himself and they positively rejected his claims, declaring allegiance to an archbishop of their own, the Bishop of Caerleon-upon-Usk. 'Be it known unto you,' they said, 'we are subject to the Church of God, and to the pope of Rome, and to every godly Christian, and to love every one. But other obedience than this we do not know to be due to him whom you name to be pope.' The Norman Conquest brought England into closer relationship with the Continent and the pope. The English Church, united under Archbishop Theodore, had regarded the pope as the first bishop of Christendom, with whom its bishops were joined in Christian fellowship. *The English Church had been peculiarly a national one, with practically no outside authority which it was bound to obey.* The English selected their own bishops. The Church made its own canons, which needed no other authority. The Norman Conquest brought about a change. The pope had blessed the enterprise of William of Normandy in coming over to England, which was subdued in a few years. Before William's disciplined soldiers, armed with sword and bow, the English, with their more primitive weapons of axe and javelin, went to defeat. The Normans were Christians, but with a Roman training. Their priests and bishops had been educated in the Roman theology. Therefore they brought a Roman element to England. A number of the old bishops and clergy were removed, and Normans were placed in their sees and parishes. Two Roman legates came over, and at the Synod of Winchester, Stigand, the old archbishop, was deposed. This was the beginning of a series of important interventions in English affairs on the part of the papacy."

Nothing could be clearer than the unanimous judgment of these noted historians that whatever authority and power were claimed and exercised by the Roman Church in England was *not by right of law or constitution of the Church or the realm of England nor* according to universal tradition in the Church at large nor in accordance with Scriptural teaching, but that it was *encroachment* and *usurpation* to be successfully resisted and totally removed later without affecting the identity of the English Church or its loyalty to the primitive Apostolic Christianity.

Translation of Holy Scripture

An important part of the Reformation work in England was the translation of the Scriptures into the native tongue. This, we recall, was done by Wycliffe about two hundred years before. And in this generation William Tyndale was laying foundations by fine scholarship and noble spirit for that inestimable blessing upon the Anglo-Saxon world of the Word of God in its own tongue and in wonderfully beautiful version, for Tyndale's translation of the New Testament (1525) and a considerable portion of the Old Testament constitutes the real basis of our authorized version so dear to the hearts of millions. To a learned man of his day Tyndale declared: "I defy the pope and all his laws. If God spare my life, ere many years I will cause a boy that driveth the plow to know more of the Scriptures than thou dost."

After Tyndale's work, came the translation of the Bible by Miles Coverdale, a bishop, in 1535, then Matthew's Bible in 1537 and the Great or Cranmer's Bible in 1538. All of this was the work of sons of the English Church. And of its value one historian thus writes: "The 'open Bible' in the greatest of all idioms and its strong clear English, had passed into our household talk, and fixed the standard of our language. But it did more than this. Breaking down the middle wall of partition that had been raised by the mediæval Church, it once more brought God down from heaven to earth, and enabled all men of good will to approach God himself. On the imperishable canvas of the Gospel narrative men could see once more Jesus Christ as He actually lived and spoke to men. They could gauge the extent to which the Catholic Church had departed from primitive Christianity. Our English Bible, unlike any other vernacular version of the Scriptures, has also, in the words of Bishop Westcott, the seal of martyrdom upon it. Of those to whom we owe it, Tyndale, Rogers and Cranmer died triumphant deaths, martyrs to the faith. Coverdale barely escaped the same doom." (Patterson, p. 235.) Now by the authority of the convocation, the Scriptures in the Mother tongue were to be read at each service on Sunday and holy days, with a lesson from the Old Testament and a lesson from the New Testament at each service—a custom still in vogue to the great edification of the people.

Let us observe in passing, how the leadership in these matters was taken by and acknowledged to be in the Church and not by or in parliament or the king. Let us not forget either what a vast debt of gratitude the whole English-speaking world owes to the Church of England for the Word of God in its own tongue. It was due to her initiative that the shackles of a dead and non-understandable language were struck from the Bible, and due to the learning, the work and heroic sacrifice of her sons that it was sent forth among the people in such form as could be read and known by them, as source of comfort, as a light to guide their feet safely through this world into the next and especially as the means of knowing Christ Himself as He was in His days on earth. And also to the great consecrated scholars of the English Church in other times they owe chiefly all the notable translations of the Sacred Scriptures into our tongue. Therefore, the evaluation of the English Bible by all English-speaking Christians should be the measure of their gratitude to the old Mother Church of the Anglo-Saxon peoples.

Then came also the revising of the service books. The first portion of the Prayer Book to receive attention was that which is called the "Sarum Breviary," being revised by convocation in 1516, 1531, and 1542, the first two revisions being before Henry's divorce. In the latter year, a committee was appointed to revise thoroughly the Breviary and translate it into English, omitting all reference to the bishops of Rome, which had crept in after the time of papal interference, and abolishing the invocation of saints. The first portion of it to appear was the Litany, being published in 1543. The entire Prayer Book was revised and given to the Church in the subsequent reign, and is known as the first Prayer Book of Edward VI, published in 1549. In subsequent revisions, changes of more or less importance have been made, but substantially the book as it stands in the English Church to-day, and as it is in our Church in this country, with some necessary and other changes, is the same as that of 1549.

Henry VIII and the Church of England

Perhaps it is well for us to discuss here the claim of Henry VIII to the headship of the English Church that has given rise to some misunderstanding by thoughtless and only partially informed people. This seems to be the foundation of the misunderstanding in their minds: That as he was the head of the English Church, he therefore founded the Church. It would be an idle waste of time to discuss such a matter if all were well-read in the history of the English Church and nation, particularly during the sixteenth century. Hence let us be as brief as possible. Henry tried to be recognized as the unconditional head of all elements in his realm. He had, as many other rulers of his time and before his time, the theocratic idea that he was ruler by Divine Right, and therefore his authority was superior to that of any one else. He did not get the acknowledgment from the Church of his supremacy in the unconditional manner in which he desired it. A statute was framed which spoke of the Church of England and its clergy of which "the king alone is protector and supreme head." This, of course, was meant in opposition to the claim of the pope to have jurisdiction in England, but because the acceptance of such a form would lead to possible misunderstanding, the English clergy represented in convocation refused to accept that form without qualifications and made the claim read: "The English Church and clergy, of which we recognize His Majesty as the protector and supreme ruler, and *so far as is allowed by the law of Christ,* the supreme head." That is as far as the convocation would go; "so far as the law of Christ would allow," the English monarch was to be the protector and head of the English Church, and not any foreign potentate, secular or religious. The bishops of the convocation of York objected to the term "supreme head" on the ground that it was ambiguous and might be taken as implying spiritual power in the king. To meet this objection, in the words of Mr. Wakeman: "Henry wrote personal letters to them repudiating any such meaning, and explaining that the true interpretation of the words was that they acknowledged the existence in the crown of a power to see that the spiritual authority discharged its functions for the good order and peace of society. On this, the formula was accepted." . . . "The recognition of the king by the convocations in 1531 as supreme head of the Church and clergy as far as is allowed by the law of Christ, and the recognition of this title by parliament in 1534, in the words 'only supreme head on earth of the Church of England,' obviously do not of themselves confer any greater powers upon the crown than it had been in the habit of exercising. If we may take the explanation which the king gave to the northern convocation of the meaning of the phrase 'supreme head' as expressing his real intentions at that time, it is quite clear that Henry did not even intend them to confer any new powers. He brings them distinctly within the principle of supervision. And in his "History of the Christian Church" Prof. G. P. Fisher writing of the passing of the Act of Royal Supremacy in Henry VIII's time tells us (p. 351): "But the government, in passing the Act of Supremacy, drew up a document in which that act is declared to signify that the sovereign has only 'such power as to a king of right appertaineth by the law of God; and not that he should take any spiritual power from spiritual ministers that is given to them by the Gospel.' "

We record these facts simply because they are facts, and throw some side lights on the matter under consideration, but they do not affect the essence of it. Had convocation and parliament granted the desire of Henry in every detail it would have had no bearing whatever on whether or not he founded the Church of England. He found it with an age of many centuries and, therefore, he could not have founded it, no matter what might have been the privileges and prerogatives assumed or acknowledged as his. That is plain enough. Is it not? The following from the pen of Dr. R. W. Lowrie is not only bright, but also a succinct and true statement of historical facts:

"Did Henry VIII found or find the Church of England? If he found it, he could not have founded it. He certainly found it; for he did find it, it being there when he came to the throne. If he found it, this is not that he founded it; for while one may find, he cannot found that which already has an existence. While then he may be called a finder, he cannot be called the founder of the English Church. The founder he could not be because he found it. If he had not found it he might have founded it. To say 'he did found it' would be bad English, as well as false history. We can only say that 'he did find it'—found it in England, and left it in England. He found the identical Church of his fathers and forefathers—a rich find for anyone, monarch or subject, prince or peasant. If he had not found it, he never could have founded it, in all the excellence which it then possessed—its heritage from the earliest days, before a Henry was on the throne."

In view of the history of the time and the identity of the Church and the nation at that time in England, we can readily understand the meaning of this phrase, "the Head of the Church." And it must appear that nothing but pure ignorance, or thoughtlessness or deliberate and dishonest misrepresentation, which we greatly dislike to impute to anyone, could possibly lead one to think or say that because this qualified acknowledgment was given to Henry VIII that he was to be accounted the founder of the Church. The fact is that Henry was able to secure a great deal less from the English Church in this respect than Constantine received from the early Church or Charlemagne in the ninth century from the Continental Church, or Charles V from the German Church. We recall, of course, that Constantine summoned the first General Council of Nicea, and that he presided over its deliberations. No such authority was ever claimed by Henry VIII over the English Church, far less was it granted. In regard to Charlemagne, we are told by the historian Robertson (Vol. III, p. 127) : "In spiritual as well as in temporal affairs, the Emperor, Charles the Great, was regarded as the highest judge beyond whom no appeal could be made. In authorizing the canons of Adrian's collection he omitted that canon of Sardica which prescribed in certain cases a reference to the bishop of Rome. While he cultivated friendly relations with the popes, while he acknowledged them as the highest bishops and often consulted them and acted on their suggestions, the authority by which these were enforced on his subjects was his own; nor did the popes attempt to interfere with the powers which he claimed."

And Lord Bryce in "The Holy Roman Empire" (p. 62) says, "There are letters of his (Charlemagne's) extant in which he lectures Pope Leo in a tone of easy superiority, admonishes him to obey the holy canons, and bids him pray earnestly, for the success of the efforts which it is the *monarch's duty to make for the subjugation of pagans and the establishment of sound doctrine throughout the Church.* Nay, subsequent popes themselves admitted and applauded the despotic superintendence of matters spiritual which he was wont to exercise and which leads some one to give him playfully a title that had once been applied to the pope himself, *'Episcopus episcoporum.'* " Shall it be said then, because he, claiming this authority in the Church, even though it was conceded by the popes themselves, that he founded the Church in the Holy Roman Empire? Or shall it be said because Constantine presided over the first General Council, and in a measure was regarded as the head of Christendom, that he founded the Christian Church; and because Charles V likewise claimed authority and headship of the Church in the German Empire that he was therefore the founder of the Church there? We see that just a little research into history reveals the absurdity of such a claim in behalf of Henry in regard to the English Church—a claim which we are certain he would most emphatically have repudiated himself. And Ranke, "History of the Popes" (Vol. III, p. 120), tells us that Louis XIV made the same claim as to the Church in France.

Milman ("Latin Christianity," pp. 180, 181, 185) gives us a very striking illustration of the emperor not only claiming but acting as the practical head of the Western Continental Church, calling councils and removing and setting up popes. The emperor is Otho the Great. The following is the record: "The emperor summoned an ecclesiastical council; it was attended by the archbishops of Aquileia (by deputy), of Milan, of Ravenna, and Hamburg; by two German and two French metropolitans; by a great number of bishops and presbyters from Lombardy, Tuscany, and all parts of Italy. The whole militia of Rome assembled as a guard to the council round the church of St. Peter. The proceedings of the council mark the times. Inquiry was made why the pope was not present. A general cry of astonishment broke forth from the clergy and the people—'The very Iberians, Babylonians, and Indians have heard the monstrous crimes of the pope. He is not a wolfe who condescends to sheep's clothing; his cruelty, his diabolical dealings are open, avowed, disdain concealment.' The calmer justice of the emperor demanded specific charges. Darker charges followed, mingled with less heinous in strange confusion; charges of adultery, incest, with the names of females, one of his father's concubines, another a widow and her niece; he had made the Lateran palace a brothel; he had been guilty of hunting; charges of cruelty, the blinding of one dignified ecclesiastic, the castrating another, both had died under the operation; he had let loose fire and sword, and appeared himself constantly armed with sword, lance, helmet and breastplate. Both ecclesiastics and laymen accused him of drinking wine for the love of the devil; of invoking, when gambling, heathen deities, the devils of Jove and Venus. He had perpetually neglected matins and vespers, and never signed himself with the sign of the cross."

Again Milman tells us: "The grateful, or vassal pope, Leo VIII, in a council, recognizes the full right of the Emperor Otho and his successors in the kingdom of Italy, as Hadrian that of Charlemagne, to elect his own successors to the empire, and *to approve the pope.* This right was to belong for ever to the King of the Roman Empire, and to none else.

"Early in the next year the Emperor Otho recrossed the Alps. Leo VIII died, and a deputation from Rome followed the emperor to Germany, to solicit the reinstatement of the exiled Benedict to the popedom. But Benedict was dead also. The bishop of Narni (John XIII), with the approbation or by the command of the emperor, was elected to the papacy." And Henry's own predecessor, William the Conqueror, definitely laid it down that no assembly of bishops was to ordain or prohibit anything except that which was agreeable to his will, and had been first ordained by himself. And in other ways William claimed and exercised as much or more authority over persons and things spiritual than Henry did. Yet no one claims that William the Conqueror founded the Church of England.

So the same reasoning that would make Henry VIII the founder of the English Church because he was called the head of the Church so far as the law of

Christ allowed, would lead us to say that Constantine founded the Christian Church, that Charlemagne again founded it in the Holy Roman Empire, that Charles founded it in Germany, that Otho the Great founded it again, and that Louis XIV founded it in France. For these had the unqualified acknowledgment of their control, which Henry never had. A queer freak indeed would this make the Christian Church—a creature of many births.

This leads us to speak not only of the historical inaccuracy of the claim that Henry VIII originated the English Church, but also the essential absurdity involved in the very idea. It is a fundamental law of human nature that man will not accept the leadership in religion of one whom he knows to be immoral and wicked. Every Englishman knew the evil of Henry's life, and therefore it would have been a contradiction of all the fundamental things in the human heart and mind and in human experience if he, a man, wicked, licentious and immoral, and known to be such, could be the leader in any spiritual movement, much less the founder of a Church. However narrow and bigoted Luther and Calvin might have been judged by some, men believed in the purity of their lives and the sincerity of their convictions, and so they were ready to listen to them and to follow them.

Again, Henry VIII's religious views did not accord with those of the Reformers of the English Church. Henry set forth what were called the "Six Articles." The points in those articles were: Transubstantiation, Compulsory Celibacy, Masses for the Dead, Communion in one kind, and Compulsory Confession to priests.

Every one of these things the reformed Church of England repudiated in that day and has repudiated ever since. And Henry ordered Anne Ascue beheaded because she would not subscribe to them. And there stands to-day, a stone shaft in the city of Oxford, bearing its mute and undeniable testimony to some of the reforming leaders in the Church of England—martyred because of their opposition to these very things. In substantiation of the above we quote these words of Patterson (p. 289): "Thus transubstantiation, private masses for the dead, the whole theory and practice of indulgences, the witholding of the cup from the laity, compulsory confession, compulsory celibacy of the clergy, the doctrine of purgatory, were rejected. A purer faith and practice were laid down." And Wakeman (p. 271), and Boyd-Carpenter (p. 200), give exactly the same testimony.

Then to the subject of Transubstantiation Mr. Patterson gives rather full notice. It is interesting, and timely and profitable, we believe, to recall his exact words (p. 242): "The *Roman doctrine of Transubstantiation* was given its final definition by the Council of Trent in 1563. The theory had established itself in the thirteenth century. It was not held in the early ages of the Church, and therefore to declare it 'catholic' *is bad history*. It is also part of a relatively obsolete philosophy (that of the Schoolmen). The Schoolmen, pressing into the service of the Church the Aristotelian philosophy, drew a distinction between the substantia, or 'essence,' of a thing and its 'accidents.' According to the Roman theory, the 'accidents,' of the bread and wine (e. g., their feeling to the touch and their appearance to the eye) remain the same after the prayer of consecration, while the substance, or essence, is changed to the Body and Blood of Christ. The whole doctrine as formulated in the Catechism of the Council of Trent *is grossly materialistic.*" And again on p. 243 he writes: "The view taken by the Church of England concerning the Sacrament of Holy Communion is this. She has explicitly rejected the doctrine of Transubstantiation (Article 28) as 'repugnant to the plain words of Scripture,' and giving rise to many superstitions. She has implicitly (but not explicitly) rejected the so-called Zwinglian view which reduces the Sacrament to a merely commemorative rite. Within these external limits she allows a considerable latitude of belief. . . . The authoritative teaching of the Church of England must, however, be taken from her own formularies. "In these she affirmatively lays down—

"(a) That there is a presence of Christ in the ordinance to the worthy receiver. 'To such as rightly, worthily, and with faith receive . . . the Bread which we break is a partaking of the Body of Christ' (Article 28). 'The Body and Blood of Christ are verily and indeed taken and received by the faithful in the Lord's Supper' (Catechism).

"(b) That the wicked partakers of the sacrament in no wise are the partakers of Christ (Article 29).

"(c) That the presence of Christ to the worthy receiver is spiritual. 'The Body of Christ is given, taken and eaten in the Supper only after an heavenly and spiritual manner.' 'The means whereby the Body of Christ is received and eaten in the Supper is Faith' (Article 28).

"The Church of England may be said to retain the doctrine of a real presence. But the presence taught by her is of a spiritual nature, and something quite distinct from a corporeal presence of Transubstantiation. The most real things in life are spiritual, not material.

"To maintain a real presence is only incompatible with the formularies of the Church if a presence other than spiritual is intended."

How illogical, even ridiculous, therefore, it is for anyone to maintain that a man could be the founder of an institution that denied the things for which he stood, an institution whose teachers and leaders died rather than acknowledge those things, and an institution that taught at the same time, and has taught and practised ever since, things in plain and direct opposition to those which he stoutly maintained? Henry also made provision for private masses to be said in behalf of his soul after death—a wise precaution indeed in his case, if there were any efficacy in such things!

CHAPTER XII

THE CHURCH OF ENGLAND AGAINST THE EXCESSES OF THE REFORMERS

We cannot lose sight of the influence of foreign Reformers on the Church of England. As the leaders of the English Church were desirous to cast out all of those mediæval superstitions and errors in doctrine and worship, as well as in polity, so were they just as anxious to retain everything that was Scriptural, primitive and Apostolic. It has been said that "their object was not to revolutionize, but to reform; not to get as far away as possible from the Church of Rome, or any other church, but by retracing the steps whereby the primitive Church of England had fallen from herself, to return to Catholic faith and practices." All of this was clearly set forth in the Preface of the first Prayer Book of Edward VI in 1549. And it continued to be the underlying purpose actuating the Church throughout all the years of the Reformation in England even up to the culmination of the movement in the days of Elizabeth, who herself wrote to some Roman Catholic princes "that there was no new faith propagated in England; no new religion set up but that which was commanded by our Saviour, practised by the primitive Church, and approved by the Fathers of the best antiquity." Then again the "same principles are distinctly and authoritatively set forth in the 30th

Canon Ecclesiastical, which says: 'So far was it from the purpose of the Church of England to forsake and reject the Churches of Italy, France, Spain, Germany, or any such-like Churches, in all things which they held and practised, that, as the Apology of the Church of England confesseth, it doth with reverence retain those ceremonies which do neither endamage the Church of God nor offend the minds of sober men; and only departed from them in those particular points wherein they were fallen both from themselves in their ancient integrity, and from the Apostolical Churches, which were their first founders.'" Daniel, (p. 30.)

On the other hand, the Continental Reformers who came from Switzerland and Germany had to be checked to prevent their influence from casting out some things from the Constitution and worship of the Church that English Church people have ever held as both dear and essential. Many of the foreign Reformers were rash and obtrusive men who seemed unable to distinguish between what should be retained and what should be eliminated. Some of those who settled in England were much dissatisfied with the limited extent of the changes made in the Church's Liturgy, and it was just as necessary for our English forefathers to fight against their influence as it was to stand firm for the cutting away of Roman and mediæval beliefs. Calvinistic and papal tyranny and errors had to be resisted alike. Truly it has been written: "The essence of the Puritan demand from first to last had consistently been to make the *Church itself Puritan,* not merely to find a footing for Puritanism within its borders." And Wakeman says (p. 346): "Arguments there may be to show that Puritanism was better than the Church—there are none to prove that the two systems were compatible one with the other. The English government and the English nation had to choose between them, and the Hampton Court conference marks the choice which they made. The Church Catholic was to remain the religion of Englishmen, and, if the Puritans wished to supplant it, they must do so by force alone." It is indeed a matter of great thankfulness on our part that the English Church, clergy and people, were given the guidance of the Spirit to keep their judgment clear, and grace to stand firm. Nothing else could account for their course.

The progress of the Reformation was halted by the accession of Mary to the English throne. She was a papalist and endeavored to restore the influence of the pope and all of the accessories that naturally go therewith. The martyrdom of Ridley, Latimer and Cranmer, to whose memory was erected that monument in Oxford to which we have referred, showed how strongly this reaction was resisted. It was one of those passing incidents that so often belong to a great movement.

The progress of the movement was resumed under Elizabeth. The principles that were adopted for guidance in the reign of Elizabeth were, as we have seen above, the same as those which had characterized the previous generations and had stood for the clear faith, national independence and catholicity of the Church. No doctrine was to be regarded as heresy unless the Scriptures or decisions of the Four Councils declared it to be so. The effort was now, as it was in the time of the Hatfield Synod, as in the first part of Henry's reign and all through Edward's reign, simply to *restore* what had been lost, and to cut away those things that had grown as carbuncles upon the body. The test of orthodoxy was to be the decisions of the great General Councils of the whole Church of Christ.

A thing of striking character and importance occurred in the reign of Elizabeth, showing the continuity of the English Church in a most undeniable fashion. The Prayer Book had been revised in 1559. Pius IV was then the bishop of Rome. He examined the Book and declared that "he found nothing in it contrary to sound doctrine and pure faith," and would authorize it if Elizabeth would receive it from him. She declined to do so on the ground that he had no jurisdiction whatever in England—in either Church or State. Then came Pius V to the papal throne, and after losing all hope of winning England to the Roman obedience issued his bull of excommunication in 1570, forbidding use of the Prayer Book which all—Romanists and others—had been using for 11 years and which his papal predecessor had offered to ratify as correct in doctrine and discipline if Elizabeth would receive it at his hands, recognizing him as the Vicar of Christ. There were at that time 9,400 clergy in England. As Elizabeth refused to receive the Prayer Book from him, the pope excommunicated her, and placed England under papal interdict, and attempted to turn her subjects from allegiance to her. Let it be remembered, however, that the Book had been in use from 1559 to 1570, in which latter date, the pope issued his denunciation. Out of the 9,400 clergymen in the Church of England, 189 obeyed the instructions of the pope, set up new altars and gathered around them new congregations. We ask, in all reason and fair-mindedness, who were the dissenters and schismatics—the 9,211 clergymen who remained in the same rectories, ministering at the same altars and serving the same congregations, using the same vestments and the same liturgy; or the 189 who went out and ministered in new buildings and to strange congregations? Whatever schism there is in England to-day between the historic branches of Christianity, lies at the door of the Roman Church. It is they who separated, and not those who remained as they had been and where their forefathers in the faith and the flesh *had worshipped for century after century before them*. We remember that a fully organized branch of the Apostolic Catholic Church was in the British Islands centuries before Gregory and Augustine were born. We recall that, because of this, Wakeman declares that, "Gregory had no possible right" to place the British bishops under Augustine's authority. And further, "The Roman Catholics were the *first religious body to separate from the national Church and to form their own organization outside of it*. Obloquy and persecution bound them together in a way which nothing else could have done. Their ostracism from the national life tended to make them into a foreign-minded clique, and at times rendered them a political danger. But from first to last their loyalty to the crown, save for the few years of Jacobite intrigue, has been as conspicuous in England, in spite of much provocation, as the want of it has been remarkable in Ireland." Bishop Boyd-Carpenter also writes: "The Romanists had been in some measure willing to conform at first but the *pope ordered them to become Non-Conformists."* (P. 224.) Recall also Gore's "Anglo-Catholic Movement To-Day" (p. 31) : "So the dogma of the papal supremacy and infallibility, as something substantially belonging to the Catholic tradition as held from the first, is plainly contrary to the facts of history. It was never part of the Eastern tradition of the Church. *And the faith which accepts such a claim has really to triumph over history.* Thus the Roman development of Catholicity is a development which has narrowed its scope and meaning, by its constant accentuation of authority and by its centralization. In these tendencies it does not represent the New Testament spirit or the spirit of the early Church : it has made the Roman communion impossible for many, and many of the best men, who would have been at home in the undivided Church ; and *it is responsible in very large measure for the divisions of Christendom."*

The force of all this was recognized by an English Roman priest, Father Humphreys, who lecturing some years ago said, "The Church of England is the pre-Reformation Church in this country. We are a mission straight from Rome." In concluding the remarks concerning this incident, it is well for us to say that the messenger sent by the pope to tell Elizabeth that he would agree to all the changes the English had made in the Liturgy, in the appointment of bishops, in the translation of the Scriptures and all else if only his supremacy might be recognized, was not allowed to land in England. As has been pointed out, this circumstance proves that the chief struggle between Eng-

land and Rome was for the right of a national Church
to be free from alien jurisdiction, and that no new
faith was imposed on the nation in the sixteenth century, even the pope himself admitting the same.

There comes to mind at this time an excellent pamphlet recently written by Rev. S. C. Hughson, O.H.C.,
from which we quote: "The study of the case shows
that the English Church repudiated the pope's claim
to universal authority in 1534. If the Anglican Church
was founded by Henry, this was the year in which he
must have founded it. Clement VII, who was pope
at the time, did not make the slightest effort to with-
draw Catholics from the Church of England. If he
believed that Henry had established a new Church in
which grace could not be found, surely he must have
initiated instantly an effort to secure the Sacraments
for England, or else stand convicted of the crime of
allowing his spiritual children to go on receiving the
false Sacraments of this Church. He made no protest
whatever. He did not send a single priest to England.

"At last in 1570, *thirty-six years* after Henry VIII
had, according to the present papal claim, founded the
Church of England, despairing of inducing the English
ever again to bow their necks to the yoke of Rome,
Pius V excommunicated Elizabeth and all who adhered
to the Church of England. Now for the first time those
who adhered to Rome were told that it would be sin
to communicate at English altars.

"Thirty-six years! During this period millions had
been born, baptized, confirmed, shriven, had received
their Communion regularly at Anglican altars; had

finished their course, and, fortified by the last Sacraments, had gone out into the other world;—and pope after pope had regarded it as a thing to be permitted without question that all these faithful souls, hungering for the Bread of Life, should be fed by the shepherds of a Church which Rome now declares to be the evil device of the most wicked king who ever sat on England's throne.

"Seven popes reigned contemporary with this early Reformation period. They knew what was going on, and they were well content to leave their people to the spiritual mercies of a Church which we are now told was Henry's creation.

"Let it be noted that it is claimed that these men were infallible rulers of the universal Church, with the responsibility for the world on their souls. And yet not one of them had addressed himself to the work of rescuing England and English Catholics from the pretensions of this Church which they now claim had been conceived in iniquity and born in sin."

Sometimes a question is raised as to the proper succession of the Anglican episcopate in the sixteenth century, it being claimed that Parker, made archbishop of Canterbury in Elizabeth's reign, was not properly consecrated. There is, of course, absolutely no ground for such a charge, except in the desire of some to invalidate the succession of the Anglican episcopate, and the readiness often manifested to forge documents and to bring in false testimony wherever it could be effective for the purpose of discounting that succession. We only stop here to say that the consecration of Parker took place in Lambeth Palace, December 17,

1559, in the presence of a goodly congregation. The ceremony was held within the altar rails and was participated in by William Barlow, consecrated bishop of Asaph; John Scory, consecrated in 1551 as the bishop of Chichester; Miles Coverdale, translator of the Bible, and bishop of Exeter in Edward's reign; John Hodgkins, suffragan bishop of Bedford appointed in the reign of Edward. (For adequate treatment of this and other matters pertaining to validity of Anglican orders see M. W. Patterson pp. 286-295).

In summarizing this period, let us say that the continuity of Church organization during the period when the Tudors reigned seems as clear as historical facts can make a thing, and that all of the statutes passed in those reigns were brought about expressly to preserve such continuity, and explicitly disclaim any intention of breaking that continuity, and with the exception of the monasteries and nunneries not a single corporation was dissolved; and these institutions were dissolved by those having authority to do so, and because of internal conditions. "The Church's corporate life remained unbroken, the same orders—bishops, priests and deacons—retained their jurisdiction and administered the same laws as before. The bishops still sat in the House of Lords by the same title as before. The convocations continued to sit concurrently with parliament as before. The Church never lost her identity, only corruptions were cut away." The old Church stood forth more beautiful than ever before. No new Church was founded. As Mr. Wakeman has written: "The essence and power of the Church of England since the Reformation lay not where Cromwell sought for it, not in the power of the Church to influence, not where Elizabeth and James the First tried to place it, in the power that the Church gave to and derived from the Crown, but where Hooker and Laud and George Herbert found it—in the right of the Church to the prestige and the teachings of the Church of the Apostles and of the Middle Ages." A fair appeal to history thus demonstrates that however great may have been for a time her helplessness in the hand of the Crown, however severe the buffetings of discordant opinion that she had to endure in order to change her book of worship and in part remodel her ways, nevertheless she preserved unimpaired the faith and discipline of the Catholic Church.

During the seventeenth century the struggle of the Church was against the ultra-Protestant element, the inordinate influence of Calvin, Zwingli and Luther. And in her fight for the maintenance of Catholic principles against Protestant negations, her leader was William Laud, archbishop of Canterbury. He, together with such men as Lancelot Andrews, bishop of Ely, and Richard Hooker, pastor of the Temple Church in London, formed a band of men whose object it was to resist the progress of Calvinistic principles as seen in Presbyterianism; by the appeal to history, reason and Scripture, to demonstrate that episcopacy is an Apostolic form of government, and that the Church of England in her organization, discipline, doctrine and liturgy is directly connected with the Apostolic Church by unbroken lineage; and that her rejection of papal influence and authority did not put her out of harmony with other branches of the Holy Catholic Church. And they showed that the doctrines of the Church of England are more than a system of negations, that they are based upon Holy Scripture, are in conformity with the Conciliar standards of the Christian Church, and are in accordance with enlightened reason and approved by inward conviction. The Church will never be able to measure in due proportion the debt that she owes to these men. We to-day are under obligation as great to them for preserving the historical continuity, the Apostolic character of the Church against the onslaught of ultra-reforming negations and destructions as we are to men like Latimer, Colet, Ridley and Cranmer for cutting away mediæval superstitions and errors, and resisting papal usurpations.

It was unfortunate that the Stuart monarchs were aligned as closely as they were with the fortunes of the Church. The people's displeasure visited upon the monarchy extended to the Church of the monarchy. The Independents when they arose to ascendancy, slandered the Church and grossly ill-treated the clergy because of their political associations. Cromwell and his Independent followers allied themselves with the Presbyterians in their opposition to the Church, and together they secured and held power over the Church for awhile. That, however, no more caused the destruction of the Church than the usurped authority of Rome did in earlier days. Many of the bishops and clergy were deprived of their rights as were also the laity, but they never acquiesced in the deeds of the Independents and Presbyterians, and when the Church regained her authority and position she treated the dissenting ministers much more charitably and with far greater broadmindness, going so far indeed in some cases as thereby to invite criticism of the importance she placed upon the Orders of her ministry.

Then under James the Second, other troubles came— troubles of the sort that forced the Church of England to make another fight for the prevention of the re- introduction of mediæval ways and of the restoration of the papal usurpations. Our leaders at that time, men whom we might say saved the day for the Church of England, were Bishops Trelawney, Lake, Ken, White, Lloyd and Turner. These were imprisoned for the stand they took in regard to the Church, but they won; and we owe to them very deep gratitude for their splendid and heroic stand in her behalf. Bishop Boyd-Carpenter (p. 318) pays this tribute to the spirit and work of these men: "The pulpits resounded with expositions of the Reformed faith. The errors of Rome were publicly refuted. It was no mere 'No popery' howl. It was the conscientious effort of men who desired to warn their flocks against dangers which came with royal support and Jesuit intrigue. Ken, the devout, peace-loving, cultured Ken, was foremost in this effort. His preaching drew thousands as he led men's minds to dwell on what they owed to the Reformation, and to realize how needful it was to cleave to that faith which their fore- fathers had won back for them." He further says that such men as these furnished the foundations for the Anglo-Catholic movement in its true beginnings as seen in the great Caroline Divines (p. 421). "These grave and learned men, who had held firmly to historical Catholicity, had known and declared that Roman teach- ing was both unscriptural and uncatholic. They held by the faith of Bishop Ken, who believed in *the pure Christian faith as it was before all Roman and Puritan innovations."*

The troubles of the Church were not yet at an end, however. When William and Mary came to the throne in 1689, the Protestant extremists renewed their attack upon her, but her leaders were enabled to steer her safely through and in quieter times she began to build up her own life and extend her missionary endeavors. As indicative of the way the Church of England desired to maintain unquestioned her continuity with the great past, the House of Convocation refused to accept the term "Protestant" at the opening of the reign of William III because it was feared that it would be misconstrued, and that it might appear that the Church of England was in the same class with the new religious organizations that had just come into being on the Continent.

Not only was the Lower House of Convocation jealous of the Church's clear title to continuity with the past, but all sections of the Church were very anxious to have her teaching unimpaired by any false doctrines, and whenever any of those in her ministry, whether among the bishops or other clergy, were guilty of questionable opinions or open defiance of her teaching, those in authority were quick to repudiate such teaching and to censure such teachers.

As an excellent summary statement applicable at this point we quote these words of Wakeman (pp. 370–1) as applying to the time of the restoration of Charles II: "There were plenty of questions as to the exact shape which the settlement of religion should take, whether changes should be made in the Prayer Book, what relief should be afforded to tender consciences; but that the religion of England was no longer to be Presbyterian or Independent, but was to be that of the Church, there was no question at all. When Charles II was crowned king of England in Westminster Abbey, Juxon was there as archbishop of Canterbury to crown him. It required no public act to abolish the various ordinances by which the Church had been superseded and persecuted. In the eye of the law they were unconstitutional acts of a rebel government and had no legal validity. Just as Charles II returned to what was rightfully his in the twelfth year of his reign, so the *Church returned to what was rightfully* hers in the eighteenth year of her suppression. According to the theory of the Restoration, all that had intervened had been *an illegal usurpation,* and could confer no rights. Wren, bishop of Ely, came out of the prison in which he had languished for twenty years. Piers of Bath and Wells, Skinner of Oxford, Roberts of Bangor, Warner of Rochester, and King of Chichester came forth from their exile or their retreat to resume the government of the dioceses from which they had been driven by force. Frewen, bishop of Lichfield, was placed in charge of the Northern province, and Brian Duppa moved from Salisbury to Winchester. The bishops simply resumed their functions as rulers and leaders of religion in England, without waiting for any act on the part of the State to authorize them to do it. *Just as there had been* no *act of the nation reconstituting the Church at the time of the Reformation in the previous century, so there was no act of the nation restoring the Church at the time of the Restoration.* The Divine Society had indeed passed through a period of severe crisis. In altering its relations to the papacy it had considerably modified its own teaching and its own worship. It had fallen under the tyranny of the State. It had been conquered and driven into exile by the armed power of Puritanism. But through all these crises its continuity had been carefully preserved. Its law, its organisation, its theory remained essentially unaltered. It had maintained beyond question the due succession of its bishops, and as a necessary consequence the validity of its Sacraments. It claimed that in its alterations of teaching and worship it had only brought itself into closer union with the Church of the Apostles and Fathers. So when the season of persecution passed away and constitutional government once more took the place of military rule, the Church came forth from its hidingplace to discharge the spiritual functions which it had been for a time obliged to suspend, to resume its ancient traditions, to claim its ancient rights, to take up again its solemn duty of guiding the English nation along the way of salvation according to the purpose of God."

It would be very interesting to follow at some length the fortunes of such societies as the "Society for the Promotion of Christian Knowledge" and the "Society for Propagating the Gospel in Foreign Parts" and also the movement under the inspiration of the Wesleys and Whitfield, and other events of the eighteenth and nineteenth centuries, but space permits only brief references to a few of them—sufficient, however, we hope to be of value in setting before the reader the existence of "the seven thousand" in England's Israel that never bent the knee to ecclesiastical, secular or wordly Baals.

The Wesleys and Others

The first of the Georges came to the throne of England in 1714. George I was a Lutheran prince, a foreigner by birth and speech. The four Georges reigned through a period of 115 years. During their reigns the temporal welfare of the nation progressed very rapidly, but the whole Georgian era has been termed the siesta of the English Church. And one writer tells us that "that is a very mild way of putting it." It was, as most readers know, a period of great spiritual indifference and apathy, and a time of considerable infidelity. But on the other hand, there were those who were devoutly earnest and nobly spiritual, among whom we might name William Law who through his "Serious Call to a Devout and Holy Life," published in 1726, exercised a very wide and wholesome influence and served to bring professing Christians to a finer sense of their responsibilities as disciples of Christ. And about this time Oliver Goldsmith, too, wrote his poem, "The Deserted Village" and in it, perhaps the reader will remember, he gives this picture of the faithful parson:

> "Thus to relieve the wretched was his pride,
> And e'en his failings leaned to virtue's side;
> But in his duty prompt at every call,
> He watched and wept, he prayed and felt for all;
> And, as a bird each fond endearment tries,
> To tempt its new-fledged offspring to the skies;
> He tried each art, reproved each dull delay,
> Allured to brighter worlds, and led the way."

There were others who were standing out as powerful champions of the faith, and sounding the voices of the prophet and the scholar as Bishops George Berkeley and Joseph Butler, calling to repentance and renewed allegiance to the God of truth and love. And Dr. Jeremy Taylor was still exercising a deep and wide influence through "Holy Living" and other books.

While Bishop Butler's writings—particularly his "Analogy of Natural and Revealed Religion"—have had a profound effect in America as in other countries, as is the case also of Jeremy Taylor's books, yet as Berkeley, then Dean Berkeley, lived in our country a while and showed deep personal interest in our development, for a fuller notice and appreciation of him and his work, we commend to the reader the Rev. Dr. C. C. Tiffany's "History of the Protestant Episcopal Church" (pp. 282–286):

"The influence of Berkeley has not yet died out. His is still a name to conjure with in matters educational. The town wherein stands the University of California is named in honor of him. His name is given to the Divinity School of Connecticut at Middletown, and to various preparatory schools throughout the country, notably those in New York and Providence. The Berkeley Prize which he founded in Yale College is one of the most coveted in the university at New Haven. There, a college hall bears his name, and a stained-glass window stands as his memorial in the college chapel. His interest in America continued active after his return to Europe. He frequently corresponded upon topics of education with our prominent professors, and wrote shortly before his death to President Clap: 'The daily increase in religion and learning in your seminary of Yale College gives me very sensible pleasure and an ample recompense for my poor endeavors to further those good ends.' His interest in America was continued by his son, the Rev. George Berkeley, whose influence both in Scotland and England in securing an American episcopate was as great as, if not greater than, that of any other single man."

The Wesleys

Among the well known country clergy of the first quarter of the eighteenth century was Samuel Wesley, Rector of the Church of England parish in Epworth, Lincolnshire. Undoubtedly his greatest fame came from the fact that he was the father of John and Charles Wesley. Both of these sons, after being educated in the University of Oxford, became clergymen, John being ordained in 1725, and Charles in 1735. John Wesley was very much affected by Jeremy Taylor's "Holy Living" and Law's "Serious Call" to which we have just referred. They both impressed him with the necessity of living a deeply religious life. And his father, Samuel Wesely, was a sincere promoter of the devotional part of the Church's life, and was always a stalwart friend of any society organized for emphasizing that part of the Church's ministrations. These facts show that both John and Charles Wesley had been trained from infancy in the old Mother Church of England in an atmosphere and system of spiritual fervor of which they have been erroneously considered the originators. While at Oxford, these two brothers spent much of their spare time in giving religious instructions in the charity schools, the jails, and work-houses; and generally, by their life and conversation, tried to spiritualize other students of the University, who might have caught the materialistic spirit of that age. The leadership of the guild among the young men of Oxford contemptuously called the "Holy Club," was offered to John, and he accepted it with alacrity. Because the members of the club tried to set a good example to those around them, they were much ridiculed by those who used profane language; and one of the nicknames by which the new society was known was the term "Methodist." It has been observed that it seems strange now to read that their "Method" consisted in a most strict observance of all that the Prayer Book demands from conscientious sons of the Church of England, but there can be no doubt of it. They fasted on all the appointed days and communicated every Sunday or Holy Day. They also denied themselves of every luxury and amusement in order to save money for beneficent deeds.

Soon after the death of their father, both John and Charles went with General Oglethorpe to the Colony of Georgia, Charles as the General's secretary and chaplain, and John as a missionary being sent by the Society for Propagating the Gospel in Foreign Parts, especially to the Indians, but actually became Rector of Christ Church, Savannah. They were not very well received in Georgia, because they were too strict in imposing the discipline of the Church and were rather too ritualistic for the people of the colony.

McConnell in his "History of the American Episcopal Church" (p. 163) thus describes John Wesley's activities in Savannah: "There he began at once to carry into practice his pronounced ideas of Church order and discipline. He multiplied services; emphasized the fast and feast days of the Church; refused to allow parents to stand, and insisted that none but communicants could be sponsors; insisted upon Baptism by immersion as being the primitive mode; repelled from the Holy Communion all who had not been baptized by an episcopally ordained minister; insisted upon making priestly inquisition into the lives of all who offered to come to the Lord's Table. No place more ill adapted to his rubrical rigor could have been found than the Georgia colony was. He quickly estranged his people by his malapropos zeal. From estrangement, the feeling against him soon passed into active hostility."

They returned to England, and John began to be impressed with the conviction that he ought to go up and down England striving to reclaim the people from spiritual apathy which was settling down upon the nation like a blight. Up to 1739 the pulpits of the Church of England were freely open to him, but the excesses of Methodism became such that these opportunities were more and more restricted. In five years after Wesley started to organize his movement he had 45 preachers and a little over 2,000 people attached to it. He, himself, preached from two to four times every day and travelled about 4,500 miles a year. And in 1790 or about 40 years after his movement had its definite start he had 511 preachers and 120,000 members. Some one writing about him remarked: "It is not too much to say that in the eighteenth century England no single figure influenced so many minds and no single voice touched so many hearts." The purpose of both the Wesley brothers was, through their Society, to organize a powerful auxiliary to the Church, and not to establish something that would be *outside* of the Church. Charles Wesley died in 1788 and was buried in the Church yard of the English Church, and just before his death said, "I have lived and I die in Communion of the Church of England, and I will be buried in the yard of my Parish Church." And John in 1790, just before his death, published these words: "I hold all the doctrines of the Church of England, I love her Liturgy, and approve her plan of discipline, and only wish it could be carried out." And just a few years before, he had written a pamphlet, "Twelve Reasons Against Separating From the Church of England." And in 1789, just two years before his death, he said: "None who regard my judgment or advice will separate from the Church of England."

However, Wesley performed an act in his private bed room on September the 2nd, 1785, which ultimately led to the separation of the Methodists from the Episcopal Church. For at that time and place, in solemn manner, he set apart Rev. Dr. Coke as Superintendent of the Methodists in America and authorized him to appoint the Rev. Francis Asbury to a similar position, and further authorized them to ordain elders for administering the Sacraments. This latter he did on the principle that a presbyter might ordain presbyters. And later when these Superintendents styled themselves "bishops," Wesley vehemently protested, but it was too late. The seed sown was bearing its natural fruit.

Further evidence of Mr. Wesley's attitude toward Methodist separation may be seen in a correspondence between Dr. Coke and Bishop White of Pennsylvania. See Bishop White's "Memoirs" pp. 408–9.

Bishop White also tells in "Memoirs of the Church" (p. 200) of a conversation which he had with the Rev. Charles Wesley when he was in England: "The author had also carried a letter from the Rev. Mr. Philmore to the Rev. Charles Wesley, and had a conversation with him on the same subject. He expressed himself decidedly against the new course adopted, and gave the author a pamphlet published by his brother and himself in the earlier part of their lives, against a secession from the Church of England, which, he said, was at that time proposed by some. And he remarked that the whole of the pamphlet might be considered as a censure on what had been done recently in America."

Two Important Societies

About the beginning of the eighteenth century two very important societies were organized, and began to operate in the Church of England, the first being what is generally called the S. P. C. K., which letters stand for the Society for the Promotion of Christian Knowledge. It was founded on May 8, 1698, by a clergyman by the name of Dr. Bray, and four laymen, Lord Gilford, Sir H. Mockworth, Justice Hook and Colonel Colchester. The Society rapidly increased in numbers and in strength, and there grew out of it another that has been the source of wonderful inspiration and effectiveness in spreading the Gospel of Christ. The latter is known as the S. P. G., meaning the Society for the Propagation of the Gospel in Foreign Parts. This Society was organized to relieve the S. P. C. K. of the necessity of sending men and women abroad, the original Society being responsible for providing the literature and other educational machinery connected with the missionary work of the Church. The active work of the S. P. G. commenced in June, 1701, and it has gone on increasingly throughout all the years since then. It rendered very marked and wide-spread service to the American Colonies, greatly promoting Christianity among them. Our debt of gratitude as members of the Episcopal Church in the United States to Dr. Bray, the founder of the Society for Propagation of the Gospel in Foreign Parts, and to the Society itself is so great that they should be ever held in affectionate remembrance by us. On this account as well as for its historical interest and value we incorporate here these words of Dr. Tiffany (pp. 280–282) : "In less than forty years after this, when by the independence of the United States the former colonies were cut off from the assistance on which they had relied so long, a brief summary of what the Society had done in seventy-five years gives the following results. It had maintained 310 ordained missionaries, had assisted 202 central stations, and had expended 227,454 pounds, or nearly a million and a quarter of dollars. It had stimulated and supported missions to the Negroes and the Indians as well as to the White colonists. Its labors were chiefly in those colonies where the Church was not established;

and the contrast between the results of the voluntary and the government effort is markedly in favor of the former.

"Since its cessation of labors in the United States the Venerable Society has on three separate occasions shown its sympathy with the Church it nurtured so long by handsome gifts of money to the corporation of St. George the Martyr in New York, to Bishop Tuttle's mission to the Mormons in Salt Lake City, and to the Church in Maine. In recognition of its invaluable services an alms-basin was presented by the American to the English Church at the one hundred and seventy-first anniversary of the Society, held in St. Paul's Cathedral, July 4, 1872. At the time of the first Lambeth Conference of Anglican Bishops throughout the World, in 1868, Bishop Littlejohn, of Long Island, at a missionary conference given by the Society, gave utterance to the sentiments of all American hearts when he said:

" 'For nearly the whole of the eighteenth century this Society furnished the only point of contact, the only bond of sympathy, between the Church of England and her children scattered over the waste places of the New World. . . . It is therefore with joy and gratitude that we, the representatives of the American Church, greet the Venerable Society on this occasion as the first builder of our ecclesiastical foundations, and lay at her feet the golden sheaves of the harvest of her planting. . . . May God speed the work of this Society in the future as in the past! The greatest, the most enduring, the most fruitful of all missionary organizations of Reformed Christendom, may it continue to be in the years to come, as in those which are gone, the workshop of churches, the treasury of needy souls all over the world!' "

Again, in 1883, the General Convention acknowledged the congratulations of the Society in a message of which the following words are an extract: "At the close of the first century of our existence as a National Church we acknowledge with deep and unfeigned gratitude that whatever this Church has been in the past, is now, or will be in the future, is largely due, under God, to the long-continued nursing care and protection of the Venerable Society." Other societies came later, the Church Missionary Society founded in 1799, which has been a powerful instrument in carrying the Gospel to many parts of the world, although originally intended for work in Africa; then came the Bible Society in 1804 for the distribution of the Scriptures; and the National Society for giving the children of the poor both secular and religious education, according to the principles of the Church of England.

The Oxford or Tractarian Movement

At the close of the first generation of the nineteenth century another Movement was initiated in the Church of England which, like the Wesleyan Movement, had as its inspiration deep spiritual earnestness, but the mode of expression was somewhat different. This Movement was commonly known as the Oxford or Tractarian Movement, the first designation coming from the place of its origination, namely, the University of Oxford; and the second, from the fact that during the development of the Movement there was issued a large number of tracts on the history, the doctrines and practices of the Church. It really was sort of complement to the revival of spiritual life in the Movement under the Wesleys and Whitfield. It has sometimes been misunderstood as having for its sole or chief object the restoration of external observances, ornate ceremonial and symbolism that had characterized the public worship of the Church of England in former times. There was something of that in the Movement, but its inspiration was far deeper and its scope far wider and its purpose far more exalted. The leaders of the Movement made a very strong appeal to the authority of the undivided ancient Church. Their effort was to make the national Church of England more truly Catholic, not by the introduction of new features, but by the restoration of those elements that had characterized the Church in former generations, and that were latent in its very constitution, but had been somewhat overshadowed by excitement incident to the Reformation. They taught, for example, that episcopacy or the three-fold ministry of bishops, priests and deacons pertained, not only to the *bene esse,* but to the *esse* of the Church, that is, not only to the well being, but to the being of the Church as it was seen in Apostolic times and days immediately following, and they sought to deepen the spiritual life through emphasis upon the Sacramental system of the Church.

The Movement is said to have had its real beginning in a sermon preached by John Keble at Oxford in the year 1833. Keble was a fine scholar possessed of a lovely character and noble gifts as a poet, as seen in his "Christian Year," which awoke and still awakes new music in the hearts of thousands. He was born and reared in the Church of England and loved her with a passionate love to the day of his death in 1866. His famous sermon was followed by the publication of a series of pamphlets called "Tracts For the Times." They were short, but clear and incisive statements bearing upon the polity, doctrines and worship of the Church. Along with the issue of these Tracts came sermons preached by John H. Newman in St. Mary's Church, Oxford. Toward the close of 1834 Edward Pusey, a noble character and a distinguished professor of Oxford University, joined the Movement and gave to it much weight. But there were certain new angles forming that had the tendency to obscure the original viewpoint and to sweep aside the originally controlling party. This new party within the Oxford Movement was under the leadership of William George Ward, and the sympathies of most of its members seemed toward the Roman Catholic idea of Christianity. Newman became unsettled and finally seceded to the Roman Communion in 1845, causing a decided reaction against the Movement, his defection being taken by some as the logical outcome of it, and not without some reason, in as much as he was a conspicious figure and leader in its early development.

But such men as Keble and Pusey stood firm on the original foundation of the Movement and enabled it to preserve its true balance and to continue its steady progress along sane lines. Its influence reached beyond the Church of England and extended throughout the Anglican Communion. It had its champions in our own American Church, they being typified by such a man as Dr. DeKoven. No doubt this Movement, like most things that have the human element in their origination and development, had its weak points, but it had also the things that should readily commend it, for it recalled to the minds of men great and forgotten truths. It rallied to it the learning, culture, and intellect of England and of other lands, and helped to produce that wholesome mind in the Church that stands ready to assimilate the results of the ripest scholarship and the most searching scientific investigations when accompanied by the spirit of reverence in searching for the truths of the Eternal. And it can hardly be successfully disputed that the Movement counted for much in the change that took place in the religious life and work in the Anglican Communion since the middle of the nineteenth century, the general average of worship being raised to a higher dignity, the ministrations to the poor and the distressed being more diligent and more intelligent, educational facilities being multiplied, the Church's vision being broadened and its ability to lay hold upon the affections of the people being increased.

For some time the Missionary enterprise of the Church received new emphasis and additional inspiration. Noble heroes like George Selwyn, John C. Patterson and James Hannington—the latter two being martyrs to the cause of Christ for the sake of their brethren who knew Him not—going to far away savage tribes, equalling the devotion of the Apostles themselves in fervid zeal and personal sacrifice. And about this time also Reginald Heber was sent as a missionary bishop of India, and the Church that was sending out some of her finest men to other people naturally began to grow in grace and strength at home.

In the latter part of the eighteenth century the Sunday School came into existence. We suppose that most people know that the Sunday School had its origin in the Church of England and that Mr. Raikes, a worthy tradesman of Gloucester, and a communicant of the English Church, and Mr. Stock, one of the clergy of that city, were the originators in 1780 of what has become such a force among the young people of this and other lands.

Of the Church of England in such times these lines were written seemingly inspired by the spirit that she was manifesting and the work that she was doing:

"Bulwark of a mighty nation, see the Church of England stand,
Founded on the Rock of Ages, hope and glory of our land;
Nursing Mother of our freedom, sowing truth from door to
    door;
Watching o'er the young and aged, Church alike of rich and
    poor."

And these lines recall some others that have recently fallen under our eyes, namely:

"Our Mother, the Church, hath never a child
    To honor before the rest,
And she singeth the same for mighty kings
    And the veriest babe on her breast;

And the bishop goes down to the narrow bed
    As the ploughman's child is laid,
And alike she blesseth the dark-brow'd serf,
    And the chief in his robe arrayed.

She sprinkles the drops of the bright new-birth
  The same on the low and the high,
And christens their bodies with dust to dust,
  When earth with its earth must lie."

Nor can we omit here the following beautiful little poem composed by the late Bishop A. C. A. Coxe of Western New York:

"I love the Church, the Holy Church,
  The Saviour's spotless bride,
And O, I love her palaces,
  Through all the world so wide.

"Unbroken is her lineage,
  Her warrants clear as when
Thou, Saviour, didst go up on high,
  And give good gifts to men.

"Here clothed in innocence they stand,
  Thine Holy Orders three,
To rule and feed Thy flock, O Christ,
  And ever watch for Thee.

"I love the Church, the Holy Church,
  That o'er our life presides,
The birth, the bridal, and the grave,
  And many an hour besides.

"Be mine through life to live in her,
  And when the Lord shall call,
To die in her, the Spouse of Christ,
  The Mother of us all."

Important Summary of Facts

Before leaving the continuous record of the Church in England and taking it up in our American land, we wish to give a very brief summary of outstanding facts which should seem beyond dispute. First, it is a fact that however and by whomsoever it was founded, the Church was in Britain at a very early period, with its own liturgy and its full-fledged ministry culminating in the episcopate. It is a fact that she was independent of all outside authority. It is a fact she was sufficiently prominent to be the object of fierce persecution under the Roman Emperor Diocletian, and was sufficiently eminent and respected to be asked to send representatives to the great Councils of the Church held on the Continent from 314 onwards. It is a fact that this Church, zealous and known on the Continent for its orthodoxy, was driven by heathen invaders from what we now know as England into Wales and Ireland. It is a fact that in her new home she set up centers of learning and missionary enterprise, sending her sons and grandsons into Ireland and Scotland and thence down into England in the seventh century. It is a fact that when Augustine with his forty Roman monks came in 597, they found this old Church with her own bishops, priests and abbots, with her liturgy and customs different from those of Rome, and having lived her life entirely independent of all outside authority. It is a fact that she refused to allow the claims of obedience to Rome set forth by Augustine. It is a fact that each set of Christians then went their own way and did their work as best they could. It is a fact that the permanent results in evangelization effected by Augustine and his companions were confined chiefly, if not entirely, to the County of Kent. It is a fact that the missionaries of the old British-Celtic Church evangelized by far the larger part of England, and all of Ireland and Scotland. It is a fact that the papacy was constantly extending its claims of jurisdiction and that after the Norman Conquest, followed by a large importation of foreign bishops, abbots, deans and rectors, papal encroachments increased in both the Church and the realm of England and that the pope exercised both influence and power there for several centuries. And it is also a fact that such exercise of power was usurped jurisdiction and not according to the constitution or ancient customs of the Church in Britain. It is a fact that such unwarranted encroachments and their consequences were from time to time resisted through the centuries and finally repudiated and definitely terminated by constitutional authority and by constitutional methods. Can any one with any show of historical accuracy deny any one of these facts? If not, it would seem clear that when the English Church in the sixteenth century rejected such unwarranted impositions, placed upon her by the forgery of others and ignorance of her own, and by foreign invasion—military and ecclesiastical,—as well as by royal and papal greed and ambition, she was expressing her own inherent life and setting forth her identity with her former self, the same essential self that refused the yoke of Rome in Augustine's day. And the Anglican Church to-day has no "position" assumed artificially, but is in her true position as an independent national Church, one through the ages, and Catholic in faith and order, which position and character are hers by reason of the facts just stated, notwithstanding the theories and prejudices of men that may be to the contrary. Facts are solid and remain. Theories and prejudices are shaken and pass away.

We trust that through the foregoing pages it has been made clear to the reader that throughout these troublesome times from the sixteenth to the eighteenth and nineteenth centuries, the Church of England, fighting boldly, bravely against foes on all sides, was undaunted and marched steadily under the banner of Apostolic order, primitive faith, national independence, resting securely upon the Scriptures, the three Creeds, and the General Councils of the undivided Christian Church as the guides of her faith and the tests of her orthodoxy and order. Here she stands, holding in one hand all the precious things of the Scriptures and the ancient teachings and customs of the Church, and in the other, all the inspiration and the advantages that came from the reviving of the minds and the spirits of men in the mighty movement of the sixteenth century and those other movements in the succeeding centuries, so constituting a Church for which we can give intelligent and devout thanks to Almighty God, and in which we can find our fellowship extending back generation after generation to the Magna Charta and on back to Alfred the Great, to Theodore, to Aidan, Cedd, Eborius, Resitutus, and yet back to St. Paul, St. John and St. James, yea even to Jesus Christ our Lord, and find in it also the springs of present inspiration for renewed life and hope and ever increasing zeal in behalf of our Divine Master and those whom He came to help and to save.

CHAPTER XIII

THE EPISCOPAL CHURCH IN THE UNITED STATES

First Services in English

It is interesting to note that the first religious services held in this country in the English language were conducted by clergymen of the Church of England and were Prayer Book services. Some probable, and some positively known instances, will now be given. Rev. B. F. De Costa in his historical sketch of the Colonial Churches published as a preliminary to Bishop White's Memoirs (p. vi) says: "On St. John Baptiste Day, June 24th, 1497, John Cabot, in advance of Columbus, discovered the mainland of America, which he called *Prima Vista*. Beyond question he had some chaplain or other minister of religion with him in his ship, the 'Matthew,' of Bristol. This led to other voyages by Englishmen and in 1504 there is an entry in King's privy purse of two pounds paid 'to a preste (priest) that goeth to the new Island.' . . .

"Then with Frobisher on the voyage of 1578, came the first known representative of the Reformed Church of England, 'Maister Wolfall, Minister and Preacher,' who was charged 'to serve God twice a day, with the ordinary service usual in the Church of England.' In the Countess of Warwick's Sound they landed, and Wolfall 'preached a godly sermon' and celebrated also a Communion, 'the first English Communion recorded in connection with the New World.'

" 'This Maister Wolfall being well seated and settled at home in his own country, with a good and large living, having a good honest woman to wife and very towardly children, being of good reputation among the best, refused not to take in hand this painfull voyage, for the only care he had was to save soules, and to reforme the Infidels, if it were possible, to Christiantie: and also partly for the great desire he had that this notable voyage so well begunne, might be brought to perfection; and, therefore, he was contented to stay there the whole yeare if occasion had served, being in every necessary action as the resolutest men of all. Wherefore, in this behalfe may rightly be called a true Pastor and minister of God's word, which for the profite of his flocke spared not to venture his owne life.' "

Dr. Tiffany tells us (pp. 4–5): "The first charter granted for the establishment of an English Colony on American shores was that which Sir Humphrey Gilbert received from Queen Elizabeth, June 11, 1578, which prescribed by letters patent 'for the inhabiting and planting of our people in America.' It was ordered that the laws and ordinances of the settlement 'be, as near as conveniently may, agreeable to the laws and policy of England, and also that they be not against the true Christian Faith and Religion now professed in the Church of England.' This expedition proved fruitless. A second voyage was undertaken in 1583, and this reached St. John's, which was taken possession of; and here a few laws were promulgated for immediate observance, one of which provided that the religion of the colony 'in publique exercise should be according to the Church of England.'" This account is recorded not because it was a successful effort to colonize but to show the religious element in the enterprise. Rev. Francis Fletcher of Drake's ship, the "Pelican," read prayers from the Prayer Book on the Pacific coast in 1579. A great stone cross in the Golden Gate Park in San Francisco commemorates this event.

In 1587 a colony under John White of 150 people including for the first time women as well as men arrived at Roanoke instead of Chesapeake Bay as intended and Thomas Hariot preached to the Indians of Roanoke and administered the Sacrament of Baptism for the first time on American soil in the English language. Manateo was the first Indian convert, and Virginia Dare was the first child born of English parents in America to be received into the Episcopal Church. Then soon after the destruction of the Armada in 1603 two English ships under the command of Martin Pring landed at Plymouth Harbor in Massachusetts, and remained there for six weeks. While it is not definitely stated, still the probability is, that in accordance with the universal custom in England in those days, they had prayers and the service of English sailors is, as is well known, that of the Book of Common Prayer. Consequently, "it may be said with moral certainty that the Prayer Book was used in the neighborhood of Plymouth Rock, while William Brewster was still living in Scrooby, and William Bradford was still attending the parish Church of Austerfield, England." And Dr. Tiffany says of Pring and his expedition: "He thus became acquainted with the land of the Pilgrims seventeen years before the Pilgrims came; and here the service of the Church of England was celebrated in advance of the Puritans, who on these shores afterwards rejected it" (p. 9). And then in 1605 Sir George Waymouth visited the coast of Maine and set up a cross on one of the adjacent islands to show that Christian men had been there, and Rosier distinctly declares, "a public good and true zeal for promulgating God's holy Church, by planting Christianity, to be the intent of the honorable setters forth of this discovery." And Dr. Tiffany makes this comment: "The short-lived colony is, however, worthy of note, because the claim of the English to the possession of the territory of New England rests upon this settlement. It is interesting, moreover, as a witness to the performance of the service of the Church of England as the first religious worship in the region afterward to become the land of the Pilgrims." (p. 10.) From the year 1605 onward, the agency of Churchmen in colonization is evident. April 10th, 1606, Sir Ferdinando Gorges, in connection with Sir John Popham, both members of the Church of England, obtained by royal charter a tract of country extending from Nova Scotia to the Carolinas. The same year a ship was sent out under Pring to complete the survey of Waymouth; while, June 1st, 1607, The "Mary and John" and "The Gift of God" sailed for Maine with upwards of a hundred colonists. The ships were separated during the voyage, but met in August at the Island of Monhegan near the Kennebec.

Historians have dwelt upon the religiousness of the

Plymouth Pilgrims who spent their first Sunday on Clark's Island, faithfully observing the day; but the men of the "Mary and John" and "The Gift of God" were not less duteous than those of the "Mayflower." Landing upon this romantic and well wooded isle, then clothed in primeval forests fragrant with the perfume of the pine and the hemlock mingled with the odor of the wild rose, they set up their simple altar under the shadow of a tall cross that had been planted previously and which was seen by the voyager afar. There they celebrated the service of the Church in simplicity and faith. We copy the memorandum verbatim:

"Sondaye beinge the 9th of August in the morninge the most part of our holl company of both our shipes landed on this Illand the wch we call St. George's Illand whear the cross standeth and thear we heard a sermon delyvred unto us by our preacher guinge God thanks for our happy meetinge and saffe aryvall into the contry & so retorned abord aggain."

The preacher was the Rev. Richard Seymour, a minister of the Church of England, to whom belongs the honor of having preached the first sermon known to have been delivered in New England. On the 19th of August, a site was selected for the colony at the mouth of the Kennebec, and the work of building a fort was commenced. This occasion was also solemnized by a sermon, showing that the undertaking was conceived in the spirit of the Psalmist, "Except the Lord build the house, they labor in vain that build it." The fort was finished together *with a chapel, and dwelling houses;* and here the services of the *Church of England* were celebrated. This was a regularly officered community, established upon a moral and legal basis.

Permanent Settlements

1. Jamestown, Virginia

While these earnest, high minded, but unsuccessful efforts by the English were being made in other sections, English Christianity had already been permanently established in Jamestown, beginning on May 13, in the year 1607. In the previous year, James I had chartered the Virginia Company. Operating under that company, a band of men set out for the American Continent on New Year's Day of 1607. The names of the ships in which they sailed are "The Discovery" "The Godspeed," and "The Susan Constant"—names which, as Dr. Hodges points out, seem to shadow forth the spirit both of religion and adventure in which these emigrants were seeking to set up a new home in a foreign land. The council of that colony was composed of Edwin Wingfield, Captain John Smith, John Ratcliffe, John Martin and George Kendall. The chaplain was Robert Hunt, a pious and courageous divine of the English Church. Although the expedition was undertaken partially as a commercial enterprise, it had also a missionary purpose and was sent forth in a religious spirit which indeed seemed to be uppermost in the minds of both the colonists and the incorporators of the enterprise. As evidence of the latter, it is recalled that Rev. Richard Hakluyt, a prebendary of Westminster Abbey, and later archdeacon and also a noted geographer and writer of his day, was one of the influential movers in securing the patent for colonizing Virginia, and one of the four persons to whom the king granted the first charter of the company, which was dated April 10, 1606. In his capacity as historian he has written: "To the Jamestown colonists the prime object of colonization is to plant the Christian religion." And before the expedition left England for Virginia an ordinance was passed, under the sign-manual of the king and the privy seal, which contained the following declaration: "That the said Presidents, Councils, and the Ministers should provide that the Word and service of God be preached, planted, and used, not only in the said Colonies, but also, as much as might be, among the savages bordering among them, according to the rites and doctrines of the Church of England."

According to the spirit of these documents and the feeling evidently in their hearts they built on the first day a fort for their protection and then provided a place of worship next. "I well remember," writes Smith in his "Advertisements for the Unexperienced Planters of New England," "wee did hang an awning (which is an old saile) to three or four trees to shaden us from the sunne, our walles were rales of wood, our seats unhewed trees, till we cut plankes: our pulpit a bar of wood nailed to two neighbouring trees. This was our Churche till wee built a homely thing like a barne, set upon crotchets covered with rafts, sedge and earth; so were also the walles, that could neither well defend wind nor raine. Yet we had daily Common Prayer, morning and evening, every Sunday two sermons, and every three months the Holy Communion, till our minister died. But our prayers daily, with an homily on Sundaies, we continued two or three yeares after till more Preachers came."

This shows that a determined religious spirit pervaded the whole colony. It is also a fine illustration of lay services in the Church when the people are Providentially deprived of the services of an ordained minister.

Of the chaplain and his services Dr. Tiffany thus writes (p. 14):

"The chaplain was alive to the duties of his calling from the first moment. On June 21st, five weeks after the landing, the first celebration of the Eucharist took place in the English colonies of America. That was the day preceding Captain Newport's return to England for supplies, and the day following Captain Smith's admission, after much turbulent bickering, to membership in the council. Beneath a rude sail upheld by the logs fresh cut from the forest, the first Communion was celebrated in Virginia as the Sacrament of peace. It was the third Sunday after Trinity, 1607, and the exhortation of the Epistle for that day, 'All of you be subject one to another, and be clothed with humility,' was certainly apt to the occasion.

"The history of the Virginia Colony, apart from its bearing on the development of the Church, lies, of course, beyond the province of this volume; but Chaplain Hunt seems to have been always the mainstay of the colony. Captain Smith, who soon came to the front, made him his chief reliance in pacifying quarrels and maintaining the spirit of the colonists. It is recorded that no one ever heard him murmur or repine. He did not survive many years; but he lived long enough to leave behind him a memory redolent of devotion and sagacity, and an influence which secured for some time a succession of ministers of a like character to his own."

We know that the colony suffered severely from the hostilities of the savages, from the inexperience of the settlers and from the lack of food and medicines. One of their number said, "Had we been as free from all sins as from gluttony and drunkenness, we might be canonized for saints." Captain Smith and Chaplain Hunt were the two leading spirits—a man of the fort and a man of the Church—leading the colony in all things pertaining to their welfare. But the cold and the lack of provisions and the increasing deaths, as well as the hostilities of the savages, greatly reduced the number and the spirit of the colony until at last they were ready to give up and return home. However, as they started out of the James River into the Atlantic Ocean, they caught sight of the ships of Lord Delaware, who was coming to their relief. Consequently they turned back and decided to start over. Just as soon as they landed, they knelt in prayer, all joining in silent thanksgiving to God for the mercy of their delivery. They then went to the church and the Rev. Mr. Buck of the Delaware Colony preached and offered praise and prayer. So with these acts of devotion, and calling on the name of God, they began to live their lives anew and to re-enter upon the enterprise that they were about to abandon. And there in the wilderness, as they had done from the beginning, they continued their daily services in the Church.

It is of interest and historical value to note that

among the names of the grantees of the second charter
of this colony (May 23, 1609), occur those of James
Montague, Bishop of Bath and Wells; Robert Cecil,
Earl of Salisbury, and Francis Bacon, Abbot, the
Bishop of London, and afterward Archbishop of Canterbury; the bishops of Lincoln and Worcester;
Sandys, the pupil of Hooker; and John and Nicholas
Ferrar; and again Hakluyt, whose interest never
flagged. And in the third charter (March 12, 1611), we
find the names of the archbishops of Canterbury, three
other bishops, the dean of Westminster Abbey and
seven other clergymen of the English Church.

The clergy of the English Church were not only instrumental in originating and launching the colonization of Virginia but they were its unfailing friends
and supporters. As illustrating this statement, I quote
these words from a sermon of Rev. William Crashaw
preached before Lord Delaware, Governor of the
Colony, on February 21, 1609: "To you, right honorable and beloved, who engage your lives in this business, who make the greatest ventures and bear the
greatest burdens; who leave your ease and pleasant
homes and commit yourselves to the seas and winds for
the good of the enterprise; you that desire to advance
the Gospel of Jesus Christ, though it be with the hazard
of your lives, go forward in the name of the God of
heaven and earth, the God that keepeth covenant and
mercies for thousands; go on with the blessings of
God, God's angels and God's Church; cast away fear
and let nothing daunt your spirits—remembering what
you goe to doe, even to display the banner of Jesus
Christ, to fight with the devil, and the old dragon, hav-

ing Michael and the angels on your side; to eternize your own names, both here at home and amongst the Virginians, whose apostles you are, and to make yourselves most happy men, whether you live or die; if you live, by effecting so glorious a work; if you die, by dying as martyrs and confessors of God's religion."

And it is significant that Delaware or De la Warr did not assume command of the colony until after the Divine Service in the Church conducted by Master Burke. And among the earliest acts of the colony were provisions for maintaining and extending the Gospel.

The following facts concerning the Rev. Alexander Whitaker, an English clergyman, will show how the spiritual side of the enterprise appealed to the clergy for action. Mr. Whitaker was the son of Dr. Whitaker, regius professor of Divinity at Cambridge University, and author of the Lambeth Articles, a man of renown in his time. His son, Alexander, is described as "a master of arts of five or six years standing in Cambridge," and as "competently provided for, liked and beloved where he lived, rich in possession and more in possibilities." "Yet," the story continues, "he did voluntarily leave his warm nest and to the wonder of his kindred and the amazement of them that knew him, undertook this hard but heroical resolution to go to Virginia and help beare the name of God to the Gentiles." He came with Sir Thomas Dale in May, 1611, and served with great zeal and ability until 1617, when he was drowned in the James River. And it was he who baptized the famous Indian girl Pocahontas. And again, the papers of instruction to the Company declared that "the way to prosper and achieve great success is to make yourself of one mind for the good of your country and your own, and serve and fear God, the Giver of all goodness, for every plantation which our Heavenly Father hath not planted shall be rooted up."

In 1619 the first representative assembly in America was held in the Episcopal Church at Jamestown, the exact date of assembly being July 30th, and the session was opened with the prayer by Mr. Buck, "That it would please God to guide and sanctify all of our proceedings to His own Glory and the good of the plantation." Then immediately after the establishment of the colony, they began planning for the education of the children of the natives. But of course that included instruction in the Catechism of the Church of England. As Dr. Tiffany writes (pp. 21–22) : "The interests of education were not neglected. Measures were passed looking for the foundation of a college, and specific directions were given that from the children of the natives, 'the most towardly boyes in witt and graces of nature be fitted for the college intended for them,' that they *might be missionaries* to their own people. The college was intended for the English as well as the Indians. In response to an address to the archbishops, fifteen hundred pounds was received for the college; and the Company instructed Yeardley to plant a university at Henrico, and allotted ten thousand acres of land for its endowment. Further sums were also received; one, a bequest of Mr. Nicholas Ferrar, Sr., a merchant of London, of three hundred pounds, 'to be paid when there shall be three of the Infidels' children placed in it'; also twenty-four pounds, 'to be distributed to three discreet and godly men in the colony which shall honestly bring up three of the Infidels' children in the Christian Religion and some good course to live by.' Bishop King, of London, collected and paid a thousand pounds to the Henrico college. The sum of five hundred pounds was forwarded to the treasurer, Sir Edwin Sandys (son of the archbishop of York and pupil of Richard Hooker), for the education of Indian children from seven years of age until twelve, after which they were to be taught some trade until they were twenty-one, when they were to be admitted to equal privileges with the native English of Virginia. Numerous gifts of Communion plate and linen, of Bibles and Prayer Books, were sent out for the use of the college and Church; and Thomas Bargrave, a clergyman, gave his library to it. Rev. Mr. Copeland, chaplain of an East-Indiaman, a little later collected a sum for the establishment of a public free preparatory school, for which the company allotted a thousand acres of land for the support of a master and usher. Mr. George Thorpe, 'an exemplary man, of good parts and well bred,' accepted the headship of the college from a desire to help *on the conversion of the Indians.*" It is interesting to note that the appreciation of learning by our English forefathers in New England which led to the founding of Harvard College in 1636 had also moved the Jamestown Colony previously, in 1621, to the same purpose—the founding of a college. Mr. John Fiske writes: "It is a just and wholesome pride that New England feels in recalling the circumstances under which Harvard College was founded, in a little colony but six years of age, still struggling against the perils of the wilderness and the enmity of its sovereign. But it should not be forgotten that aims equally lofty and foresight equally intelligent were shown by the men, who from 1619 to 1624 controlled the affairs of Virginia. Their desire and plan were to establish a university for both English and Indian youths." This Virginia institution, we thus see, was to be a college of religious education, that is, a university under the control of the Church where the religious element and spirit in education were given due and prominent recognition.

The New England Settlement

Let us now consider the permanent settlements in New England. In spite of several efforts to found colonies in New England in the latter part of the sixteenth and the first years of the seventeenth centuries yet down to the year 1620 there does not appear to have been any permanent English settlement along the coast. Nevertheless the influence of the Popham Colony was not lost, as it paved the way for fresh operations. In this connection too, it must be noticed that the work in New England and in Virginia was one, both colonies being under the general Council of Thirteen. Reserving therefore, the Virginia Colony for separate notice, let us point out the fact that New England was settled under the authority of the same company of Churchmen who prosecuted the work in the South.

It may be said that when the Plymouth Pilgrims landed in 1620 no English settlement was known upon the coast, but this is not a technical question. At the time they landed one branch of the work was established in Virginia, while the necessary steps had already been taken to carry on the work in New England. Experiments had been made, and the company was now ready for permanent work. The seed was sown, even though no green blade had appeared above the soil in token of the coming harvest.

This leads to the consideration of the fact that the men who had labored for the Popham Colony and for the twelve years following maintained ships in New England defending their interests and repelling intruders, had secured a new patent, signed by the king in November 1620, putting them in absolute possession of the territory from 40° N. to 48° N. They were entitled to the patent for various reasons, and especially in consideration of what they had done to protect the coast against the French. But for this fact the settlement at Plymouth might have been an impossibility. It was under this new patent that throngs of emigrants poured into New England. From the patentees, who were known as the "Plymouth Company," *the Leyden Pilgrims received authority to settle*. Sailing for the region of the Hudson, a storm drove them to Cape Cod, whence they went to the place which in 1616 had received the name of "Plymouth," from no less a Churchman than Prince Charles. At Plymouth, however, they were intruders; but the company at home, which was composed of *loyal Churchmen,* recognizing the merits of the men thus Providentially cast within their jurisdiction, consented to allow them to remain; and, September 9th, 1621, gave them a charter to the lands which they occupied. The charter was signed, among others, by Sir Ferdinando Gorges, who took a lively interest in the establishment of the Plymouth settlement, notwithstanding he disapproved of the principles entertained by leading spirits at that place. The people at Plymouth experienced little else but kindness and courtesy from the Churchmen who controlled affairs in connection with New England. This kindness was generally reciprocated by the Plymouth people, who were of a gentler disposition than the men of Massachusetts Bay. They *never denied their indebtedness* to the Plymouth Company, and it has remained for some of their descendants to undervalue the work of those Churchmen who warmed the Pilgrim Colony into life.

Mr. DeCosta observes: "In 1622, so thoroughly had the idea of colonization taken possession of the best men in the Church of England, that the archbishop of Canterbury ordered a collection to be made 'in all the several parishes within the Kingdome of England,' in aid of the colonization of Newfoundland; and a copy of Whitbourne's book on the subject was printed and sent to every parish. It is therefore, idle to fancy that colonization resulted from the wrong-headed treatment of a kind of wrong-headedness. The time for the conquest of the wilderness had come."

In the vicinity of Massachusetts Bay, Churchmen were the first colonists. As early as 1622, Thomas Morton established himself at Merry Mount; and in 1622 and 1623 colonies were attempted at Weymouth. Indeed, Sir Ferdinando evidently intended to secure the ground to the Church. In the company of 1623 came the Rev. William Morrell, who had been appointed an ecclesiastical commissioner. While in the country he composed a Latin poem on New England, translating it into English. This poem abounds with missionary aspirations. Again, long before Winthrop and his company came to settle Boston, the three peninsulas of the harbor had been taken possession of by Churchmen. At Charlestown dwelt Thomas Walford, afterwards banished, and who became the first Church warden in New Hampshire. At East Boston Samuel Maverick lived in his fort; while at Boston the Rev. William Blackstone, alone in a little cottage, led a quiet, contemplative life. Blackstone had been on the ground a number of years, and apparently came out with authority from the New England Company. The intentions of Sir Ferdinando respecting the ecclesiastical character of the colony that he expected to establish have been recognized. Some indeed have made these intentions a ground of complaint, showing that his policy was insisted upon, after it became impracticable. From this it appears that he and his brother Churchmen were earnestly engaged in promoting the colonization of New England. It was also contemplated that the colonists going thither would remain in the Church of England however they might modify certain usages. When Endicott came over to Salem with his company in 1628 there was no apparent sign of separation; and the Rev. Ralph Smith, being suspected of a tendency that way, that is, of having "a difference of judgment in some things from other ministers," was refused a passage by the Company, until he had given satisfactory assurance respecting his conduct while within the Company's jurisdiction. Their language on leaving home was, "Farewell, Church of God in England, and all Christian friends there! We *do not go to New England as separatists from the Church of England,"* etc.

Winthrop's company of 1630, on leaving England, likewise disavowed all designs of separation; and in writing to remove "suspicions and misconstructions of their intentions," declare that they "esteem it an honour to call the Church of England from whence wee rise our deare mother."

Again Mr. DeCosta says: "Attention is called to these points for the purpose of indicating the fact that *New England owes her origin to the Church.* The company holding the patent of the country was composed of men devoted to the Church of England, and the colonists of 1629 and 1630 would not have been allowed to sail, if it had been supposed that they would have proved disloyal to their own principles; yet the defection came. Winthrop himself joined the standard of the men who revolted against him and refused the ordinances of religion until he engaged heartily in the rebellion. This case is one of the most curious in ecclesiastical annals."

To this we add the following from Dr. Tiffany (p. 91): "The party in the Reformed English Church who especially emphasized individual religion became known as 'Puritans.' The Puritan founders of Massachusetts had at home belonged to the Established Church. Their ministers were Episcopalians until the policy of Laud was brought to bear against them. They believed firmly in a union of Church and State, and in the suppression of all schisms, provided theirs were the church, and that the suppression of schism were entrusted to their hands." They strove for their

especial tenets with the earnestness of men who felt
that they had a great reality at stake. The old feeling of
hostility to Rome was awakened toward the Established
Church. There was no idea or true comprehension of
toleration in the mind of any party in the Church. The
Puritans were forced by Queen Elizabeth to be present
at their parish church. The parliament under Cromwell
sentenced to one year's imprisonment any one who for
the third time made use publicly or privately of the
Book of Common Prayer.

From these records pertaining to the English settlements both North and South it appears that the Church
of England very earnestly advocated the colonization
of America as a missionary enterprise and encouraged
her ministers and people to enter upon it. It also appears that due to the efforts and generous attitude
of her sons the colonization of New England was
made possible both by those who separated from her
and by those who, when leaving English shores professing love and loyalty to her, yet changed their attitude on this side of the ocean. It is further plain that
the Virginia colonists were imbued with a true missionary spirit and religious earnestness.

Religious Settlement in the Various Colonies

We present a brief summary of outstanding facts
in the early religious settlements of each of the other
colonies. In doing so, we use freely the work of Mr.
DeCosta and Drs. Tiffany, McConnell and Dalcho,
for the most part using their exact words, but sometimes not. We commence with New Hampshire on

the North and proceed down to the Carolinas and
Georgia in the South.

New Hampshire

In the New Hampshire Patent, under Mason, a
Churchman, religious liberty was early enjoyed; and
when Walford went thither, in 1631, the services of
the Church were inaugurated, Richard Gibson being
the minister in 1638. In 1640 a parish was organized,
being the first regular organization of the Church
known to have been effected in New England. New
Hampshire takes the precedence while Thomas Walford, the despised blacksmith, appears as the first
New England Church warden. St. John's, Portsmouth,
now represents the ancient Church of "Strawberry
Bank." When, however, New Hampshire was an-
nexed to Massachusetts the people were oppressed. The
Royal Commissioners came to the relief of those who
had been denied the use of Common Prayer, the Sacraments, "decent burial of the dead," and the rights of
Freemen.

Massachusetts

Although we have discussed the original religious settlements in Massachusetts, the later developments in
Colonial times are so important that it seems well to
resume the record commencing with the year 1662.
At this period Cromwell had fallen, and Charles II
had ascended the throne. June 28th, 1662, the king
addressed a letter to the Massachusetts authorities,

which was of the nature of a proclamation, enjoining freedom for Churchmen to "use the Book of Common Prayer, and perform their devotions in that manner." The Rev. Joshua Moody of Portsmouth thought this "a very tremendous thing to us," and for a long time the Congregational party sought the means of eluding the command. In 1664, four commissioners were sent over by the king to inquire into the general administration. One of these commissioners was Samuel Maverick, who had been obliged to leave Boston and go to England, on account of his Churchmanship. Maverick and his associates, finding that the letter of the king had been disregarded, demanded, among other things, that his co-religionists "should no longer be fined for not attending the religious meetings as they had hitherto been," and that they should "let the Quakers alone." They also demanded that the restoration of the royal family should be celebrated by an annual thanksgiving as at home, which was agreed to. In New England, at this period, thanksgiving days were irregular and sporadic, the festival which was finally established being the outgrowth of customs observed in the Church of England. With respect to toleration, however, the Massachusetts authorities were amusingly evasive and well-nigh impertinent. Their answer was, "as to ecclesiastical privileges they commended to the ministry and the people here the Word of the Lord for their rule." Thus unfavorable was their reply, though when visited by the Royal Commissioners, their co-religionists of Connecticut, in theory, accepted toleration. It was clear that Massachusetts must soon yield. Drake says, "It was not until 1664 that the Church service was performed in Boston without molestation." In 1665, the commissioners had a chaplain with them, but there was no place of worship in Boston for Churchmen. In 1667, however, the general court being unable to stand the pressure, it was ordered, that no person should be hindered from performing the Church of England service; yet, such was the local hostility, that, as late as 1682, it was necessary for Randolph to assure the archbishop of Canterbury that clergymen of the Church would not be interfered with.

Early in 1685, a great change took place in the colony. Its charter was then taken away by James II, who set up a royal government, appointing Joseph Dudley President. May 15th, 1686, he arrived in the "Rose Frigate." With him came the Rev. Robert Ratcliffe, a clergyman of the Church of England, and the first parochial minister of Boston. The same day the organization of a parish was effected, when Dr. Benjamin Bullivant and Mr. Richard Banker were elected wardens. It was voted to take up a collection "every Sabbath day after evening sermon," while the archbishop of Canterbury and the bishop of London were requested to favor "our Church." The first collection, made Sunday, June 20th, when services were commenced, amounted to 3 pounds and 11 shillings. A room was taken in the Town House, and movable pulpit and twelve benches were ordered. Mr. Ratcliffe was voted a salary of 40 pounds per annum; while a "sober and fitt person," as "clarke," was to receive "for his paynes 20S. a weeke." Thus humble was the beginning, though at the time there appear to have been several hundred persons in the colony favorable to the Church. Dunton, the bookseller, describes Ratcliffe as a preacher. The next place of meeting was the Exchange, where, at the Wednesday and Friday meetings, Mr. Ratcliffe could overhear the citizens outside referring to "Baal's priest," while from the Congregational pulpits the Church prayers were called "leeks, garlic and trash." Randolph in his letter to the archbishop of Canterbury gives a vivid picture of the condition of things, and coolly proposes that the "three meeting houses of Boston," should pay "twenty shillings a week, apiece," to support the Episcopal service.

December 19th, 1686, Sir Edmund Andros superseded Dudley, and the 23d of March, 1687, he demanded the keys of the "Old South Meeting-house," that the Church service might be celebrated. Judge Sewall, with the committee, waited upon the Governor and he refused, but on the 25th, Good Friday, Andros ordered the sexton to open the doors and ring the bell. This, of course, was a plain case of usurpation. On February 10th, the funeral of Lady Andros took place at the "Old South," the ceremonies exciting great attention. About this time Mr. Ratcliffe was interrupted at the funeral of Lilly by a deacon of the "Old South." April 18th, 1689, Andros was deposed by the people, and Randolph, Warden Bullivant, and others, were thrown into the fort. Upon the accession of William and Mary they were sent to England with Andros for trial. Ratcliffe and Clarke also disappeared, but in the meantime a wooden church had been built. In 1694, it was still without pews. The Rev. Samuel Myles was on the ground July 1st, 1689. He went to

England in 1692; and a Mr. Smith and a Mr. Hatton officiated until his return, July 24th, 1696.

In 1702, Dudley reappeared in Boston, now as Governor of Massachusetts, and while a vestryman of the Church attended the Congregational Communion at Roxbury. In 1710, "Queen's Chapel" was enlarged, and the people addressed the Queen with respect to the appointment of bishops, saying that about eight hundred persons were attached under the Rev. Mr. Cutler, formerly president of Yale College; and in 1729, Mr. Price succeeded Mr. Myles at what had become "King's Chapel." Services were commenced at Newbury, Marblehead, and other places. We do not wish, however, to pursue these matters in detail, but simply to indicate the general course of events. Price was appointed commissary, and was succeeded by Dr. Caner, who served until the Church was closed at the commencement of the Revolution; though it should be noted that the church was rebuilt of stone in 1749. Trinity Church had also been established, the pulpit being supplied by the clergy of the Chapel and Christ Church until 1740, when Mr. Davenport became minister; who, in turn, was succeeded by Messrs. Hooper, Walter, and Parker, the latter being connected with the Church from 1774 until his death in 1804.

At Christ Church, Cutler, who died in 1765, had for his successors Messrs. Greaton, Byles, Lewis, and Montague. Dr. Cutler had four hundred regular attendants at the service. This ancient church contains the first chime of bells cast for America, and the first monument erected to Washington. From the tower was hung out the signal lantern on the eve of the battle of Concord and Lexington.

During the Revolution, services were maintained at Christ Church and Trinity, but at "King's Chapel" they were suspended March 10th, 1776. Caner, who was a royalist, left the city upon its evacuation by the British troops, taking with him the records, the vestments, and the plate, the latter amounting to two thousand eight hundred ounces of silver, the gift of three crowned heads. The records were returned in 1805, but the vestments and plate were not found. This brings us to an event that should be touched upon—the loss of this building to the Protestant Episcopal Church which was rebuilt of stone.

It appears that the Chapel remained closed until 1777, when the proprietors granted the use of it to the congregation of the Old South Church, so unjustly treated by Governor Andros. This congregation held possession gratuitously for about five years, at the end of which time, their own house, which had been taken as a training school for Burgoyne's cavalry, was repaired. They left the Chapel in February 1783; but during the previous summer a number of the old proprietors concluded to re-establish services. September 8th, 1782, they invited Mr. James Freeman, of Walpole, to officiate as lay reader for six months. The invitation was sent through the wardens, Dr. Thomas Bulfinch and James Ivers. Mr. Freeman entered upon his duties October 18th, 1782; and the Episcopal and Congregational Societies appear to have held joint occupancy until the latter removed the following February. April

21st, Mr. Freeman was elected minister on a salary of two hundred pounds. At this time the wardens say, "The proprietors consent to such alterations in the service as are made by the Rev. Dr. Parker; and leave the Athanasian Creed at your discretion." These alterations were simply such as the changed political condition of the country demanded. The congregation appears as an Episcopal organization, Mr. Freeman, for whom Episcopal ordination was contemplated, carefully abstaining from the assumption of priestly functions. It has been claimed that in the summer of 1784 "King's Chapel" and its lay reader were supposed to be in harmony with the Church. It has also been claimed that at that time the parish received a notice from Bishop White of the action of the Church in Pennsylvania, of May 25th, 1784. At least a copy of "The Broadside," a pamphlet sent to the Colonial churches, came into the possession of Mr. Freeman. This document states that the Pennsylvania convention empowered its committee "to correspond and confer with representatives of the Episcopal Church in the other states, or any of them, and assist in forming an ecclesiastical government." It may perhaps be conceded that this communication, signed in autograph by Bishop White, was addressed officially to the parish of "King's Chapel," but of this there is no proof. If, however, they were thus invited to share in the deliberations, it was with the distinct understanding that the doctrine and Orders of the Church of England were to be adhered to without question, as the principles of "The Broadside" state. Under the circumstances, therefore, such an invitation would have been proper. The

Church welcomed all who came in accordance with the principles recognized; which, in substance, were endorsed by the convention in Massachusetts, September 8th, 1784. New England, however, was not represented at the primary General Convention, held at Philadelphia, September 27th, 1785.

Rhode Island

The first white man who established a permanent home in Rhode Island was the Rev. William Blackstone, who, as we have already seen, left Boston in the spring of 1635, and took his way into the wilderness, eventually selecting for his abode a place called "Study Hill," on the banks of the Blackstone River, and now included within the boundary of Attleborough, Massachusetts. Anticipating Roger Williams as a colonist in Rhode Island, he excelled that stern man in gentleness of manners and sobriety of speech. Williams, who is held up as a pattern respecting religious toleration, *denounced* the hearing of the Church of England clergy as sinful; but Blackstone was kindly to all, and may even be regarded as the founder of Rhode Island. At "Study Hill" he was something of a recluse, but it is known that he exercised his vocation, and occasionally preached in Providence, where he was the first representative of the Church of England. Prior to 1700 some families attached to the Church settled in Narragansett County. They worshipped in private houses until 1706, when the Rev. Christopher Bridge became their minister. McSparran says that he officiated in a little church at Newport in 1707. In 1717 the Rev. Mr.

Grey of the Propagation Society officiated in Narragansett. The first Church record commences April 14th, 1718. In 1730, the Attorney General, Updike, was baptized in the Petaquamscut River, by immersion, Mr. McSparran officiating. This clergyman served the Church in Rhode Island until 1757. The advent of Dean Berkley, however, constituted a great feature in the colonial history of the Church in Rhode Island. He reached Newport in 1729, and left in 1731, but his visit produced marked results. His donations of books to the libraries of Yale and Harvard proved very important, and the weight of his character was felt for a long period. Mr. Fayerweather, the successor of McSparran, labored with good results; though, having his scruples, he sided with the king when the Revolution dawned, and his church was closed. The last record made by him was dated November 6th, 1774. He died in 1781. Toleration prevailed in Rhode Island, yet in 1722–3, in Bristol, twelve Churchmen were imprisoned by the Connecticut authorities for refusing to pay dues for the support of the non-episcopal minister, Mr. Nathaniel Cotton. In 1775, the Propagation Society maintained three or four clergymen and a schoolmaster in Rhode Island, and they struggled on through the Revolution, but at its close the Church was very feeble.

Connecticut

The Connecticut Congregationalists formed a compact body in Church and State; but, in 1665, the Royal

Commissioners were assured that the local authorities would not interfere with those who might desire to maintain public services, according to the Book of Common Prayer. It was not, however, until 1708 that the "Act of Toleration" was passed. Nevertheless at Stratford, in 1690, there were a few Churchmen. When Keith and Talbot came over as missionaries, curiously enough, they were entertained by the Congregational minister at New London, who spoke kindly of the Church, and treated them with much civility. In 1705, Mr. Muirson settled at Rye, then in Connecticut, and in 1706, he went with Colonel Heathcote to Stratford on a missionary tour, where a local officer stood in the highway and threatened them with a "fine of five pounds." Mr. Muirson died in 1708. From this time the work went on with great success, and, in 1722, President Cutler of Yale College, and six others, assembled in the College Library declared for Episcopacy, having been led to this course by the study of books which they found upon the shelves. The community was astounded, but the Congregationalists could not undo the work. Cutler, Johnson and Brown embarked for England, and received Orders. With the growth of the Church a corresponding increase of hostility was developed. In 1742, there were fourteen churches built or building, the Rev. Roger Price, as commissary for New England, supervising the work. There were at that time seven clergymen in the province. At this period Whitfield introduced an element of discord, but in 1747, the undue excitement was followed by corresponding depression.

About the year 1763, Mayhew and others of Boston commenced the discussion of episcopacy and were replied to by Archbishop Secker, who showed clearly that the system was not aimed, as the Congregationalists taught, at the subversion of popular rights. As early as 1766, twelve of the clergy assembled at Stratford and addressed the Bishop of London in favor of the episcopate. They did so again in 1771. In 1774, the report of Goodrich "makes the Episcopalians about one in thirteen of the whole number of the inhabitants." With the approach of the Revolution, Connecticut experienced the same troubles that overtook other colonies, and such Churchmen as Seabury and Samuel Peters were roughly used. Seabury of Westchester, on account of certain writings, was arrested and held a prisoner for some time, being finally released. Peters, of Hebron, did not find the people so lenient, and finally fled the country, while others of the clergy fell under popular displeasure, owing to their devotion to the crown. As the work progressed, churches were closed, desecrated, or burnt, notably at Fairfield and Norwalk. Mr. Leaming, one of the most prominent of the clergy, fled to New York, and Beach and Kneeland died, *Seabury taking duty as chaplain* in the British service. At the close of the war, however, something remained. When the smoke rolled away, on the last week of March, 1783, ten out of the fourteen parochial clergy who held their places, assembled at Woodbury to reorganize; and in due time Dr. Samuel Seabury was sent to England with a view to Episcopal Consecration, which he received from the Non-jurors, November 24th, 1784, these Non-jurors being bishops of the Church in Scotland.

New York

In 1609, Henry Hudson, with a mixed crew of English and Dutch, made his voyage up the river which bears his name, his voyage having originally been projected under French influence, though he was advised to search for a strait to India in the region of the Hudson by Captain John Smith. Henry Hudson was an Englishman and a *communicant of the Church,* though the Dutch reaped the fruit of his voyage of 1609.

It appears that the first permanent agricultural colony in New York was undertaken by the Dutch in 1623, who maintained the ascendency until 1664. During the Dutch rule, religious freedom prevailed, and Father Jogues the Jesuit was hospitably received when in distress. Dutch toleration, in theory, nevertheless was designed for "Calvinists." In the year 1700, a law was passed against Jesuits and all Roman Catholic ecclesiastics, and against those who harbored them. Still Romanists were entitled to the private enjoyment of their opinions, their public services not being rendered legal until the period of the Revolution.

In 1664, the Dutch surrendered to the English, and thereafter the British army chaplains were accustomed to hold services in the fort at the Battery, occupying the chapel in common with the Dutch. The latter, by the terms of the surrender, were guaranteed "liberty of their consciences in divine worship and church discipline"; but Protestants alone were allowed to hold service. "Indian powawowing and devil worship" were nevertheless forbidden. Governor Nicolls in 1665, and

Lovelace in 1670, levied taxes for the support of a minister in each town, who was to be selected by a majority of the people, who, of course, were Dutch. In 1683–84, the Duke of York, a Roman Catholic, made ample provision "for liberty of conscience to all Christians, and provided also for the maintenance of the ministry of all Christian Churches." In this the duke was strictly impartial, and under his successor, Dongan, the same policy was continued. The Lutheran, Dutch and French religious societies were equally free from taxation. In 1683, the Assembly had reaffirmed the duke's policy; and in 1691, an act was proposed for "settling the Ministry." This work, however, was not completed until 1693, during the administration of Governor Fletcher. Under this act, freeholders were to elect two Church wardens and ten vestrymen, who were to levy taxes for the maintenance of the ministry and the poor of their respective places, though these officers were not wardens nor vestrymen in the Episcopal sense. Nevertheless the Church party considered it a partial victory; though it is argued, that as the Assembly contained but a single Churchman, the act was not intended for the sole benefit of an Episcopal establishment. Accordingly, in New York, February 12th, 1694, the majority of the wardens and vestry voted that the minister should be a Dissenting minister, while three days after, the Rev. John Miller, though licensed by the bishop of London, was refused the benefit of the act by the Council. Nothing was done until January 19th, 1695, when the wardens and vestry elected Mr. William Vesey, who appears to have been elected by Dissenters. The Governor declared that the establishment of Dissenters was a contravention of the act, though the Assembly had maintained the contrary. Two years, therefore, passed before the matter was adjusted. March 19th, 1696, ten members of the Church of England, several of whom were "vestrymen" of New York, were granted leave to purchase a piece of land for a church, and July 23d, they were authorized to collect funds and commence building. These men appear to have acted for the "Managers of the Affairs of the Church of England in the City of New York," a body in existence in 1693. Next, November 2nd, 1696, Mr. William Vesey appeared before the wardens and vestry, accepted an election, and agreed to go to England to obtain Orders and return at the first opportunity. Mr. Vesey now appears to have changed his views, some said with unworthy motives, and passed from the Presbyterian to the Episcopal ranks. Money was raised for his travelling expenses, and he went to England and was ordained in 1697. The Church wardens continued in the interests of Episcopacy; and in the same year, an act was passed by the Assembly, assigning to the rector of Trinity Parish, New York, and his successors all the benefit that was intended by the act of 1693. In this manner was the Church of England established in New York, if it was established. Missionaries soon began to come over.

In 1701, the Propagation Society commenced its work, when an address forwarded to the managers showed that neither in the province of New York nor on Long Island was there any "Church of England." Nevertheless, the French Church received some help from Mr. Vesey and the Ministry Act was interpreted in its favor. It has been mournfully said "that the period of religious freedom" closed with the previous century. The Church had indeed been put in power, but things were not so bad as some have represented. Dissenters were not treated with more rudeness than were Churchmen themselves under Lord Cornbury, who, however, behaved badly towards the Presbyterian minister at Jamaica, where the people were divided about the title to the church building.

In 1704, an act was passed to raise one hundred pounds annually for the rector of Trinity Church, while the Ministry Act was continued down to 1784, when it was abolished, and Episcopacy lost the peculiar privileges formerly possessed. During the continuance of the Act, under Lord Cornbury, several Presbyterians were annoyed. In 1707, Makemie and Hampton were arrested as strolling preachers; but Churchmen, like Moore and Brooks, were also proceeded against as having no proper authority for the exercise of their vocation. The people, however, universally disapproved of Cornbury's arbitrary proceedings. Churchmen were in the minority, though the law was on their side; and when the Presbyterians organized, they proved a pushing people, incessantly laboring to circumvent the Episcopalians, who, upon the whole, could show a tolerably fair bill of grievances.

The Church grew slowly in the colony of New York, and when the Revolution dawned became more or less disorganized. When, in 1776, the British evacuated New York City, Inglis of Trinity Church, remained, continuing in a firm, if not defiant manner, to pray for the king. This was finally put an end to by the soldiers. In 1783, the property of Trinity was committed to the care of a board of nine responsible trustees. In 1784, the Rev. Messrs. Bloomer, Moore, and others were on the ground to join in the reorganization of the Church at large.

New Jersey and Delaware

In New Jersey, the proprietary government was kindly to all denominations of Christians. About 1695, some of the East Jersey proprietors addressed Compton, Bishop of London, requesting the services of the Church; and the Rev. Edward Perthuck was sent over near the close of 1698. He commenced services at Perth Amboy, though he did not remain permanently. Queen Anne's instructions to Lord Cornbury, in 1702, enjoined the maintenance of worship and the Sacraments according to the Book of Common Prayer, ordered the building of churches and a provision for the maintenance of the clergy. He was to prefer none who could not produce the certificate of the bishop of London. Accordingly, he proceeded against various clergymen who officiated contrary to law; and the Assembly of New Jersey, October 24, 1707, reproached him in their address, because one minister of the Church of England was "dragged by a sheriff from Burlington to Amboy" and afterwards confined like a malefactor in "another government."

In 1732, the Rev. George Keith came out, and the Rev. John Talbot was associated with him. Through their efforts a church was established at Burlington, the present St. Mary's. In 1704, Mr. Brook was missionary at Elizabethtown, and Vaughn in 1709, with Halliday in 1711. Perth Amboy lost some of its importance when the Governor moved to Trenton. The history of the Church at Amboy gives a fair idea of the progress made elsewhere. St. Mary's, Burlington, also serves a similar purpose, exhibiting the career of Talbot, though there appears to be no evidence that the Church can accept the Episcopal character claimed for him. He never performed any act of a bishop, and he denied that he ever attempted to exercise any supervision of his brethren.

In Delaware, as in Pennsylvania, the Swedish Church appeared first, colonizing the west side of the Delaware in 1636–37. In 1703, Keith visited Delaware, and in 1704, the Rev. Thomas Crawford was sent over as a missionary by the Propagation Society. In 1726, there were four churches. In 1792, the Swedes were merged in the Protestant Episcopal Church.

Pennsylvania

The Church of Sweden was first upon the ground in Pennsylvania, and about 1646, the Rev. Mr. Printz built a church at Tinicum. In 1657, Borell was made Provost. In 1677, the Block House was built on the site now occupied by the Gloria Dei Church. It was used for public worship. In 1681, Penn obtained his charter, which stipulated that any of the inhabitants desiring the services of the Church of England should be entitled to a minister or ministers approved by the bishop of London. In 1695, Christ Church, Philadelphia was built, and the Rev. Mr. Clayton was appointed minister. In the year 1700, Mr. Evans was sent out; and, in 1702, Keith and Talbot arrived. In 1707, Mr. Rudman, of the Swedish Church, served Christ Church, the regular minister being absent. In 1711, while Christ Church was being enlarged, the congregation worshipped in Gloria Dei Church, and Swedish hymns were sung in the service. Later, the Propagation Society made an appropriation for the Swedish ministers who served vacant English churches. In 1712, it is said, the "Surplice" was first mentioned at Christ Church. In 1716, Rev. Mr. Evans was made minister at Oxford and Radnor, in addition to his duties at Christ Church, of which he was rector seventeen years. In 1724, the congregation invited Dr. Richard Welton of Burlington to take charge of Christ Church. It has been stated that this person was consecrated a bishop by the Non-jurors, but the case appears dubious. In 1750, Christopher Gist went through Western Pennsylvania as an explorer and did something to call attention to Church services. In 1731, there appear to have been about seven clergymen in the colony, of whom five were missionaries of the Propagation Society. In 1760, a Convention of the clergy was held in Philadelphia, and missionary reports were read. Dr. Jenney, Dr. William Smith and seven other Pennsylvania clergy were present. In 1763, Whitfield preached in Christ Church. In 1770, the last Swedish missionary, the Rev. Nicholas Collin, of Upsal, came over to Gloria Dei Church, and, eventually, the Swedes became a part of the Protestant Episcopal Church. In 1772, the Rev. William White commenced his labors in Philadelphia as deacon at Christ Church and St. Peter's. December 3rd, 1775, Mr. White was elected chaplain to the Continental Congress, and the members of the Church in Philadelphia entered heartily upon the work of achieving American Independence. July 4th, 1776, it was resolved, at the house of Mr. Duché, to omit the prayer for the king. April 15th, 1779, Mr. White was elected rector of Christ Church and St. Peter's. The Church struggled on through the Revolution; and in November 1783, with Drs. Morgan and Blackwell he took measures which led to the Primary Convention of May 24th, 1784. This convention was attended by about twenty-five delegates from sixteen parishes. Six principles were drawn up and recommended.

Maryland

Maryland was colonized by Calvert, known as Lord Baltimore, who arrived March 25th, 1634, the majority of the people being Protestants, while the leaders were Roman Catholics. Religious liberty was proclaimed, and the Church of England was protected. Father White, a Jesuit, stood at the head of his co-religionists, but he enjoyed no special favor. The Puritans were invited by Lord Baltimore to become a part of this happy family. In 1648, the lieutenant governor was obliged to take oath not to trouble or molest any believer in Jesus Christ on account of his religion. Under Cromwell, Maryland was seized by the Protestants, and Roman Catholics were disenabled as to voting. In 1691, Maryland was made a royal colony, when the

Assembly established the Church of England, imposing a tax of forty pounds of tobacco on each person to create a fund for building and repairing churches. At that time, according to some, there were sixteen, and according to others, three clergymen in the colony. In 1695, Dr. Bray was made commissary. In 1714, the Church was in a very depressed condition. In 1716, Wilkins and Henderson were appointed commissaries, and in 1720, the bishop of London did something towards reviving the Church. At his suggestion, Mr. Colebatch was nominated by the clergy as suffragan bishop, upon which an act was passed by the legislature, then more or less hostile, to prevent the candidate from leaving the colony. Thus the scheme failed. The legislature still continuing inimical, Bishop Gibson, the bishop of London, became inactive, and Henderson ceased acting as commissary. The Roman Catholics now revived, and the Baptists were active. In 1763, the legislature, weary of the irregularities that characterized many of the clergy, reduced their salaries; and, in 1769, Governor Eden ordered that the clergy should no longer meet together to act on matters connected with the Church, declaring that they were beyond the control of any bishop. When the Revolution approached, the Church in Maryland experienced the same evils that overtook co-religionists in other colonies. The Rev. Jonathan Boucher and a third of the clergy sided with the crown. Ultimately, quite all the churches were closed, and the clergy, for the most part, left the country. After the Revolution, the legislature secured to the Church the properties previously held.

Virginia

As in the case of Massachusetts, much has been said in previous pages about the religious establishments in Virginia. Nevertheless we feel it important and that it will be quite interesting to the reader to add briefly some facts in her religious history up to the Revolution. In 1621, under Sir George Yeardley, a memorable approach to constitutional government was made by the colonial Assembly. Such was the success of the colony, that Bacon compared its growth to that of a mustard seed; while the Spanish ambassador in England feared that, if the work continued to succeed, it would endanger the Spanish possessions in the West Indies and Mexico. At this period, however, the people of Plymouth were in danger of starvation. Fortunately, at the time they reached the place of their abode, the colonization of the whole country had been resolved upon, and they obtained the benefit of the general determination.

In 1629, under the administration of Sir John Hervey, the Assembly ordained strict conformity, under pains and penalties. One man was excommunicated forty days "for using scornful speeches and putting on his hat in church." While Archbishop Laud was in power, statutes were framed to prevent Nonconformists from coming to Virginia. This severity only served to excite opposition where there was none, and, in 1642, application was made to the people of Boston, who sent three ministers to Virginia. These men were quickly silenced, though Winthrop says that certain people resorted to them in private houses. In 1648, there were one hundred and eighteen Dissenters in Virginia. Many of them were "clapt up in prison." Under Cromwell, Churchmen in turn were humiliated, though their services were tolerated, and Virginia became a refuge for persecuted royalists. In 1662, under Charles II, the Church was re-established by law, and religious liberty declared for all except Quakers, there being at this time about fifty parishes. Under the second James there was great uneasiness respecting popery; but with the accession of William and Mary, confidence was restored. The Rev. Mr. Temple served as the representative of the bishop of London prior to 1689, and was succeeded by Dr. Blair, who was appointed the commissary, being empowered to visit the parishes, deliver charges, and in some cases to administer discipline. He was eminently useful, and founded the College of William and Mary. In the year 1700, Virginia revealed a kindly spirit, receiving the French Protestant refugees and exempting them from taxation. In 1722, the inhabitants were almost exclusively members of the Church of England. In 1731, Presbyterianism was introduced and in 1740, Whitfield appeared as a clergyman of the Church. About 1765, the Baptists came. In 1771, the commissary, the Rev. Mr. Camm, called several meetings of the clergy to address the king in behalf of an American episcopate. The more than one hundred churches of the colony were thinly represented; but finally the clergy agreed to address the bishop of London, instead of the king. There was opposition also to the immediate establishment of Episcopacy, and, though the legislature favored the movement, it failed. In 1772, the Methodists began to preach in Virginia; and in 1776, the Church was disestablished by the legislature, though the *Methodists stood* by the Church, opposing disestablishment. Then followed the period of depression, which prevailed at the time when the case of Virginia is taken up in the narrative of Bishop White. May 18th, 1785, the first Convention of the Protestant Episcopal Church assembled, thirty-six of the clergy and seventy-one laymen meeting at Richmond. There is much in the colonial history of Virginia to mortify Churchmen, and the shortcomings of their own brethren at that period should serve to moderate the severity of their judgment of Non-Conformists.

North Carolina

The name Carolina appears to have been first applied to the region which it designates, in honor of *Charles IX* of France, by *the French Huguenots,* who settled in Florida as early as 1562. The name, however, was formally given to the territory by Charles I of England, in honor of himself, when in 1629, he made a grant of it to Sir Robert Meath. No settlement was made under this grant; and in 1663, Charles II apportioned the region to eight lord proprietors, including among them the Earl of Clarendon, the Duke of Albemarle, and Lord Ashley Cooper, afterward Earl of Shaftesbury. In 1665, he gave another charter, greatly enlarging the territory, and two settlements, the Albemarle and the Clarendon, were started. Before the first charter, in 1663, a small company of Dissenters had migrated from Virginia to the Chowan River, which formed the nucleus of the Albemarle settlement, to which a governor, William Drummond, was appointed by Sir William Berkeley, Governor of Virginia. Some English colonists in 1665 came over from the Barbados to the Cape Fear River and formed the nucleus of the Clarendon, or southern, settlement; and their leader, John Yeamans, was appointed the governor. Freedom of religion was guaranteed in these charters to all who did not disturb the peace; and the proprietors were at pains to make liberal offers to New Englanders and any others who might choose to migrate to their possessions.

It was in 1669 that the proprietors adopted "The Fundamental Constitution of Carolina," framed by the philosopher John Locke in conjunction with the proprietor Lord Shaftesbury, his intimate friend. It proved to be an impracticable system of government, with whose general features, as they were never carried out, this history is not concerned. Its religious features are interesting as it contained, contrary to Locke's wishes, a provision for the establishment of the Church of England, the building of churches, and the maintenance, through acts of the Parliament, of its ministry. Thus, either by the charters of Charles II or the constitution of Locke, the Church of England was "by law established."

The Clarendon colony did not flourish; and after its disappearance there were two colonies, Albemarle on the North and Ashley River Colony on the South, respectively North and South Carolina. The settlers at Albemarle were reinforced by emigrants from New England who were not Churchmen; and the Quakers were in sufficient force, though not numerous, by 1672 to be visited by George Fox. In 1729, the one Province of Carolina was divided into two, thereafter known as North and South Carolina. The real history of the Church in North Carolina begins with the efforts of the S. P. G., although in 1701 the Assembly constituted four parishes in the Albemarle settlement and one in Bath and appointed a vestry in each. Under this act one church was built at Edenton. In 1703, Messrs. Keith and Talbot tried to visit this region as representatives of the S. P. G., but made little headway on account of swamps and marshes and poor conveyances. In 1708, Gordon and Adams were sent by the Society as permanent missionaries and to them were assigned the parishes laid out in 1701. After one year Gordon, discouraged by hardships and the distractions among the people, returned. Adams remained until his death in 1710 and did a remarkably fine work, it being said of him, "He left more communicants in Currituck than could be found in most of the neighboring parishes of Virginia, where there had long been a settled ministry." But he declared in the last years of his life, "Nothing but my true concern for so many poor souls, and my duty to those good men who reposed this trust in me, could have induced me to stay in so disorderly and barbarous a place where I have undergone a world of trouble and misery both in body and mind."

Until the Revolution the people asserted through their legislature that the Church of England was the Church in North Carolina, and her leading men, repelled by the narrowness of the Dissenters, felt that the Episcopal Church was an essential part of a well ordered commonwealth. This province had a number of men of high character as missionaries sent by the English Society for Propagation of the Gospel in Foreign Parts. Among them may be mentioned Rev. Messrs. J. Garzia of St. Thomas, Bath, 1741; James Moir, St. James, New Hanover, 1737–1767; Clement Hall, the second native, the first having been Rev. John Boyd, to enter the ministry of the Church. He went to London for ordination and returned in 1744 and did a marvelous work for 15 years, dying in 1759; Alexander Stewart, 1753, another consecrated man who accomplished fine things, one result of his labors being to induce Messrs. Peter Blinn and Nathaniel Blount to take up the work of the ministry. They both served the Church in North Carolina long and faithfully.

We close this notice of the Church life and activity in North Carolina with these words of Dr. Tiffany: "It is to be noted in the case of North Carolina that while the English government established the Church, its revenues came entirely from the Assembly of the province. Native taxes furnished such means as were given it by the State; and these, supplemented by voluntary contributions, constituted its entire support. The English government furnished neither bishop nor revenue; though too high praise cannot be given to the Venerable Society, which so long and so generously contributed to the maintenance of the missionaries whom it sent or adopted."

South Carolina

The Church really had an earlier and better start in the Southern Carolina Province than in the Northern.

While the charter for the original united colony establishing the Church of England as the Church of the colony applied to both sections, in the Southern portion there was a more vigorous activity on the part of the people in behalf of the Church. Dr. Frederick Dalcho, the highest authority on history of the Episcopal Church in South Carolina during the Colonial period, in his book on the same published in 1820 says:

"The first Episcopal Church in Carolina was built in Charles-Town about 1681 or 1682. But little of it is known. It was 'large and stately' and was surrounded by a neat white palisade. Mrs. Blake, wife of the Governor, subsequently contributed liberally towards its adornment.

"The Church having begun to decay, and being too small for the increasing population of the town, an act of the Assembly was passed, March 1, 1710 or 1711, for building a new church of brick. This was erected on Church Street, and is the present St. Philip's Church. The old wooden church was taken down in 1727. The town was divided into two parishes by an act of Assembly, June 14, 1751. All south of the middle of Broadstreet was formed into a separate parish, called St. Michael's, and its church was built upon the spot on which the old St. Philip's stood."

From him we quote also this extract from an act passed by the General Assembly of the Province, March 10, 1696:

"VI. And whereas several of the present inhabitants of this country did transport themselves into this Province, in hopes of enjoying the liberty of their consciences according to their own persuasions, which the Royal King Charles the Second, of blessed memory, in his Gracious Charter, was pleased to empower the Lords Proprietors of this Province, to grant to the inhabitants of this Province, for to encourage the settlement of the same; Be it therefore enacted that all Christians which now are, or hereafter may be in this Province (papists only excepted), shall enjoy the full, free and undisturbed liberty of their consciences, so as to be in the exercise of their worship, according to the professed Rules of their Religion, without any Let, Molestation or Hindrance, by any Power, either Ecclesiastical or Civil whatsoever: Always provided, that they do not disturb the Public peace of this Province, nor disturb any other in the time of their worship."

The first minister of the Church in the colony was Rev. Atkin Williamson, 1680, the second was Rev. Samuel Marshall, 1696, the third Rev. Edward Marston, who caused quite a lot of disturbance and was called "the incendiary and pest of the Church." And now a most godly and zealous minister was appointed by the Venerable Society in 1702 to succeed Mr. Marston. This man was Rev. Samuel Thomas, the first appointee of the S. P. G. for South Carolina. Unfortunately, he lived only four years after his appointment, and because of his character and his works his decease was taken as a great loss to the Church in the Province. Dr. Dalcho writes thus of him: "He died, much lamented for his sound Doctrine, exemplary Life and Industry; after having laid a good Foundation for his Successors to carry on the Work he had begun." He was succeeded by Rev. Dr. Francis Le Jau as rector of the old Church at Goose Creek, who labored with similar zeal and devotion.

Before this division of the Province into North and South Carolina thirty-eight clergy had been settled in the various parishes of the common colony; and between that time and the Declaration of Independence ninety-two more came out to South Carolina alone. Many other parishes, about twenty in all, had been formed in the Province soon after that established by Mr. Thomas at Goose Creek, among which were St. John's in Berkeley; Christ Church, near Craven County; St. Thomas's and St. Denis's on the Cooper River; and many others in various parts of the present State. Some of the clergy who came out to minister to these parishes felt the climate severely, and died or returned to England. A large majority, however, remained, and were, on the whole, steady and consistent in the discharge of their duties.

As we observed that a perusal of "The Virginia Colonial Churches" showed that the list of vestrymen of the Episcopal Church in Virginia contained names famous in State and Nation, so also is it the case with Dalcho's "Historical Account of the Church in South Carolina." For on the vestry lists we find such names as Rutledge, Middleton, Pinckney, Singleton, Izard, Colleton, Marion, Moultrie, Sumpter, Gadsden, Lynch, Richardson, Manning, Miles, Elliott, Glover, Heyward, Drayton, Jenkins, and many others.

The effects which resulted from the establishment of the Church of England by law in this Province, are thus described by the accurate and impartial historian of South Carolina: "The religious establishment which enjoyed so many and such highly distinguished privileges, was mildly administered. A free toleration was enjoyed by all Dissenters. The law which excluded them from a seat in the Legislature was soon repealed by the Provincial Assembly. The friendship of the Mother Church, the patronage of Government, and the legal provision for clergymen, though partial and confined to one sect, were useful as means of introducing more learned ecclesiastics than would probably have been procured by the unassisted efforts of the first settlers. Religion assumed a visible form, and contributed its influence in softening the manners of dispersed colonists, who, from the want of schoolmasters and clergymen, were in danger of degenerating into savages. It was the means of introducing about an hundred Episcopal clergymen into the country, who were men of regular education and useful in their profession, who generally became settlers, and left families. It also contributed to the introduction of a number of Bibles, and other books on religious subjects, which either formed parochial libraries, or were given away by missionaries of the English Society for Propagating the Gospel. The establishment also procured an influx of several hundred pounds sterling annually into the country, for the maintenance of Episcopal clergymen, in aid of their Provincial legal salary. For these benefits resulting from the establishment, the country was, in a great measure, indebted to Governor Sir Nathaniel Johnson."

Georgia

Georgia was colonized by Oglethorpe in 1733, the archbishop of Canterbury and many of the clergy of England making contributions in aid of the work. The Rev. Dr. Herbert came as missionary, and brought a quantity of religious books contributed by friends. The Rev. Samuel Wesley gave a chalice and paten. Herbert was succeeded by Channey, and the latter by the Rev. John Wesley, who reached Georgia in February, 1736, accompanied by his brother Charles, who was secretary and chaplain to Oglethorpe. John Wesley was at this time *a very rigid Churchman,* and his views of duty finally brought him into collision with some of the people. This led to his flight from the colony, of which we have written elsewhere. George Whitfield came out in 1737, and founded an Orphan House, Norris being a co-worker with Whitfield. The Church grew, and in 1758, was established by law.

When the Revolution dawned, Georgia had but few settled clergymen. Some of these took sides with the crown and left the country. One of the first acts of the legislature, however, after the war, was to recommend measures to maintain public worship.

In Colonial Times

The Church, however, throughout the entire Colonial period was greatly handicapped because she had no resident bishop. Petitions almost innumerable from missionaries, eminent laymen and Convocations of the clergy were made to the English authorities asking for a bishop for the American colonies. But for one reason or another, the petitions were not granted. The result was that very few native sons of America went into the ministry of the Church, as not having a bishop in this country, they would be required to make the long and dangerous voyage to England for ordination. Consequently, the ministry of the Church was filled by men from abroad, who did not understand the conditions in the colonies and whom the colonists could not fully understand. This, of course, was a great handicap to the growth of the Church in every way. For not only did it keep down enthusiasm among its own people, but it failed to attract those on the outside and made missionary work almost an impossibility. While on the other hand, the religion of the Dissenters, not depending in its principles upon any other authority than that which was represented in this country, was uninterrupted in its progress, and drew sons of the settlers into its ministry. They, unhampered by such conditions, were making great progress, while the Church of England, fettered by the conditions mentioned above, was either standing still or making slow progress. This same circumstance, that of having its ministers, largely if not entirely, supplied by men of English birth and rearing, caused the Church to be much misunderstood and even attacked at the time of the Revolution. The English clergy, to a large extent, were naturally Loyalists and left the country after the signing of the Declaration of Independence, or else were Tories while they remained.

Before passing out of the Colonial period to that of the National it may be well for us to recall that outside of Virginia and Maryland, where the Church was strongest, there were four church buildings before the close of the seventeenth century: St. Philip's in Charleston, South Carolina, erected in 1692; King's Chapel in Boston in 1689; Christ Church, Philadelphia, in 1695 and Trinity Church, New York, in 1698. It is important to repeat in connection with the New England settlement that while the Pilgrims who landed in 1620 were Separatists from the Church of England, the settlers who landed at Salem in 1630 were members of the Church of England. As they were leaving their native shores they said, "Farewell, dear England. Farewell, the Church of God in England and all Christian friends there. We do not go to New England as Separatists from the Church of England, though we cannot but separate from the corruptions of it, but we go to practise the positive part of Church reform and to propagate the Gospel in America." And Winthrop, the Governor, wrote: "We desire that you would be pleased to take notice of the principal body of our company as those who esteem it our honour to call the Church of England, from which we rose, our dear mother, and we cannot part from our native country where she especially resideth without much sadness of heart and tears in our eyes, and acknowledging that such degree that we have obtained in salvation we have received it in her bosom and sucked it from her breasts."

During the eighteenth century, the missionary society known as the Society for the Propagation of the Gospel in Foreign Parts was zealous in sending its missionaries to various parts of the American Colonies and caused many churches to be founded within their borders.

The reader, no doubt, recalls what we have already written about this. And it is also to be recalled that the colonists were great promoters of Church schools and colleges. Some of their efforts resulted in the establishment of William and Mary College in 1693, the College and Academy in Philadelphia, now the University of Pennsylvania, King's College in New York, now known as Columbia University. And everywhere where there was any real strength there was the effort to extend the Church through schools and colleges.

George Whitefield

We cannot pass on without mentioning the effort known as the "Great Awakening" under the leadership of George Whitefield and the influence of the great revival under John Wesley. These men were of the Church of England. We recall, of course, that John Wesley was for a time the rector of Christ Church in Savannah, Georgia, and partly because of his "High-Church" proclivities had an uncomfortable time in that province. The testimony he bore concerning the brethren in the Colony of South Carolina is very interesting. In writing of their clerical conference he said: "There was such conversation for several hours on Christ and His Righteousness as I have not beheld in any visitation in England or hardly on any other occasion." Whitefield succeeded Wesley as the rector of the Savannah parish. He founded a school for orphans, and established Bethesda College nine miles from Savannah. This has been called "the most interesting and valuable act of Whitefield in Georgia." Throughout the remaining thirty years of his life he was devoted to its interests, raising eighty thousand dollars for it, of which he gave sixteen thousand himself. But it became evident to him and to others that he was pre-eminently a preacher, and to that calling he henceforth unreservedly gave himself. He had a wonderful ability to appeal to the emotions of people, and by such appeal to move them to acceptance of Christian allegiance and to deep consecration of their energies to the cause of religion.

Of course, a man of Whitefield's methods of appeal while attracting a certain sort of people would as certainly repel others. His tremendous emphasis upon the emotional side of religion would naturally alienate men of quieter ways, who were influenced more by calm reflection and settled conscientious convictions, and to whom display of their deeper feelings is distasteful. Consequently, we can understand the situation as outlined by Rev. Dr. Timothy Cutler, formerly President of Yale College, who had changed from the Congregational to the Episcopal Church. Writing under date of September 24, 1743, he says: "Whitefield has plagued us with a witness, especially his friends and followers, who themselves are like to be battered to pieces by that battering-ram they had provided against our Church here. It would be an endless attempt to describe that scene of confusion and disturbance occasioned by him,—the division of families, neighborhoods, and towns, the contrariety of husbands and wives, the undutifulness of children and servants, the quarrels among teachers, the disorders of the night, the intermission of labor and business, the neglect of husbandry and of gathering the harvest. Our presses are forever teeming with books, and our women with bastards, though regeneration and conversion are the whole cry. The teachers have, many of them, left their particular cures, and strolled about the country. Some have been ordained by them as Evangelizers, and have their Armor-bearers and Exhorters; and in many conventicles and places of rendezvous there has been checkered work, indeed, several preaching, and several exhorting and praying at the same time, the rest crying or laughing, yelping, sprawling, fainting, and this revel maintained in some places many days and nights together, without intermission; and then there were the blessed outpourings of the Spirit!

"When Mr. Whitefield first arrived here the whole town was alarmed. He made his first visit to Church on a Friday, and conversed first with many of our clergy together, belied them, me especially, when he had done. Being not invited into our pulpits, the Dissenters were highly pleased, and engrossed him; and immediately the bells rang, and all hands went to lecture; and this show kept on all the while he was here.

"After him came one Tennent, a monster! impudent and noisy, and told them they were all damn'd, damn'd, damn'd; this charmed them, and in the most dreadful winter I ever saw people wallowed in the snow night and day for the benefit of his beastly brayings; and many ended their days under these fatigues. Both of them carried more money out of these parts than the poor could be thankful for.

"All this turned to the growth of the Church in many places, and its reputation universally; and it suffers no otherwise than as religion in general does, and that is sadly enough."

Dr. Coke and Bishop White Correspond

Dr. Coke, one of Wesley's associates and whom Mr. Wesley had appointed Superintendent of the Methodists in America after the Methodist movement had attained considerable proportions both in numbers of lay people and preachers, made overtures to Bishop White for a union between the Methodists and the Episcopal Church. We feel sure that the reader will enjoy the following extract from the letter of Dr. Coke to Bishop White:

"You, I believe, are conscious that I was brought up in the Church of England, and have been ordained a presbyter of that Church. For many years I was prejudiced, even I think to bigotry, in favor of it; but through a variety of causes or incidents, to mention which would be tedious and useless, my mind was exceedingly biased on the other side of the question. In consequence of this, I am not sure but I went further in the separation of our Church in America than Mr. Wesley, from whom I had received my commission, did intend. He did indeed solemnly invest me, as far as he had a right so to do, with Episcopal authority, but *did not intend,* I think, *that an entire separation should take place.* He, being pressed by our friends on this side of the water for ministers to administer the Sacraments to them (there being very few of the clergy of the Church of England then in the States), went further, I am sure, than he would have gone, if he had foreseen some events which followed. And this I am certain of—*that he is now sorry for the separation.*

"But what can be done for a reunion, which I much wish for, and to accomplish which, Mr. Wesley, I have no doubt, would use his influence to the utmost? The affection of a very considerable number of the preachers and most of the people is very strong towards him, notwithstanding the excessive ill usage he received from a few. My interest also is not small, and both his and mine would readily, and to the utmost, be used to accomplish that (to us) very desirable object, if a readiness were shown by the bishops of the Protestant Episcopal Church to reunite. . . . Shall I be favored with a private interview with you in Philadelphia? . . . We can then enlarge on these subjects."

In response Bishop White wrote a most kindly letter to Dr. Coke in which he said: "I shall be very happy in the opportunity of conversing with you at the time proposed." It seems that the two had three conferences without practical effects. Bishop White discusses the matter in the "Memoirs of the Church" and we deem it of sufficient interest and importance to reproduce here what he says (pp. 196–199):

"To guard against misconstruction, at some future time, of the correspondence between Dr. Coke and the author, he records it here.

"In the spring of the year 1791, the author received from that gentleman a letter, containing a plan of what he considered as a union of the Methodistical Society with the Episcopal Church. The plan was, in substance, that all the Methodist ministers at the time in connection, were to receive Episcopal ordination, as also those who should come forward in future within the connection; such ministers to remain under the government of the then superintendents and their successors. Dr. Coke's motive to the proposed union, as stated in his letter, was an apprehension entertained by him, that he had gone further in the separation than had been designed by Mr. Wesley, from whom he had received his commission. Mr. Wesley himself, he was sure, had gone further than he would have gone, if he had foreseen some events which followed. The Doctor was certain that the same gentleman was sorry for the separation, and would use his influence to the utmost for the accomplishment of a reunion. Dr. Coke's letter was answered by the author with the reserve which seemed incumbent on one who was incompetent to decide with effect on the proposal made.

"It happened that Dr. Coke, before he received the answer to his letter, hearing of the decease of Mr. Wesley, the news of which reached America during the short interval between the dates of the two letters, set off immediately from Baltimore for Philadelphia, to take his passage for England. On reaching this city and calling on Dr. Magaw, he was much disappointed on hearing of the early answer, lest it should fall into the hands of his colleague—Mr. Asbury. He visited the author, in the company of Dr. Magaw, and in speaking of the above incident, said, that although he hoped Mr. Asbury would not open the letter, yet he might do so, on the supposition that it related to their joint concern. The conversation was general, and nothing passed that gave any ground of expectation of a re-union on the principle of consolidation; or any other principle than that of the continuing of the Methodists as a distinct body and self-governed. In short, there were held out only the terms of the letter, in which there does not seem to be contemplated any change in the relation of the Episcopal Church to that Society, except the giving of them access to the Episcopal congregations, while there was sufficient security provided to prevent the clergy of the latter from having access to congregations of the Methodists. At least, it is here supposed that these things would have been unavoidably the result.

"The author saw Dr. Coke twice after this; once, by appointment at Dr. Magaw's, where nothing material passed and again alone at the author's house, where Dr. Coke read a letter which he had written to Bishop Seabury similar to that which he had written to the author, but with the difference of his suggesting to Bishop Seabury as follows— that although the Methodists would have confidence in any engagements which should be made by the present bishops, yet there might in future be some who, on the arrival of their inferior grades of preachers to a competency to the ministry, would not admit them as proposed in the letter; that to guard against the danger of this, there would be use in consecrating Mr. Asbury to the episcopacy; and that although there would not be the same reasons in his (Dr. Coke's) case, because he was a resident of England, yet, as he should probably, while he lived, occasionally visit America, it would not be fit, considering he was Mr. Asbury's senior, that he should appear in a lower character than this gentleman. These were, in substance, the sentiments expressed; and on reading this part of the letter, he desired the author to take notice that he did not make a condition of what he had there written. There was no comment, and he proceeded.

"In this conversation he said that Mr. Asbury had opened his letter, but he had heard nothing from him on the subject. With this interview all intercourse ended. Dr. Coke soon afterward embarked for England, and was reported to have had an interview with Mr. Asbury somewhere down the river on his journey to the ship. The author avoided speaking on the subject until the Convention in 1792, and then mentioned it only to the bishops, towards whom there was understood to be a latitude."

The matter was brought up in the House of Bishops at the General Convention of 1792 by Bishop Madison of Virginia. While reunion with the Methodists was especially in the mind of Bishop Madison, his proposition which passed the House of Bishops and was rejected in the House of Clerical and Lay Deputies was couched in general terms. The proposition was as follows:

"The Protestant Episcopal Church in the United States of America, ever bearing in mind the sacred obligation which attends all the followers of Christ to avoid divisions among themselves, and anxious to promote

that union for which our Lord and Saviour so earnestly prayed, do hereby declare to the Christian world, that uninfluenced by any other considerations than those of our duty as Christians, and an earnest desire for the prosperity of pure Christianity, and the furtherance of our Holy Religion, they are ready and willing to unite and form one body with any religious society which shall be influenced by the same Catholic spirit. And in order that this Christian end may be the more easily effected, they further declare that all things in which the great essentials of Christianity or the character-istic principles of their Church are not concerned, they are willing to leave to future discussion; being ready to alter or modify those points which, in the opinion of the Protestant Episcopal Church, are sub-ject to human alteration. And it is hereby recom-mended to the State conventions to adopt such measures or propose such conferences with Christians of other denominations, as to themselves may be thought most prudent, and report accordingly to the ensuing General Convention." It seems such a pity that some method could not have been provided for reconciling the dif-ferences, and another conclusion arrived at than the unfortunate one reached. For the people who had been moved by the Great Awakening could have contributed much to the spiritual life and zeal of the Episcopal Church, and the Church could have contributed the very things that the other brethren needed.

The Revolution and Immediately After

We come now to consider the days of the American Revolution. While the Church was, as we have pointed out, greatly handicapped by the fact that most of her clergy were Englishmen, and so became Loyalists, still the backbone of the Revolutionary movement as far as its personnel is concerned was constituted of men of the Episcopal Church. In this connection we recall that three-fourths of the signers of the Declaration of Independence were sons of the Episcopal Church; that the man who wrote that immortal document, Thomas Jefferson, was educated at a Church college and was a son of the Episcopal Church; that Richard Henry Lee, who moved the adoption of the Declaration of Independence, was also a son of the Episcopal Church; that the Continental Congress which adopted it was opened with prayer by Rev. Jacob Duché, rector of Christ Episcopal Church, Philadelphia; that Patrick Henry, the fountain of inspiration in those stirring times, was a son of the Episcopal Church; that George Washington, the man who led the forces that made good the Declaration of Independence, was a son of the Episcopal Church, as were also a large number of the country's other military leaders in the Revolution; and that Benjamin Franklin, one of the most stalwart supporters and effective aids to the country in those perilous days, was a son of the Episcopal Church; and Robert Morris, great genius in the field of finance, who, by his moral support and his aid in providing the means for material supplies, contributed greatly to the success of the American army and the winning of the country's freedom, was a son of the Episcopal Church. And from the steeple of Christ Episcopal Church, Boston, were hung the lanterns on the night of

April 18th, 1775, that guided Paul Revere in his famous ride from Boston to Concord.

Thomas Jefferson and Benjamin Franklin

From time to time something is said about the religious affiliations of Thomas Jefferson and Benjamin Franklin. We wish to say here that in "Virginia Colonial Churches" it is stated that of the five men composing a committee to revise the laws of the Commonwealth of Virginia and that brought in an act providing for religious freedom, every one of them, Jefferson, Pendleton, Wythe, Mason and Lee, "were on the list of vestrymen of St. Anne's Parish," although the records do not show that Jefferson was active as the others were. And we have seen a copy of a letter from one of his relatives asserting his faithful attendance at the services of the Church and telling of his carrying his prayer stool to the church, attached to his saddle bag. From the same volume, "Virginia Colonial Churches," we quote the following (p. 56):

"The bishop of Southern Virginia, in an address delivered in St. John's Church on its 150th anniversary, June 10th, 1891, stated this very remarkable fact: speaking of Richard Randolph, who superintended the building of St. John's Church in 1741, and Edmund Randolph, who represented the Church in the first convention of the diocese, both of them vestrymen, he says: 'These men were great-grandsons of one of the earliest members of your parish. A simple, strong, true man he must have been; out of his loins sprang three great men. He was the ancestor of Chief Justice

Marshall, the greatest jurist of America. He was the ancestor of Thomas Jefferson, the greatest political thinker of America. He was the ancestor of Robert E. Lee, the greatest soldier of America.' "

The ancestor of these three men lived in this parish, on the river, just below Richmond.

No one can read such books as the one just referred to without realizing that Thomas Jefferson was born in the Church, his spiritual environment was that of the Church from infancy to maturity and there can be no doubt that his character was largely moulded by her principles and her breadth of spirit. But the clincher on the whole matter is found in Mr. Jefferson's own words. In answer to an application for financial assistance to a certain religious denomination he wrote under date of August 10, 1823, the following: "The principle that every religious sect is to maintain its own teachers and institutions is too reasonable and too well established in our country to need justification. I have been, from my infancy, a member of the Episcopalian Church, and to that I owe and make my contributions. Were I to go beyond that limit in favor of any other sectarian Institution, I should be equally bound to do so for every other, and their number is beyond the faculties of any individual. I believe, therefore, that in this, as in every other case, everything will be better conducted if left to those immediately interested. On these grounds I trust that your candor will excuse my returning the inclosed paper without my subscription; and that you will accept the assurance of my great personal respect and esteem.

"Th. Jefferson."

While reading this volume on the history of the Church in Virginia one is struck with the identity of the names of leaders in both Church and State and Nation. For the Church's vestries carry such names as Randolph, Peyton, Pendleton, Nelson, Meade, Lee, Washington, Henry, Tyler, Marshall, Harrison, etc.

As to Franklin, we quote these words from Tiffany (p. 215): "During Dr. Jenney's rectorship of Christ Church, the College and Academy of Philadelphia, since developed into the University of Pennsylvania, was founded and opened in 1749, some five years before the opening of King's College, New York. Benjamin Franklin, a *vestryman of Christ Church,* was the chief mover in the matter, and had received Bishop Berkeley's suggestions regarding it. Three-fourths of the trustees were members of the Church of England; and they, with Franklin, were strongly desirous of securing Dr. Johnson, of Stratford, Connecticut, as rector of the institution."

And when the time came for the adoption of the Constitution, the Nation turned for leadership to the men of the Episcopal Church, for he who wrote that immortal document, described by an English author of note as "The greatest instrument that ever came from the mind of man at one time," Alexander Hamilton, was a son of the Episcopal Church, as was also his great collaborator, James Madison; and the man who was its chief expounder for thirty years, John Marshall, was a son of the Episcopal Church; John Jay and Elbridge Gerry, John Rutledge, C. C. Pinckney and Thomas Nelson—men of light and leading in those days—were sons of the Episcopal Church; and two-thirds of the members of the Constitutional Convention were sons of the Episcopal Church. And hence it is readily seen that the part which the Episcopal Church played in the establishment of this country as a Nation was not only an honorable and exceedingly prominent part, but also out of all proportion to the size of its membership. Let us recall here these words of the late Dr. R. H. McKim: "John Fiske, the Massachusetts historian, has told the world that there were five great men of that epoch who may be said to have made the Nation—Washington, Jefferson, Hamilton, Madison and Marshall.

"Now all five of these makers of the Republic were sons of the Episcopal Church.

"It is not then too much to say that this Church led the way in the making of the Republic. It was her voice, through these her sons, that taught the people the first rudiments of liberty. It was her influence that was most puissant, through these great men, in establishing our free institutions.

"Let the historian who would estimate the place which the Anglo-Saxon Church ought to occupy in the annals of the Republic, let him, I say, look at the stature of the patriots whom the Episcopal Church gave to the Revolution. Let him observe that they are not only among the giants of that remarkable epoch. They are the greatest of the giants!

"And then let him ask himself how the story of the Revolution and the rise of the Republic would have read, if the names of Peyton Randolph, Richard Henry Lee, Thomas Jefferson, Patrick Henry, John Jay, James Madison, Alexander Hamilton, John Marshall and George Washington were blotted from our annals.

"The answer to that question will gauge the debt of America to the Anglo-Saxon Church," or what we call in this country, the Episcopal Church.

Notwithstanding all this, however, immediately succeeding the Revolution the Episcopal Church in America was in serious trouble, not only because her clergy, for the most part, had been Loyalists, but because by reason of their removal she was without many ordained leaders and had no bishops. For a fuller description of the situation we turn to Bishop White: "On a retrospect of the low condition in which the Episcopal Church has been left by the Revolutionary war: of her clergy, reduced almost to annihilation; of the novelty of the business arising out of the existing crisis; of the despair of many, as to the perpetuating of the Communion, otherwise than in connection with an establishment, from which it was forever severed; of an unwillingness to recognize such a severance, although brought about by the Providence of God, and the recognizing of it as agreeable to a prominent principle in the institutions of the parent Church; of a difficulty, to be done away only by legislative acts, which perhaps it would be impossible to obtain, and which we could not apply for, consistently with our civil duties; of the apprehension of conflicting opinions in different sections of the United States between which there had been hitherto no religious intercourse; of the existence of known differences, on some points; and, with all these things, of danger from selfish passions, so apt to intrude under imposing appearances, defeating the best intended endeavors in collective bodies; it must be perceived, that there were formidable obstacles to be surmounted, in combining the insulated congregations with the respective clergy of those who had any, under an indisputable succession of the Episcopacy; and with an ecclesiastical legislature, necessarily differing in form from that under which we had been from the beginning, yet the same with it in principle." Such were some of the elements of her great distress, yet the spirit of her people was indomitable and soon her clergy and people in Connecticut and Philadelphia, in Maryland and Virginia and in other parts, began to take thought concerning her future and to make efforts to secure resident bishops, so that the life of the Church might be unimpaired and her continuity with the Great Church of the past reaching through England back to the days of the Apostles might not be broken.

The National Organization of the Church

There is no authority on the subject of the organization of the Church in this country so reliable as that of him who was the leader in the undertaking, that is, Bishop William White of Pennsylvania. Before quoting his words let us recall a few facts in his life: William White, son of Colonel Thomas White and Esther Hewlings, was born in Philadelphia, March 24th, 1747. Pursuing his preparatory studies in the city of his birth, he graduated from the College of Philadelphia at the age of seventeen. At this time he had fully decided to adopt the sacred profession. After pursuing his theological studies under the guidance of the local clergy, being especially indebted to Dr. Peters and Mr. Duché, he sailed for England, where December 23rd, 1770, in the Royal Chapel, London, he was ordained deacon by Dr. Young, bishop of Norwich. Remaining in London about a year and half, he saw considerable society, meeting Goldsmith and Dr. Johnson. June, 1772, he was advanced to the priesthood by Dr. Terrick, bishop of London. He at once sailed for Philadelphia, where he arrived September 13th, soon being elected assistant minister of Christ Church and St. Peter's.

When the Revolution dawned he took sides with the Colonies without wavering. Upon the Declaration of Independence, he ceased praying for the king, and was the second person to take the oath of allegiance to the Commonwealth of Pennsylvania. September, 1777, he became chaplain to the Continental Congress. April, 1779, he was elected rector of Christ Church and St. Peter's, Philadelphia, devoting himself with much zeal to the discharge of his duties, and winning the approval of the entire community.

When the time drew near to take measures for the organization of the Church, believing that it would be impracticable to obtain the Episcopal succession from England, at least for a time, he prepared a pamphlet, entitled "The Case of the Episcopal Churches in the United States Considered," in which he proposed a provisional organization, that was to be superseded as soon as the succession could be obtained. Happily, however, the accomplishment of political independence was attended by its recognition on the part of the British Government, leaving no difficulty in the way of organization in accordance with the system of the Church of England. Nevertheless, the author of the pamphlet was misunderstood in some quarters, while, at a later period, his production was used for purposes entirely foreign to the author's intentions. The criticism excited was met by Bishop White and disarmed of force, so that no permanent harm resulted from his proposition. The Churchmanship of Bishop White was thoroughly sound, he being conservative and opposed to all doctrinal and ecclesiastical innovations.

When peace was declared, he was at once looked to as the proper person to lead in the organization of the American Church, and accordingly he was elected bishop of Pennsylvania. His own narrative gives the story of his election, and his consecration which took place in Lambeth Chapel, London, February 4th, 1787. He arrived in New York on Easter Sunday of the same year. Easter Day, 1787, will, therefore, possess a peculiar significance to the end of time. It marks the Renaissance of the American Church, of which he stood the acknowledged head until his decease which took place July 17th, 1836.

Let us now take up Bishop White's account of the organization of the Protestant Episcopal Church in the United States of America. We quote as follows (pp. 19–22):

"The first step towards the forming of a collective body to the Episcopal Church in the United States was taken at a meeting for another purpose, of a few clergymen of New York, New Jersey, and Pennsylvania, at Brunswick, in New Jersey, on the 13th and 14th of May 1784. These clergymen, in consequence of prior correspondence, had met for the purpose of consulting, in what way to renew a society that had existed under charters of incorporation from the governors of the said three states, for the support of widows and children of deceased clergymen. Here it was determined, to procure a larger meeting on the fifth of the ensuing October in New York; not only for the purpose of reviving the said charitable institution, but to confer and agree on some general principles of a union of the Episcopal Church throughout the States.

"Such a meeting was held, at the time and place agreed on: and although the members composing it were not vested with powers adequate to the present exigencies of the Church, they happily, and with great unanimity, laid down a few general principles, to be recommended in the respective States, as the ground on which a future ecclesiastical government should be established. These principles were approbatory of Episcopacy and of the Book of Common Prayer; and provided for a representative body of the Church, consisting of clergy and laity; who were to vote as distinct orders. There was also a recommendation to the Church in the several States, to send clerical and lay deputies to a meeting to be held in Philadelphia, on the 27th of September in the following year.

"Although at the meeting last held, there were present two clergymen from the Eastern States; yet it now appeared, that there was no probability, for the present, of the aid of the churches in those States, in the measures begun for the obtaining of a representative body of the Church at large. From this they thought themselves restrained in Connecticut, in particular, by a step they had antecedently taken, for the obtaining of the episcopate from England. For until the event of their application could be known, it naturally seemed to them inconsistent to do anything which might change the ground on which the gentleman of their choice was then standing. This gentleman was the Rev. Samuel Seabury, D.D., formerly missionary on Staten Island, who had been recommended to England for consecration before the evacuation of New York by the British army.

"On the 27th of September 1785, there assembled agreeably to appointment, in Philadelphia, a convention of clerical and lay deputies from seven of the thirteen United States, viz., from New York to Virginia, inclusive, with the addition of South Carolina. They applied themselves to the making of such alterations in the Book of Common Prayer, as were necessary for the accommodating of it to the late changes in the State; and the proposing, but not establishing, of such other alterations in that Book and in the Articles, as they thought an improvement of the service and of the manner of stating the principal articles of faith; these were published in a book, ever since known by the name of 'The Proposed Book.' This Book was revealed as very unsatisfactory to the Church in the States and also in some particulars to English archbishops and bishops to whom application was made for Episcopal Consecration.

"The Convention entered on the business of the Episcopacy, with the knowledge that there was now a bishop in Connecticut, consecrated, not in England, but by the non-juring bishops of Scotland. For Dr. Seabury, not meeting assurance of success with the bishops of the former country, had applied to the latter quarter for the succession, which had been there carefully maintained; notwithstanding their severance from the State in the revolution of 1688. Bishop Seabury had returned to America, and had entered on the exercise of his new function in the beginning of the preceding summer, and two or three gentlemen of the Southern States had received ordination from his hands. Nevertheless, the members of this Convention, although generally impressed with sentiments of respect towards the new bishop, and although, with the exception of a few, alleging nothing against the validity of his Episcopacy, thought it the most proper to direct their views in the first instance towards England. In this they were encouraged by information which they thought authentic, assigning for Dr. Seabury's failure these two reasons; that the administration had some apprehension of embroiling themselves with the American Government, the sovereignty of which they had so recently acknowledged; and that the bishops were doubtful how far the act of some clergymen, in their individual capacities, would be acquiesced in by their respective flocks. For the meeting of the former difficulty, it was thought easy to obtain, and there were afterwards obtained, from the executive authorities of the States in which the new bishops were to reside, certificates, that what was sought did not interfere with any civil laws or constitutions. The latter difficulty was thought sufficiently obviated by the powers under which the present Convention was assembled.

"Accordingly, they addressed the archbishops and bishops of England, stating, that the Episcopal Church in the United States had been severed, by a civil revolution, from the jurisdiction of the parent Church in England; acknowledging the favors formerly received from the bishops of London in particular, and from the archbishops and bishops in general through the medium of the Society for the Propagation of the Gospel; declaring their desire to perpetuate among them the principles of the Church of England, in doctrine, discipline, and worship; and praying that their lordships would consecrate to the Episcopacy those persons who should be sent, with that view, from the churches in any of the States respectively.

"In order that the present Convention might be succeeded by bodies of the like description, they framed an ecclesiastical constitution, the outlines of which were, that there should be a triennial Convention, consisting of a deputation from the Church in each State, of not more than four clergymen, and as many laymen; that they should vote Statewise, each order to have a negative on the other; that when there should be a bishop in any State, he should be officially a member of the Convention; that the different orders of clergy should be accountable to the ecclesiastical authority in the State only to which they should respectively belong; and the engagement previous to ordination should be a declaration of belief in the Holy Scriptures, and a promise of conformity to the doctrines and the worship of the Church.

"Further, the Convention appointed a committee with various powers; among which was, that of corresponding, during the recess, with the archbishops and bishops of England; and they adjourned, to meet again in

Philadelphia, on the 20th of June, in the following year."

The correspondence with the English archbishops having terminated favorably, some of those elected by their brethren to become their bishops, after having secured the proper credentials and testimonials, crossed the Atlantic and presented themselves to the archbishop of Canterbury. The first to do this were Rev. William White, D.D., Rector Christ Church and St. Peter's, Philadelphia, and Rev. Samuel Provoost, D.D., Rector of Trinity Church, New York.

On the 4th of February, 1787, in the chapel of the archiepiscopal palace of Lambeth, Dr. White and Dr. Provoost were ordained and consecrated bishops, by the Most Rev. John Moore, archbishop of Canterbury. The Most Rev. William Markham, archbishop of York, presented them. And the bishops who joined with the two archbishops in the imposition of hands, were the Right Rev. Charles Moss, bishop of Bath and Wells, and the Right Rev. John Hinchliff, bishop of Peterborough. Before the end of the same month, the newly consecrated bishops sailed from Falmouth for New York, where they arrived on Easter Sunday, April the 7th, and soon afterwards began the exercise of the Episcopacy in their respective dioceses.

Bishop Seabury's Consecration

As we have seen, Dr. Samuel Seabury had previously been elected by the clergy of Connecticut as their bishop, and went to England to secure consecration. Dr. Seabury was cordially received by the English ecclesiastical authorities, but there were some serious obstacles in the way of their granting his wish to consecrate him to the episcopate. Some of these were wholly political. Under the law of England, a bishop had to take the oath of allegiance to the English king and realm. Now since the United States had become an independent nation such action, of course, was impossible for any American citizen. After spending a year in fruitless negotiation in England, Dr. Seabury went to Scotland. There was no political obstacle in the way there, as there were bishops in Scotland who had not taken the oath of allegiance to the English king, and who would not, being known as Non-jurors or non-juring bishops. When William of Orange and Mary his wife were crowned king and queen in 1689, the coronation oath was amplified by parliament so as to make the king swear that he would maintain "the Protestant reformed religion established by law," which oath has been taken by every succeeding English monarch. Some of the bishops did not see their way clear to transfer their allegiance from James II to the new sovereign. Five such were deprived of their sees. These with some 400 clergymen and quite a body of laymen seceded from the National Church and made up what was called the body of Non-jurors—i. e., those refusing to take the oath—and the succession of these non-juring bishops was continued until the beginning of the nineteenth century.

The bishops of the Church in Scotland, who were also non-juring bishops as the result of the disestablishment of the Episcopal Church of Scotland by William III, very willingly acceded to Dr. Seabury's wish as representing his brethren in Connecticut, and they consecrated him a bishop in the Church of God for work in America, in the upper room of a private home in Aberdeen, Scotland, on Sunday, November 14th, 1784. The names of the consecrators were Robert Kilgour, who was the chief consecrator; Arthur Petrie, the bishop of Ross and Moray, and John Skinner, bishop coadjutor of Aberdeen. The Scotch bishops made a request of Bishop Seabury that in adopting the revision of the English Prayer Book for America, the American Liturgy should contain the Invocation and Oblation which were not at that time, and are not now, in the English Prayer Book. We shall see subsequently that this request was granted and our Prayer Book was enriched by these two noble prayers from the Scotch Prayer Book.

The second General Convention met June 20th, 1786, at which the principal business transacted was another address to the English prelates, containing an acknowledgment of their friendly and affectionate letter, a declaration of not intending to depart from the doctrine of the English Church, and a determination to make no further alterations than such as either arose from a change of circumstances, or appeared conducive to union; and a repetition of the request for the succession. Before their adjournment, they appointed a committee with power to reassemble them, if thought expedient, at Wilmington in the State of Delaware.

We recall also these words of Bishop White concerning the next two Conventions: "At the present session of the General Convention, the Constitution formed in 1786 was reviewed and newly modelled. The principal feature now given to it was a distribution into two houses, one consisting of the bishops and the other, of the clerical and lay deputies, who must vote, when required by the clerical or by the lay representation from any State, as under the former Constitution, by Orders. The stated meetings were to be on the second Tuesday in September in every third year; but intermediate meetings might be called by the bishops.

"When the Convention adjourned, it was to meet the 29th of September following; and before the adjournment, an invitation was given by them to Bishop Seabury, and to their brethren generally in the Eastern States, to be present at the proposed session, with a view to a permanent union.

"On that day the Convention reassembled, when it appeared that Bishop Seabury, with sundry of the clergy from Massachusetts and Connecticut, had accepted the invitation given them. There was laid before the Convention, and by them ordered to be recorded evidence of that bishop's consecration; which had been performed by Bishops Kilgour, Petrie, and Skinner, of the non-juring Church in Scotland. There then ensued a conference between a committee of the convention and the clergy from the Eastern States; the result of which was, that after one alteration of the Constitution at their desire, they declared their acquiescence in it, and gave it their signature accordingly.

"It had been provided in the Constitution, that the arrangement of two houses should take place, as soon as three bishops should belong to the body. This circumstance now occurred, although there were present only two of them, who accordingly formed the House of Bishops.

"The two houses entered on a review of the Liturgy, the bishops originating alterations in some services, and the House of Clerical and Lay Deputies proposing others. The result was the Book of Common Prayer, as then established and has been ever since used.

"Some canons had been passed in the preceding session; but they were reconsidered and passed with sundry others, which continue to this day substantially the same; but with some alterations and additions by succeeding Conventions.

"The next Triennial Convention was held in the City of New York, in the autumn of 1792, at which were present the four bishops already mentioned to have been consecrated abroad. Hitherto, there had been no consecration in America; but at this Convention, although nothing further was brought before them from Massachusetts relative to Dr. Bass, the deputies from Maryland applied to the assembled bishops for the consecration of the Rev. Thomas John Claggett, D.D., who had been elected bishop by the Convention of that State. Dr. Claggett was accordingly consecrated, during the session of the Convention, in Trinity Church of the city in which they were assembled, Bishops Provoost, Seabury, White and Madison officiating.

"The bishops, having reviewed the Ordinal of the Church of England, proposed a few alterations in it to the House of Clerical and Lay Deputies; principally such as were necessary for the accommodating of it to local circumstances. The Ordinal, thus reviewed, is now the established form for the consecrating of bishops and the ordaining of priests and deacons."

The Name

There has been a good deal said and written from time to time about the present name and how we came by it. We have observed that in much of the correspondence immediately following the Revolution and some of the meetings of the clergy, the Church is called simply "The Episcopal Church," but in our formularies and in our Constitution and the proceedings of the General Conventions in those days and in the correspondence with the English prelates the official name used by them and by our representatives for the most part is "Protestant Episcopal Church." There seems little doubt that the name was first formally adopted and officially used at a conference of clergy and laity of Maryland held in Chestertown November 9th, 1780. This conference was called by Rev. Dr. William Smith, shortly after his removal to the State from Pennsylvania, to consider the temporal condition of the churches subsequent to the Vestry Act of 1779. It consisted of three clergymen and twenty-four laymen, mostly delegates from churches in Kent County. Dr. Smith was chosen president. At his instigation "A Petition to the General Assembly of Maryland for the Support of Public Religion" was prepared, to be submitted to the several parishes, and, when approved, presented to the Assembly. It asked that an act be passed, in accordance with the Declaration of Rights issued by the Assembly (November, 1776), empowering the vestry and wardens of the several parishes to raise money by pew rents and other means, to restore and keep in repair the Church property. In order to appear as an ecclesiastical organization, a name was requisite. To speak of the Episcopal body as the Church of England would have been repugnant both to the loyal sentiment and the ecclesiastical prejudice of the province. It was moved, therefore, by the Rev. James Jones Wilmer, rector of Shrewsbury parish, Kent County, "that the Church of England, as heretofore so known in the province, be now called the Protestant Episcopal Church." Dr. Smith is reputed to have been the author of this name, and very likely he suggested it; but being in the chair, he could not propose it. The motion was adopted; and the name made its way everywhere throughout the Episcopal Church.

From that time on it seems that it was accepted and incorporated in our official papers, in our Prayer Book, and in our Constitution. Efforts have been made to change the name, but so far the Church has been unwilling to entertain the idea.

Intention of Continuity with the English Church

The intention of the Church in the United States to remain in union with the English Church in all essentials is made conspicuously, transparently, clear on all occasions, and cannot reasonably be doubted by any one. As a few illustrations of this we cite the fourth principle of ecclesiastical union of the Episcopal Church as adopted at the meeting in New York in

1784 which reads: "4th. That the said Church shall maintain the doctrine of the Gospel as now held by the Church of England, and shall adhere to the Liturgy of the said Church, as far as shall be consistent with the American Revolution, and the constitutions of the respective States; The fourth article in the 'Declaration of certain fundamental rights and liberties of the Protestant Episcopal Church of Maryland' adopted in August 1783 which reads as follows: 'That as it is the right, so it will be the duty of the said Church, when duly organized, constituted, and represented in a synod or convention of the different orders of her ministers and people, to revise her Liturgy, forms of prayer, and public worship, in order to adapt the same to the later Revolution, and other local circumstances of America; which, it is humbly conceived, will and may be done, without any other or farther departure from the venerable order and beautiful forms of worship of the Church from which we sprung, than may be found expedient in the change of our situation from a *daughter to a sister Church'*; the address of Clerical and Lay Deputies of the Protestant Episcopal Church to the English Prelates from which we quote, 'We are unanimous and explicit in assuring your lordships, that we neither have departed nor propose to depart from the doctrines of your Church. We have retained the same discipline and forms of worship, as far as were consistent with our civil constitutions; and we have made no alterations or omissions in the Book of Common Prayer, but such as that consideration prescribed, and such as were calculated to remove objections, which it appeared to us more conducive to union and general content than to dispute. . . .' These documents, we trust, will afford a full answer to every question that can arise on the subject. We consider your lordships' letter as very candid and kind; we repose full confidence in the assurances it gives; and that confidence, together with the liberality and catholicism of your venerable body, leads us to flatter ourselves, that you will not disclaim a branch of your Church merely for having been in your lordships' opinion, if that should be the case, pruned rather more closely than its separation made absolutely necessary."

Then the following preamble and resolution (No. 3) adopted by the General Convention meeting Wednesday, October 11th, 1786, in Wilmington, Delaware, is to the same purpose: "And whereas the clerical and lay deputies of this Church have received the most friendly and affectionate letters in answer to the said address, from the said archbishops and bishops, opening a fair prospect of the success of their said applications, but, at the same time, earnestly exhorting this Convention to use their utmost exertions for the removal of certain objections by them made, against some parts of the alterations in the Book of Common Prayer and Rites and Ceremonies of this Church, last mentioned: In pursuance whereof, this present General Convention hath been called, and is now assembled; and being sincerely disposed to give every satisfaction to their lordships, which will be consistent with the union and general content of the Church they represent; and *declaring their steadfast resolution to maintain the same essential articles of faith and discipline with the Church of England*:

"Now therefore, the said deputies do hereby determine and declare, Thirdly, That the second clause so to be subscribed by a bishop, priest, or deacon of this Church, in any of the States which have not already ratified or used the last mentioned Book of Common Prayer, shall be in the words following: 'And I do solemnly engage to conform to the doctrine and worship of the Protestant Episcopal Church, according to the *use of the Church of England,* as the same is altered by the General Convention, in a certain instrument of writing, passed by their authority, entitled Alterations of the Liturgy of the Protestant Episcopal Church in the United States of America, to render the same conformable to the American Revolution, and the Constitutions of the respective States.' "

And finally, we submit the evidence as furnished by the Prefaces of the Prayer Book as a whole, and of the Ordinal. From the Preface of the entire Book we quote the following: "The Church of England to which the Protestant Episcopal Church of these States is indebted, under God, for her first foundation and a long continuance of nursing care and protection, hath, in the Preface of her Book of Common Prayer, laid it down as a rule that 'The particular forms of Divine Worship, and the Rites and Ceremonies appointed to be used therein, being things in their own nature indifferent and alterable, and so acknowledged, it is but reasonable that upon weighty and important considerations, according to the various exigencies of times and occasions, such changes and alterations should be made therein, as to those who are in places of authority should, from time to time, seem either necessary or expedient.'

"But when in the course of Divine Providence, these American States became independent with respect to Civil government, their ecclesiastical independence was necessarily included, and the different religious denominations of Christians in these States were left at full and equal liberty to model and organize their respective churches and forms of worship and discipline in such manner as they might judge most convenient for their future prosperity; consistently with the Constitution and laws of their country.

"The attention of this Church was in the first place drawn to those alterations in the Liturgy which became necessary in the prayers for our Civil Rulers in consequence of the Revolution. And the principal care herein was to make them conformable to what ought to be the proper end of all such prayers, namely that rulers may have grace, wisdom, and understanding to execute justice and to maintain truth, and that the people may lead quiet and peaceable lives, in all godliness and honesty.

"But while these alterations were in view before the Convention, they could not but with gratitude to God, embrace the happy occasion which was offered to them (uninfluenced and unrestrained by any worldly authority whatsoever) to take a further review of the Public Service, and to establish such other alterations and amendments therein as might be deemed expedient.

"It seems unnecessary to enumerate all the different alterations and amendments. They will appear, and it is to be hoped, the reasons of them also, upon a comparison of this Book of Common Prayer of the Church of England, in which it will *also appear that this Church is far from intending to depart from the Church of England in any essential point of doctrine, discipline, or worship; or further than local circumstances require.*"

From the Preface of the Ordinal we make this quotation: "It is evident unto all men, diligently reading Holy Scripture and ancient Authors, that from the Apostles' times there have been these Orders of Ministers in Christ's Church,—Bishops, Priests and Deacons. Which Offices were evermore had in such reverend estimation, that no man might presume to execute any of them, except he were first called, tried, examined, and known to have such qualities as are requisite for the same; and also by public Prayer, with Imposition of Hands, were approved and admitted thereunto by lawful authority. And therefore, *to the intent that these Orders may be continued, and reverently used and esteemed in this Church,* no man shall be accounted or taken to be a lawful Bishop, Priest or Deacon, in this Church, or suffered to execute any of the said Functions, except he be called, tried, examined and admitted thereunto, according to the Form hereafter following, or hath had Episcopal Consecration or Ordination."

And it is also clearly seen from the contents of the Book of Common Prayer in use in the Episcopal Church in the United States that she has ever been true to the purpose, expressed in its Preface, namely, not to depart in any substantial thing from the doctrine,

Liturgy and Order of the Church of England. For the Prayer Book, which we now have in use, is substantially the Prayer Book of the English Church with such revisions as were necessary to meet the needs of our local situations, containing too, as we have pointed out, an enrichment from the Scotch Liturgy for the celebration of the Holy Communion. Being equipped, therefore, by complete independence, national organization, and with her Prayer Book revised, the Church settled down to steady life and progress.

The latter part of the eighteenth century and the early part of the nineteenth were dark days for Christians in general. Infidelity and agnosticism had gained many adherents, but the time of awakening was now at hand; and the Church shared in it. In May, 1811, John Henry Hobart was made bishop of New York, Richard Channing Moore, bishop of Virginia, Alexander Viets Griswold, bishop of four dioceses of New England, John Stark Ravenscroft, bishop of North Carolina. These men found weak and discouraged dioceses and left them strong and full of faith and expectation. And their spirit spread far beyond the borders of their own dioceses. Consequently, when the General Convention met in 1835, there was a new spirit and a broadened vision. As typical of this spirit we recall these words from a sermon preached before the Convention by Bishop McIlvaine: "The Church is a great missionary association, divinely constituted for the special work of sending into all the world the ministers and missionaries of the Word. But if such be the cardinal object of the whole Church, it must be alike the cardinal object and duty of every part of that Church, so that whether a section thereof be situated in America or in Europe or the remotest latitudes of Africa, it is alike required to attempt the enlightening of all the earth; and though it be the smallest of the local divisions of the Christian household, and though just on its own narrow boundaries there may be millions of neglected pagans swarming with the horrors of heathenism, still that little section of the Church is to embrace within the circle of its zeal, if not of its immediate labors, the destitute of all the earth." It has been said, with such words as these echoing in their ears, the members of the Convention adopted a Constitution for the guidance of the Church's Mission, in which it was declared that "this Society shall be considered as comprehending all persons who are members of the Church." And for the guidance of the committees it was declared that "the missionary field is always to be regarded as one—the world; the terms domestic and foreign being understood as terms of locality, adopted for convenience. DOMESTIC Missions are those which are established within, and FOREIGN Missions are those which are established without, the territory of the United States."

In the Convention, the principle that every baptized person is a missionary by virtue of his membership in the Church was generally accepted, and it was made a living fact by sending a missionary bishop, Jackson Kemper, to the great Northwest. And in that same year, two young men from two of our seminaries started for China. As is always the case, "the light that shines the farthest, shines the brightest at home." The accumulating missionary fervor generated by the

General Convention found utterance in the voice of Bishop Doane preaching at the consecration of Bishop Kemper. In that sermon, he said: "What is meant by a missionary bishop? A bishop *sent forth* by the Church, *not sought for* of the Church; going *before* to organize the Church, not waiting till the Church has been partially organized; a leader, not a follower, in the march of the Redeemer's conquering and triumphant Gospel; sustained by their alms whom God has blessed both with power and will to offer Him of their substance, for their benefit who are not blessed with both or either of them; sent by the Church, even as the Church is sent by Christ. To every soul of man, in every part of the world, the Gospel is to be preached. Everywhere the Gospel is to be preached *by, through* and *in* the Church. To bishops, as successors of the Apostles, the promise of the Lord was given to be with His Church 'always, to the end of the world . . .' Open your eyes to the wants, open your ears to the cry, open your hands for the relief, of a perishing world. Send the Gospel. Send it, as you have received it, in the Church. Send out to preach the Gospel, and to build the Church—to every portion of your own broad land, to every stronghold of the Prince of hell, to every den and nook and lurking place of heathendom— a missionary bishop!"

This larger vision and nobler expression of Christian love reacted upon the Church in this country and initiated a movement for larger growth and finer life than it had ever known before. So that within fifteen years after the consecration of the first missionary bishop, both the clergy and the communicant list had more than doubled. The 700 clergymen of 1835 had become 1,500, and the 36,000 communicants of 1835 had become 80,000 in 1850. And from that time forward, the progress of the Church has been marked. And she never is happier in herself nor her people stronger in their devotion to her than when under the inspiration of the Holy Spirit, they are moving unitedly forward to make the Gospel a real factor in the life of man and all the nations of the world. In this development, Church colleges and seminaries have played an important part, and the people of our generation cannot be guilty of a more suicidal policy than to desert her splendid institutions for the systematic religious education of her sons and daughters.

In the Last Hundred Years

Although it is not necessary to our purpose to add anything more as to the relationship of the Episcopal Church in the United States in the year 1943 to the Church in Apostolic times, inasmuch as we, of course, know the connection between the Episcopal Church in the United States in the year 1850 and that same Church in the same land in this present year, nevertheless, it may be of interest to mention here a few facts in the progress of the Church during the century just gone.

We recall that the General Convention of 1835, being filled with the missionary spirit, elected Jackson Kemper as Bishop of the Northwest. In obedience to the summons of the Church he accepted the call and entered upon his work. His jurisdiction had an area of over 300,000 square miles and population, roughly estimated, in 1835 of 830,000. To cover that territory and minister to those people he had one clergyman and no church in Indiana, and one church building and no clergyman in Missouri. It is hard to visualize the great and numerous difficulties and discouragements with which Bishop Kemper was confronted. But, like the Apostle Paul, none of those things moved him. And being filled with the thought that he could do all things through Christ that strengtheneth us, he moved on to his task without fear, and with great hope and courage. In 1859, when Bishop Whipple was sent as missionary bishop to Minnesota, Bishop Kemper became the diocesan bishop of Wisconsin. In speaking of Bishop Kemper, Rev. Greenough White in his little book, "An Apostle of the Western Church," asks: "What had been accomplished? Twenty-four years had passed away, and by God's blessing on the Church, he now saw Missouri a diocese, with its bishop and twenty-seven clergy; Wisconsin, his own diocese, with fifty-five clergy; Iowa a diocese, with its bishop and thirty-one clergy; Minnesota an organized diocese, with twenty clergy; Kansas just organized as a diocese, with ten clergy; and the Territory of Nebraska, not yet organized as a diocese, with four clergy; in all six dioceses where he began with none, and one hundred and forty-seven clergymen where he at first found one."

Of him his biographer has justly said: "The missionary bishop of a jurisdiction greater than any since the days of the Apostles—and St. Paul himself had not travelled as widely and as long, for Kemper had gone 300,000 miles upon his Master's service—was gone to his reward. [It is hard for us in these days of quick and comfortable travel to realize what a statement like this truly meant in Bishop Kemper's time—The Author.] Well had his life borne out the meaning of his name: 'Kemper': 'A Champion.' With the great Apostle to the Gentiles he could say: 'I have fought a good fight; I have finished my course; I have kept the faith.' "

As worthy and like-spirited contemporaries of Bishop Kemper in other sections of the country, we recall James Hervey Otey, consecrated bishop of Tennessee in 1834, and Leonidas Polk, consecrated bishop of Arkansas and the Indian Territory in December 1838, and having provisional jurisdiction in Louisiana, Mississippi, Alabama, and Texas.

Back to the Northwest we come in touch with Bishops Whipple of Minnesota and Hare of Dakota as Apostles to the Indians, and Bishops J. C. Talbot, consecrated as bishop of the Northwest in 1859, and D. S. Tuttle, consecrated in 1867, as missionary bishop to Utah, Idaho and Montana. Going beyond the Rockies we meet Bishop T. F. Scott, consecrated in 1854 for Oregon and Washington Territories and Bishop B. W. Morris, consecrated for the same territory in 1868. Further down the Pacific coast we see that stalwart nineteenth century Apostle, W. I. Kip, consecrated as bishop of California in 1853.

Then a little later, reaching up to the far North, we are brought in touch with the great missionary hero of Alaska, Bishop Peter Trimble Rowe. Then into our Island possessions, the Philippines and the West Indies, into Mexico and South America, as well as in all parts of the Old World, we find the Church sending her ambassadors to preach the Gospel in every land.

And along with this missionary activity we see increased earnestness and zeal among the people of the Church at home. As illustrations of this we find the men and boys organized into the Brotherhood of St. Andrew; we see Church clubs among the men in all parts of the country; the Laymen's League more recently organized (1932) and authorized by the General Convention, for the purpose of enlarging and intensifying the interest and activities of the men of the Church; deaconesses being trained; the Woman's Auxiliary greatly enlarging its vision and inspiring other women's organizations in the Church with a new outlook and a nobler spirit of service; the Daughters of the King faithfully endeavoring to realize their noble ideals of Prayer and Service in Christ's Kingdom; the Girls' Friendly Society with its uplifting program of real sisterliness for girls in need of fellowship and help; the earnest purpose and effort to make the Sunday School more effective in carrying out its ideals and true objects; the movement for holding the young life to the Church and for developing our boys and girls into spiritually awake and active workers in the Church; hospitals erected, schools fostered, a noble Church Pension System adopted and being carried out with wonderful success; larger interest in work among Negroes in our land and better methods for doing it, the American Church Institute for Work among Negroes leading the way.

And in many other ways, as through the inauguration of the Forward Movement by the General Convention of 1934 "to reinvigorate the life of the Church and to rehabilitate its General, Diocesan and Parochial work"; and the ten-year Program of "Forward-in-Service" launched by Presiding Bishop H. St. George Tucker and endorsed enthusiastically by the General Convention of 1940, the renewed life of the Church has been, and is now being manifested and should be ever-increasingly so, under the inspiration of her wider vision and better organization.

Prayer Book Revision

From the adoption of the Prayer Book of the Church in this country in 1789 until 1892 no revision of it, nor change in it, had taken place. A suggestion was made in 1865 for revision, but it was rejected. In 1877, the late Rev. Wm. R. Huntington, D.D., offered a resolution to the same purpose but the General Convention was not yet ready, and the resolution failed of passage. The same distinguished delegate presented a similar resolution in 1880 and it passed. And then for twelve years the Commission of bishops, presbyters and laymen wrought, the people discussed, and their bishops and clerical and lay representatives in Convention after Convention voted upon their work, which after modifications was finally approved in 1892.

Then in 1913 the General Convention sitting in the Synod House of the Cathedral of St. John the Divine in New York City passed the following resolution:

"RESOLVED: That a Joint Commission consisting of seven Bishops, seven Presbyters, and seven Laymen be appointed to consider and report to the next General

Convention such revision and enrichment of the Prayer Book as will adapt it to present conditions, if, in their judgment, such revision be necessary; Provided, that no proposition involving the Faith and Doctrine of the Church shall be considered or reported upon by the Commission; and Provided, that no proposal to change the Title-page of the Prayer Book or the Name of the Church shall be referred to said Commission."

At every Convention since then up to the Convention of October 1928, a large portion of the time and thought of the House of Bishops and the House of Deputies was devoted to considering the report of the Commission on Revision and Enrichment of the Prayer Book. The present author was a member of the Convention of 1913 and voted for the resolution quoted above. He has attended every subsequent session of the Convention, but one, dealing with this profoundly interesting and important work, and gives it as his opinion that while in some particulars the work might have been better done, yet on the whole he believes that the results obtained are good, in fact, fine. He thinks that now we have a Book of Worship more adequately expressive of the mind and heart of our generation, and therefore one that can be used with greater satisfaction and deeper sincerity. And the greater flexibility in the use of the Book is also a point greatly in its favor, and a thing for which many are truly thankful. Other revisions are bound to be made as the changes of succeeding times and the needs of the people require. We are sure that such will be made with grateful appreciation of the labors of preceding generations and with both reverent and fearless looking forward to accomplishments with a deep sense of responsibility to the future as well as to the past and present.

While writing of the Prayer Book Revision it will probably be of interest to the reader to recall the process by which such revision is effected. All changes suggested by the Commission must first be passed by a majority in both the House of Bishops and the House of Deputies, and then sent to the dioceses for such action as they see fit to take. The proposed alterations are then reported at the next General Convention and must receive a majority vote of both Houses voting by orders; that is, in the House of Deputies the roll of the clergy is called and then the roll of lay deputies. No proposal can become effective without a majority of *each* order, thus voting separately. In other words, if every bishop and every clerical deputy voted in favor of a change and the proposal lacked just one of a majority in the lay vote, the measure would fail. So likewise, if the proposed change failed by one in the House of Bishops though unanimously carried in both orders of the House of Deputies it could not pass. So again, if it failed by only one vote to command a majority of the clerical order it could not become effective though every bishop and every lay delegate in the Convention voted affirmatively. It is also interesting to note that in the case of the 1928 revision, on several occasions the bishops and clergy were in favor of certain changes, but the laymen were not. The proposal was consequently lost. This indicates the real place and power the laity of the Church hold and exercise in our affairs even in so weighty a matter as the preparing of our Book of Worship. Ours is a constitutional Church, and all elements must move together in the development of her life and in regulating her affairs, and this seems to be as it was in Apostolic days, as we pointed out in our first chapter.

The Changes in Organization

The organization of the Church has been made much more efficient within the present generation. At the General Convention in Detroit in 1919, a canon was passed creating the National Council of the Church, which acts in all administrative matters for the Church during the interim between Conventions. The Council is under the authority of the Convention, and has no original jurisdiction of its own. It may, indeed it *must,* according to the canons, prepare and present to the Convention a program for its consideration, but whatever program is finally presented to the people is the Church's own program sent forth with the authority of the Church's representatives in Convention assembled. And further it is the *Church's own program* in this deeper and truer sense—that the substance of it comes from the field itself. It represents the co-ordination of the needs of the Church in the various parts of the world and spheres of operation in which she is active.

The National Council was originally composed of twenty-four elected members and the Presiding Bishop, who is ex-officio President of the Council. Sixteen of the members of the Council were elected by the General Convention—four bishops, four presbyters, and eight laymen. The other eight elective members were chosen by the Provinces, one each—either a bishop, a presbyter, or a layman. The terms of those elected by the General Convention were for six years. Members may be re-elected.

The same Convention of 1919 provided by Constitutional amendment for the election of a Presiding Bishop for a term of six years at the expiration of the term of the Presiding Bishop then in office, the venerable and greatly beloved Rt. Rev. Daniel S. Tuttle, D.D. Heretofore the office fell to the bishop who had served in the episcopate the greatest number of years. The present plan is obviously and readily seen to be superior in wisdom and to make for efficiency in service, as well as for mercy toward our aged leaders.

The General Convention of 1934 by change of canon provided for the addition of four women to the membership of the Council. These women are *nominated* by the Woman's Auxiliary in their Triennial Meeting and are *elected* by the General Convention for a term of three years. The Council therefore as now composed (1943) consists of sixteen members elected by the General Convention on its own initiative, of whom four shall be bishops, four presbyters, and eight laymen; eight members elected by the Provinces—one by each Province—for a term of three years; four women chosen and elected as stated above; four ex-officio members, namely, the President (who is also the Presiding Bishop), the two Vice-Presidents, and the Treasurer.

The Council now has the following Departments— Home Department, with the following divisions: Domestic Missions, Christian Education, Christian Social

Relations, College Work, Youth; Overseas Department; Department of Finance; and Department of Promotion. These Departments are made up of members of the Council together with additional members of a limited number taken from the Church at large, both men and women. The work of each Department is under the direction of a Director, who has under him a staff of assistants and secretaries.

The First President of the National Council

The 1919 Convention passed the following section of canon 60:

"IV. Until a Presiding Bishop shall have been elected in accordance with the provisions of the Constitution, a Bishop shall be elected in like manner to exercise the powers assigned in this canon to the Presiding Bishop as President of the Council."

In accordance therewith the Convention elected the Rt. Rev. Thos. F. Gailor, D.D., Bishop of Tennessee, as the first President of the Council. Bishop Gailor brought to the responsibilities and duties of this high and important office the splendid qualities of a brilliant mind long trained by historical studies and wide practical experience, and of a great heart singularly loyal to the accepted truths and solid traditions of the Anglican Communion and truly devoted to the interests of our own American branch thereof. He faced many problems of serious nature, and having had no predecessor, his course was uncharted; and therefore he was forced to move guided only by his own past rich experience in the life and activities of the Church, his wide knowledge of her constituency, and by the counsel of his brethren which he was not averse to seeking, and supremely, we feel sure, the light of the Holy Spirit —Source of all true wisdom and right judgment in all things, both great and small.

As one who served under him in the Council for more than three years the author can and does bear testimony to his fairness and impartiality in the discharge of his duties both in and out of the Chair. In our opinion, the Church is under a large debt of gratitude to Bishop Gailor for the signal service rendered by him for six years as the first President of the National Council in establishing points of view from which clearer vision might be and has been had for the guidance of the Church through the coming years, and laying foundations of policy broad and secure, upon which the Church has moved and can continue to move with safety and progress in the administration of her affairs.

The First Elected Presiding Bishop

As we know, Bishop Gailor was succeeded in the office of President of the National Council by the Rt. Rev. John G. Murray, D.D., bishop of Maryland, elected by the General Convention in the city of New Orleans in 1925 as the Presiding Bishop of the Church, and ex-officio President of the Council. Bishop Murray had the distinction of being the *first elected* Presiding Bishop of the Episcopal Church in the United States. He was endowed by nature, experience, and the grace of God so abundantly evident in his character and life, for discharging ably the functions of this double office. He was indefatigable in his labors for the Church, as his love abounded more and more toward her and his Divine Master. Wherever he went, and he visited all parts of the Church, he carried a message that stirred the hearts and consciences of our people, and left a blessing behind him to the benefit of the Church and her children. The whole Church was shocked and grieved to learn of the sudden death of its beloved Presiding Bishop, while presiding over the House of Bishops in Atlantic City, New Jersey, October 3, 1929.

Other Presiding Bishops

THE RT. REV. CHARLES PALMERSTON ANDERSON, D.D.

To fill the unexpired term of Bishop Murray, the Rt. Rev. Charles Palmerston Anderson, D.D., Bishop of Chicago, was elected Presiding Bishop on the 16th ballot of the House of Bishops in a special meeting held in Bethlehem Chapel of the Washington Cathedral, Washington, D.C., November 13, 1929.

Bishop Anderson assumed the duties of this high office with earnestness, tactfulness and vigor and gave promise of able administration and fine service to the Church. However, he did not possess the physical strength that his ruddy and commanding appearance would naturally lead one to suppose, and on January 30, 1930, he passed to the fuller life and higher service accorded God's faithful servants in realms above, after serving as Presiding Bishop just a little over two months.

RT. REV. JAMES DEWOLF PERRY, D.D.

The House of Bishops was then summoned to meet
in St. James Cathedral, Chicago, Illinois, March 26,
1930, for the purpose of electing a Presiding Bishop.
In obedience to that call, the House of Bishops met at
the stated time and place, and on the seventh ballot
elected Rt. Rev. James DeWolf Perry, D.D., S.T.D.,
Bishop of Rhode Island, as the third elected Presiding
Bishop of the Protestant Episcopal Church in the
United States of America.

At the General Convention held in Denver, Colorado,
1931, the House of Bishops chose on the first ballot
Rt. Rev. James DeWolf Perry, D.D., S.T.D., as Presiding Bishop of the Church for the ensuing term of
six years. On the same day, the House of Deputies
unanimously confirmed said choice, and *so completed
the election*. (It should be noted here that the General
Convention of 1937, by canon, changed the term of office
from a definite six-year period to a number of years
dependent upon the age of the electee, the provision
of the canon stating that he "shall hold office until the
first day of January succeeding the General Convention which follows his attainment of the age of *sixty-
eight* years.")

Bishop Perry entered upon the duties of his office
with his characteristic high sense of responsibility, and
endeavored throughout his incumbency to meet and
discharge them with broad vision, deep earnestness and
fatherly spirit toward the whole Church. He gave no
evidence that he was either in mind or act a *party* man,
but always and above all else, a *Churchman,* and tried

to serve the *whole* Church as the father of a great family and with a father's comprehensive understanding and love.

The author was privileged to serve with him several years as a fellow member of the National Council, and for two years under him as Presiding Bishop and President of the Council. He bears his unqualified personal testimony to his broad-minded, far-reaching outlook upon things and situations, and his unfailing courtesy and fairmindedness as presiding officer of the Council and human head of the Church.

It is more important however, to submit the judgment of his brother bishops as expressed in a resolution adopted by them in a rising vote on October 23, 1934, which reads as follows: "Resolved that this House, expresses its affectionate appreciation of the gracious and kindly courtesy with which the Chairman has presided over its meetings." And then again in a resolution adopted October 17, 1937, the House of Bishops declared: "Resolved that this House records its gratitude to God for the great and notable service rendered the Church by the retiring Presiding Bishop, the Rt. Rev. J. DeWolf Perry, D.D., S.T.D., and offers to him its affectionate appreciation of his distinguished, wise and effective leadership during the past seven years."

Then the House of Deputies on October 12, 1937, unanimously passed by rising vote the following "appreciation of the high calibre of his service as Presiding Bishop": "The House of Deputies informs the House of Bishops that by a unanimous rising vote it desires to express to the Rt. Rev. James DeWolf Perry, D.D., S.T.D., its grateful thanks and sincere appreciation for the consecrated, constructive and devoted service which he has rendered as its Presiding Bishop since his election to that office on March 26, 1930."

As our only living ex-Presiding Bishop, Bishop Perry continues to render the Church inestimably valuable service by his unwavering loyalty to the program of the Church and devoted support of all that pertains to its welfare, particularly in matters relative to its place in the Anglican Communion. In this connection he renders service in representing our American Church in the Consultative Body of the Lambeth Conference and Inter-Church Councils abroad, and as Bishop of the Churches in Europe; also by appointment of the Presiding Bishop to represent him at important functions, as for example, the Enthronement of the present Archbishop of Canterbury, the Most Reverend Dr. William Temple, in 1942.

Rt. Rev. Henry St. George Tucker, D.D.

On October 16, 1937, the Rt. Rev. Henry St. George Tucker, D.D., Bishop of Virginia, was chosen Presiding Bishop of the Church, which action was made unanimous on motion of Bishop Perry. On the same day, in the House of Deputies the choice was unanimously confirmed, and the *election* of Bishop Tucker as Presiding Bishop *thus completed*.

Bishop Tucker, with continually renewing spiritual power, and its consequently enlarging and increasingly clarified vision, followed by wise and sustained action has been leading the Church forward in noble service. He presented to a joint session of the two Houses of

General Convention on October 11, 1940, his ten-year program for enriching the spiritual life and advancing the work of the Church. It was a wonderfully fine and inspiring vision that he unfolded to the Convention which responded with a hearty unanimous endorsement of the spirit and the program so revealed. Under his continued leadership we can reasonably look forward to further glorious things concerning "Zion, City of our God."

The Church Pension Fund

We cannot leave the subject of the organization of the Church without some reference to the Church Pension Fund. The Convention of 1913 adopted resolutions embodying the following Pension principles:

"That the Church should work toward the adoption of one pension system, covering the entire territory of the Church, and the entire scope of pension activity, and operating under definite and known rules.

"That the pension system of the Church should be so constructed as to take cognizance of the problem of the accrued liabilities.

"That the contributions and the continuing liabilities should be actuarially calculated so as to balance.

"That the assessments to support the continuing liabilities should be adjusted upon the principle of an actuarial relation between the liabilities and the benefits.

"That the principle of distribution should be so arranged that the maximum pension should not exceed $2,000 per annum and the minimum limit should be

$600 per annum. [The restriction on the maximum was removed in 1916.]

"That the Joint Commission on the Support of the Clergy be continued, with power to become a corporation and to take such other steps as may be necessary to put into operation these pension principles."

The Joint Commission was incorporated under the laws of the State of New York in 1914, and under the name of the Church Pension Fund. The matter was further endorsed by the Convention of 1916.

In the meanwhile under the able and enthusiastic leadership of Bishop William Lawrence of Massachusetts and Mr. Monell Sayre, an expert executive, the Church was being prepared for the effort to raise the initial reserve of $5,000,000. The campaign was put on in January, 1917, and to the joyous amazement of everyone the subscriptions for the reserve fund exceeded $8,000,000. And since March, 1917, the Pension Fund has been in operation and has proven to be so sound and so successful that it has become a sort of model for pension systems of other Churches and institutions that pay pensions. The co-operation secured in maintaining the system, through assessments based on the salaries of the clergy, has been nearly one hundred per cent—a truly remarkable record. The whole Church will forever be grateful to Bishop Lawrence for his masterly leadership in this matter.

Efforts Toward Christian Reunion

We call attention to another recent pronounced activity of the Church, and that is its work in behalf of the reunion of Christendom. The movement in this direction was started in the General Convention of 1886, held in the city of Chicago. At that time, "It was therefore resolved to create a Joint Commission on Christian Unity, whose policy should be to move out into the open and bear to the divided Christian world a definite message of good will and a proposal for union." Meanwhile the House of Bishops had been considering the same matter, and now announced the following declaration:

"Declaration to whom it may concern, and especially to our fellow Christians of the different Communions in our land who, in their several spheres, have contended for the religion of Christ.

"1. Our earnest desire that the Saviour's prayer that we all may be one, may in its deepest and truest sense, be speedily fulfilled;

"2. That we believe that all who have been duly baptized with water in the Name of the Father and of the Son and of the Holy Ghost are members of the Holy Catholic Church;

"3. That in all things of human ordering or of human choice relating to modes of worship and discipline, and to traditional customs, this Church is ready, in the spirit of love and humility, to forego all preferences of her own;

"4. That this Church does not seek to absorb other communions, but rather, co-operating with them on the basis of common faith and order, to discountenance schism, to heal the wounds of the body of Christ, and promote that charity which is the chief of Christian graces and the visible manifestation of Christ in the world.

"But furthermore we do hereby affirm that the Christian unity now so earnestly desired can be restored only by the return of all Christian communions to the principle of unity exemplified by the undivided Catholic Church during the first ages of its existence, which principles we believe to be the substantial deposit of Christian faith and rule committed by Christ and His Apostles to the Church unto the end of the world.

"As inherent parts of the sacred deposit, and therefore, as essential to the restoration of unity among the divided branches of Christendom, we account the following, to wit:

"I. The Holy Scriptures of the Old and New Testaments as the revealed Word of God:

"II. The Nicene Creed as the sufficient statement of the Christian faith:

"III. The two Sacraments, Baptism and the Supper of the Lord, ministered with unfailing use of Christ's words and of the elements ordained by Him:

"IV. The historic episcopate, locally adapted in the method of its administration to the varying needs of the nations and peoples called of God into the unity of His Church.

"Furthermore, deeply grieved by the sad divisions which afflict the Christian Church in our own land, we hereby declare our desire and readiness, so soon as there shall be an authorized response to this Declaration, to enter into brotherly conference with all or any Christian bodies seeking the restoration of the organic unity of the Church."

This declaration was concurred in by the Lower House, and the Joint Commission appointed and instructed to enter into negotiations in any directions which might seem promising.

Someone has said of this resolution of the Convention: "No action of so great moment, and so pregnant with possibilities, had been taken by the American Church since its organization." However that might be, no great practical results have appeared, but in such a matter as Christian Reunion, involving so much of both prejudice and conviction, traditions and old associations as well as practical problems, we cannot reasonably expect practical results in a short while, and in such a matter fifty years is indeed a short while. This action of the Convention undoubtedly brought the question of reunion to the serious attention of all Christian bodies.

And the General Convention of 1910 took another step, more thoroughly and reasonably considered, we think, in the same direction when it appointed a Joint Commission of bishops, presbyters and laymen to consider questions touching Faith and Order, and to ask all Christian Communions throughout the world which confess our Lord Jesus Christ as God and Saviour to unite in arranging for and conducting a world-wide conference on such matters looking forward to a possible reunion of all Christian people.

Through much earnest prayer and patient labor our Commission has wrought unceasingly in faith and hope for creating conditions and an atmosphere in which later on definite action may be taken to promote the reunion of the Christian world, the bringing together of the dismembered parts of the Body of our Lord, a thing

we are sure is dear to His heart as it was the earnest
prayer of His soul, a thing, too, that will not only tend
to prove that the Father sent Him (as He said) but also
become a means whereby His mission may be more easily and quickly accomplished. Under the leadership of
our Commission a world-wide Conference on Faith and
Order was held in Lausanne in the summer of 1927
with representatives from practically all Christian bodies throughout the world except the Roman Catholic
Church. The second World Conference on Faith and
Order was held in Edinburgh in 1937. These will lead
to other steps which in God's own time—how far off or
how near, we cannot tell—will bring to pass the answer
to our Lord's prayer that all His disciples "may be one,
as Thou Father art in Me and I in Thee, that they all
may be one in Us, that the world may know that Thou
hast sent Me."

The Church continues her efforts toward Christian
unity through her Commission on Approaches to Unity,
and her Commission on Faith and Order to function
henceforth through the Continuation Committee.

The Commission on Approaches to Unity reported
to the 1940 Convention that since October, 1937, it had
held three Conferences with the Department of Church
Co-operation and Union of the Presbyterian Church in
the United States of America and had been in touch
with other Communions named in the instructions of
the General Convention. Certain proposals have been
agreed upon by our Commission and the Presbyterian
Department for submission to the parent Churches for
discussion and such other consideration as they see fit
to give them.

The Commission on Faith and Order in submitting its report to the 1940 Convention reminded the Convention that it was making its tenth triennial report since its appointment by the General Convention sitting in Cincinnati in 1910; and that it was appointed "to bring about a Conference for the consideration of questions touching Faith and Order," and was charged with responsibility of seeing "that all Christian Communions throughout the world which confess our Lord Jesus Christ as Lord and Saviour be asked to unite with us in arranging for and conducting such a Conference."

The Commission reported that in the two World Conferences in Lausanne in 1927 and in Edinburgh in 1937 the whole Christian world with the exception of the Roman Catholic Communion had been drawn together in a common effort to seek unity through "the clear statement and full consideration of those things in which we differ, as well as of those things in which we are at one." The Commission further stated that: "The result has been two-fold—a notable increase in unions and steps toward union between separated Churches in all parts of the world, acting on their own initiative; and a growing sense of the reality of the Christian fellowship deeper than our divisions, which has found expression in the proposal for a World Council of Churches."

The Commission also informed the Convention that the direction of the Faith and Order Movement has passed from it to a Continuation Committee representing *all* Co-operating Churches, the Chairman of which is the present Archbishop of Canterbury (formerly

Archbishop of York), and the General Secretary, the Rev. Dr. Leonard Hodgson of Christ Church, Oxford, England. Our Church is represented by Bishops Manning, Oldham, Parsons, and Perry, the Very Rev. Angus Dun, the Rev. F. W. Tomkins and Mrs. E. A. Stebbins. The function of our Commission on Faith and Order now is to co-operate with the Continuation Committee.

It is an interesting fact in the history of the Episcopal Church in this country, that she has never been sectional. During the War between the States, she was not divided and when the General Convention met in 1862 in the city of New York, the roll call began with the Diocese of Alabama. Then in 1865 the roll was called again, commencing as before with Alabama, and was answered by North Carolina, Tennessee, and Texas in the House of Clerical and Lay Deputies, and by Arkansas and North Carolina in the House of Bishops. They had been absent only from one Convention. We take pleasure in presenting here Dr. Tiffany's description of this important episode: "At the first business session of the Convention the secretary of the House of Deputies proceeded, as he had at the Convention of 1862, to call for the Southern deputies, the roll beginning with Alabama. The general failure of response did not diminish the validity of the recognition, and the answer to the roll-call by clerical and lay delegates from Tennessee, North Carolina, and Texas gave indication and promise that the absence of the South was but temporary. Bishop Lay, of the Southwest, had joined Bishop Atkinson, of North Carolina, in Philadelphia, and they together sent an inquiry, through Bishop

Horatio Potter, to the House of Bishops concerning the terms on which they would be permitted to take their seats in the House. The bishop of Maryland, whose loyalty was as unquestioned as his greatness, moved that 'The bishop of New York be requested, to ask his brethren, in behalf of whom he had consulted the House, to trust to the honor and love of their assembled brethren.' Such courtesy and confidence were irresistible. The reunion of the Church was cemented by the charity which 'thinketh no evil.' As the Church had maintained its loyalty, so it could without peril manifest its concession; and in the service of 'thanksgiving for the restoration of peace to the country and unity to the Church' it refrained from all expressions which could wound those who were once again represented in its assembly. Some thought that too much deference was shown, but it was an indication of a spirit of reconciliation and peace. The few obstacles to complete reunion, as we have before related, were soon removed, and all traces of strife presently vanished away. The Church, which in 1859 had, by the election of Dr. Talbot as bishop of Nebraska and the Northwest, and of Dr. Lay as missionary bishop of Arkansas and the Southwest, made its jurisdiction co-extensive with the boundaries of the United States, was again one throughout the whole national domain. The consecration of Bishop Quintard for the vacant Southern diocese of Tennessee crowned the work of reunion by a most significant act; and the presence and participation in the service of Bishop Fulford, metropolitan of Montreal, contributed to a growing sense of the unity of the Church throughout the whole American continent." (pp. 503-4)

We cannot close this chapter bearing on the Episcopal Church in the United States without calling attention again to the large part that she has played in the life of the Nation. In order to bring it all together, we repeat some of the things we have already stated. The First Continental Congress called to confer about the status of our Nation and that adopted the Declaration of Independence was opened with prayer by an Episcopal clergyman, the Rev. Mr. Duché of Christ Church, Philadelphia. Three-fourths of the men who signed the Declaration of Independence were sons of the Episcopal Church. The man who wrote it, Thomas Jefferson, was a son of the Episcopal Church. The man who moved its adoption, Richard Henry Lee, was a son of the Episcopal Church. The orator, par excellence, in the beginning of the movement for American Independence, Patrick Henry, was a son of the Episcopal Church, and made his immortal speech in advocacy of the principles of the Declaration in St. John's Episcopal Church in Richmond, Virginia. The lanterns that gave the signal to Paul Revere on his immortal ride to arouse the patriots were hung from the steeple of Christ Episcopal Church, Boston. The man who led the forces that made the Declaration good, George Washington, was a son of the Episcopal Church. A large number of the general leaders of those forces were sons of the Episcopal Church. Two-thirds of the members of the Constitutional Convention were sons of the Episcopal Church. Benjamin Franklin, to whom it was given to bring in the amendment making it possible for the Constitution to be adopted, was a son of the Episcopal Church.

A most interesting event is related in this connection

that we feel bound to tell of here. The Constitutional Convention of the Country had been wrangling to an exasperating degree and in such manner as almost to destroy the hope of effecting common action and of forming a National union. The thing that was causing the greatest difficulty was the quarrel between the smaller States like Rhode Island and Connecticut on one side, and the larger States like New York and Pennsylvania on the other, over representation. The reconciling measure put into the Constitution allowing equal representation of all the States in the Senate, and representation according to population in the Lower House, was suggested by Mr. Franklin, who had previously offered a resolution calling for daily opening of the Convention with prayer to God for His guidance. The editor of "Modern Eloquence" in the eighth volume of which is found Mr. Franklin's speech on the occasion, tells us that "this speech was preserved in a copy by Madison from Franklin's manuscript." The speech is brief and is so full of interest in many ways and gives such clear and emphatic evidence of Franklin's religious convictions that we reproduce it in its entirety :

"Mr. President :—The small progress we have made, after four or five weeks' close attendance and continual reasoning with each other, our different sentiments on almost every question, several of the last producing as many noes as ayes, is, methinks, a melancholy proof of the imperfection of the human understanding. We indeed seem to feel our own want of political wisdom, since we have been running all about in search of it. We have gone back to ancient history for models of government, and examined the different forms of those republics which, having been originally formed with the seeds of their own dissolution, now no longer exist; and we have viewed modern States all round Europe, and find none of their constitutions suitable to our circumstances.

"In this situation of this assembly, groping, as it were in the dark to find political truth, and scarcely able to distinguish it when presented to us, how has it happened, sir, that we have not hitherto once thought of humbly applying to the Father of Light to illuminate our understandings? In the beginning of the contest with Britain, when we were sensible of danger, we had daily prayers in this room for the Divine protection. Our prayers, sir, were heard;—and they were graciously answered. All of us who were engaged in the struggle must have observed frequent instances of a superintending Providence in our favor. To that kind Providence we owe this happy opportunity of consulting in peace on the means of establishing our future national felicity. And have we now forgotten that Powerful Friend? Or do we imagine we no longer need His assistance? I have lived, sir, a long time; and the longer I live, the more convincing proofs I see of this truth, that God governs in the affairs of men. And if a sparrow cannot fall to the ground without His notice, is it probable that an empire can rise without His aid? We have been assured, sir, in the Sacred Writings, that 'except the Lord build the house, they labor in vain that build it.' I firmly believe this; and I also believe, that, without His concurring aid, we shall succeed in this political building no better than the builders of Babel; we shall be divided by our little partial, local interests, our projects will be confounded, and we ourselves shall become a reproach and a by-word down the future ages. And what is worse, mankind may hereafter, from this unfortunate instance, despair of establishing government by human wisdom, and leave it to chance, war, and conquest. I, therefore, beg leave to move,—

"That henceforth prayers, imploring the assistance of Heaven and its blessing on our deliberations, be held in this assembly every morning before we proceed to business; and that one or more of the clergy of this city be requested to officiate in that service."

The author of the Constitution, Alexander Hamilton, and his co-laborer in that enterprise, James Madison; its great expounder for a generation, John Marshall; Madison and Monroe and Jefferson and a large number of the other early Presidents; in our War of 1812 the man who stirred the spirit of the Nation by writing the anthem that has found its response in the hearts of our people ever since, "The Star Spangled Banner," Francis Scott Key; the leaders of our forces in the Mexican War, Generals Winfield Scott and Zachary Taylor, and their chief supporters in that struggle, Jefferson Davis, Robert E. Lee and George B. McClellan; the great hero of the Spanish American War, Admiral Dewey; General Pershing, leader of our land forces in the first World War; General Leonard Wood, the leading general of our forces at home, Admiral Sims, in command of our Navy during that War; Henry P. Davison, the great leader of the Red Cross forces during that War, and William G. McAdoo, the financial genius of that War, were all sons of the Episcopal Church.

The same is to be seen in the crisis of our Nation in 1943. As examples, we recall that our President, and or of the outstanding world characters and leaders of the day, Franklin Delano Roosevelt, is a devoted and active member of the Episcopal Church, as are our able Vice-President, Henry A. Wallace, and the great outstanding citizen and patriot, Wendell L. Willkie. These also are sons of the Episcopal Church: our only two *full* Generals in the United States Army—George C. Marshall and Douglas MacArthur—and Lieutenant General Brehon B. Somervell, Commanding General, Services of Supply; Major General Jonathan M. Wainwright, hero of Bataan; Admiral Harold R. Stark, Commander of U.S. Naval Forces, Europe; Norman H. Davis, Chairman, American National Red Cross; Sumner Welles, Under Secretary of State; Edwin R. Stettinius, Jr., Lend-Lease Administrator and Special Assistant to the President; Henry J. Kaiser, outstanding industrialist promoting the shipbuilding program and transportation of men, munitions and supplies through airplanes; Admiral William D. Leahy, Chief of Staff to the Commander in Chief of the United States Army and Navy; Brigadier Frank T. Hines, Administrator of Veterans' Affairs; General George C. Kenney; Major General Walter Hale Frank; Major General Russell L. Maxwell, Major General J. C. H. Lee; Brigadier General M. W. Clark; Brigadier General G. M. Barnes; Under Secretary of War Robert P. Patterson; Mayor F. H. LaGuardia of New York City; The Honorable John G. Winant, Ambassador to

Great Britain; Chief Justice Harlan F. Stone of the Supreme Court; Associate Justice Owen J. Roberts; Associate Justice Robert H. Jackson; Hiland Garfield Betcheller, Charles Erwin Wilson, W. Averell Harriman, and no doubt, others not known to the author to be Episcopalians.

In view of all these facts, it is clear that the Nation owes much to this Church of ours, and equally clear that there is in this Church the power to serve this people. Let it be understood that these facts are recalled, not for the sake of any boasting, but in order to show that this Church, with its roots deep in the past, with its foundation securely based on Apostolic truth and faith, order and worship, with its large vision and broad and reasonable interpretation of the Gospel to meet the varying needs of men, is charged with the responsibility to put forth every effort in the power of its people, and to use in full every precious thing in the rich treasury of her spiritual values to meet our Country's need. There can be no proper or justifying excuse for lethargy on the part of its members or for failure to do their utmost to make the Church a real factor in the life of the Nation, and as a fountain of inspiration for nobler living to be manifested first in the individual citizen, then in the corporate national life; and finally gathering up her great forces become a power for Christ and His kingdom among those nations who now know Him not.

Let us hope then, that this great old Church of ours, so thoroughly grounded in Apostolic ways, may have also full Apostolic fervor, zeal and power to serve both our Nation and the people of every land.

THE END

INDEX